Misr̶e̶p̶r̶e̶s̶e̶n̶t̶i̶n̶g England

Poetry and Nationhood Since the Second World War

COSTERUS NEW SERIES 142

Series Editors:
C.C. Barfoot, Theo D'haen
and Erik Kooper

*M*isreading *E*ngland

Poetry and Nationhood
Since the Second
World War

Raphaël Ingelbien

 Amsterdam-New York, NY 2002

Raphaël Ingelbien is FNRS research worker and
guest lecturer at UCL, Louvain-la-Neuve, Belgium.

ISBN 90-420-1123-8

© Editions Rodopi B.V.
   Amsterdam - New York, NY 2002

Printed in The Netherlands

ACKNOWLEDGEMENTS

This book is the final outcome of a project that was supervised by James Booth at the University of Hull. His constant moral and intellectual support, as well as the questions he never failed to raise about the whole endeavour, were crucial in making this book what it is, and indeed in making it possible at all. I also owe great personal and intellectual debts to my fellow student and friend Yug Chaudhry and to my tutor John Kelly at the University of Oxford. My conversations with them germinated many of the ideas that eventually led to this book. I would also like to thank various persons whose suggestions, comments and encouragements all proved valuable: David Gervais, Tim Kendall, Phyllis Lassner, Angela Leighton, George Myerson, Christine Pagnoulle, Neil Rhodes, Terry Whalen. Needless to say, the author remains solely responsible for any shortcoming that they were not able to set right, and the opinions expressed in this book do not necessarily reflect theirs.

My project was funded by the Ferens Trust and the University of Hull, where I was Larkin Memorial Scholar for three years. My work there was greatly helped by the friendliness of the staff of the English Department and of the Philip Larkin suite in the Brynmor Jones Library, and by the Philip Larkin Society's injections of cheerful enthusiasm. Victoria Carpenter's friendship and sense of humour were invaluable and steady supports through the highs and lows of scholarly life.

Earlier versions of parts of this book first appeared in different collections and journals. A shorter version of chapter one was published as "The Uses of Symbolism: Larkin and Eliot" in *New Larkins for Old*, ed. James Booth, London, 1999. Parts of chapter three and four were merged into essays that appeared as "Mapping the Misreadings: Ted Hughes, Seamus Heaney, and Nationhood" in *Contemporary Literature*, XL/4 (1999), and as "Decolonizing Ireland/England? Yeats, Seamus Heaney and Ted Hughes" in *W.B. Yeats and Postcolonialism*, ed. Deborah Fleming, West Cornwall, 2001. Parts of chapter six were reworked into two articles that were published as "England and Nowhere: Contestations of Englishness in Philip Larkin and Graham Swift" in *English*, XLVIII/190 (1999), and as "Seamus Heaney and the Importance of Larkin" in *Journal of Modern Literature*, XXIII/3-4 (2000). Acknowledgements are respectively due to Macmillan, the University of Wisconsin Press, Locust Hill Press, the English Association and the University of Indiana Press. I also thank the anonymous readers of those publications for their comments.

ABBREVIATIONS AND SHORT REFERENCES

ECP: T.S. Eliot's *Collected Poems*

HCP: Geoffrey Hill's *Collected Poems*

LCP: Philip Larkin's *Collected Poems*

Unless otherwise stated, all references to individual collections by Philip Larkin, Ted Hughes, and Seamus Heaney are to the Faber paperback editions. References to individual collections by Geoffrey Hill are to the Penguin paperback editions.

Acknowledgements are due for permission to quote from the following copyright material:

W.H. Auden: extracts from *The English Auden*, reproduced by permission of Faber and Faber Ltd.
Keith Douglas: extracts from *Selected Poems*, reproduced by permission of Faber and Faber Ltd.
T.S. Eliot: extracts from *Collected Poems 1909-1962*, reproduced by permission of Faber and Faber Ltd.
Seamus Heaney: extracts from *Wintering Out, North, Field Work, Station Island, The Haw Lantern, Seeing Things*, reproduced by permission of Faber and Faber Ltd.
Geoffrey Hill: extracts from *Collected Poems, Canaan, The Triumph of Love*, reproduced by permission of Penguin Books Ltd.
Ted Hughes: extracts from *The Hawk in the Rain, Wodwo, Crow, Gaudete, Season Songs, Remains of Elmet, Moortown Diary, Flowers and Insects, Wolfwatching, Rain Charm for the Duchy, Tales from Ovid, Birthday Letters*, reproduced by permission of Faber and Faber Ltd.
David Jones: extracts from *The Anathemata* reproduced by permission of Faber and Faber Ltd.
Philip Larkin: extracts from *The Less Deceived*, reproduced by permission of The Marvell Press; extracts from *Collected Poems*, reproduced by permission of Faber and Faber Ltd; extracts from unpublished material, reproduced by permission of The Estate of Philip Larkin.
Sylvia Plath: extracts from *Collected Poems*, reproduced by permission of Faber and Faber Ltd.

CONTENTS

INTRODUCTION

England, England. With the title of his 1998 novel, Julian Barnes once again proved that he is both attuned to contemporary debates and adept at casting them in an ironical light. In its very repetition, Barnes's title playfully acknowledges the extent to which words like England and Englishness have been discussed in recent years. Since then, a flurry of books on England has confirmed that the discussion is far from ended. From Jeremy Paxman to Antony Easthope, from Roger Scruton to Stefan Collini,[1] recent publications show that the question of England has infiltrated areas of debate as diverse as popular journalism, history, philosophy and literary theory. The question is not entirely new of course; indeed Barnes's title draws on and subverts a long tradition. W.E. Henley's jingoistic poem "England, My England" was written at the height of the late Victorian exaltation of patriotic virtues. Throughout the twentieth century, writers have appropriated Henley's phrase for purposes very different from its author's: D.H. Lawrence's eponymous short story offered a bleak view of how the Great War revealed England's sickness; the aesthete Cyril Connolly turned his nose up at England in the 1930s in an essay entitled "England, Not My England"; George Orwell spoke to and of the nation as a public intellectual in "England, Your England".[2] The present book will show that the question also resurfaced regularly after the Second World War. Coming as it does in the first years of the twenty-first century, it is itself part of a marked revival of interest of which Barnes's title is symptomatic. For if the repetition in that title may suggest overkill, it also confirms the urgency with which the question is now being asked, at a time when political developments like devolution and European integration are prompting fresh discussions about English identity. Barnes's title differs from its models in that the possessive "my" is now missing. This absence reveals the difficulty of simply identifying with England in a postmodern age, but it is also a means of recognizing that England now actively contested – in other words, ideas of England are increasingly being disputed by various claimants.

---

[1] Julian Barnes, *England, England*, London, 1998; Jeremy Paxman, *The English: A Portrait of a People*, London, 1998; Stefan Collini, *English Pasts: Essays in History and Culture*, Oxford, 1999; Antony Easthope, *Englishness and National Culture*, London, 1999; Roger Scruton, *England: An Elegy*, London, 2000.
[2] W. E. Henley, *Poems*, London, 1898; D.H. Lawrence, *England, My England and Other Stories*, London, 1998; Cyril Connolly, *The Condemned Playground: Essays 1927-1944*, London, 1985; George Orwell, *Inside the Whale and Other Essays*, Penguin, 1971.

Misreading England

Englishness has become quite a common term in literary criticism. In one sense, of course, the question of Englishness was always already implied in the very discipline of English studies. In a post-Romantic age, literature and national identity are bound to interact, and the making of a literary canon has traditionally been one of the ways in which nations have sought to define themselves. As the works of D.H. Lawrence and of his critical apologist F.R. Leavis testify, England has been no exception – although it can also be argued that, historically, ideas of England pre-date the rise of the European nation-state, and that the question Englishness therefore occupies a somewhat peculiar place in that post-Romantic tradition. The theme of Englishness was rather overshadowed in the 1970s, when (post)structuralist approaches both questioned the idea of literary canons and severed texts from their historical and cultural moorings. Since then, however, the rise of cultural studies, new historicism and postcolonial criticism have put questions of national identity firmly back on the agenda. But the increased theoretical self-awareness of those forms of criticism means that Englishness is no longer apprehended as an essence distilled by literature; instead, it is increasingly considered as an ideology informing particular texts. Following the political lessons of postcolonialism, this ideology has often been subjected to severe scrutiny: England is the centre of the Empire to which others write back; the very concept of an "English literature" is now a controversial. The dominance of the postcolonial paradigm, however, does not mean that Englishness is always equated with an oppressive Anglo-centrism. Postcolonialism has also conferred a new legitimacy on the question of national identity. Moreover, with the recent decline of other ideological issues, nationhood has recovered at least some of the political respectability which it had lost after two World Wars in which nationalism had played a prominent part. Those developments have provided a rationale for those who want to explore more positive versions of Englishness than the terminal and negative concepts to which the critique of Empire may seem to consign ideas of England. The end of that Empire, and the increasing dissociation of British and English identities that devolutionary processes are making inevitable are so many factors that have opened up fresh possibilities of redefining Englishness as an alternative to the British Imperial past.

Thus, if the aims and methods of present-day literary criticism may seem a far cry from the patriotic purposes which English studies once served, the critical debate on Englishness is still often largely normative. Many accounts are still characterized by a need to either debunk or promote certain versions of England and Englishness, in terms which are sometimes still surprisingly straightforward. Of course, few contemporary critics actually believe that Englishness is anything but a construct: most of them would fully agree with David Gervais that "England is always a country of the mind", that "the notion of a real England must always be a chimera".[3] The anti-essentialist bias of current critical modes, however, has certainly not led all critics to adopt a stance of neutrality in their analyses of Englishness. While an influential theorist of nationhood like Benedict Anderson rejects any immutable definition of what constitutes a nation, his *Imagined Communities* also stresses the productivity and the desirability of national ideals.[4] English studies are similarly characterized by a radical uncertainty as to what constitutes Englishness, but this means that "England" has become a literary site that can be actively fought over and appropriated. This is particularly true of the debate that has surrounded the works of some of the major figures in English poetry since the Second World War. The question of England has occupied a prominent place in many a body of poetic work, and the canonical wars that have been waged about the status of various poets have often coincided with attempts (sometimes implicit, sometimes unconcealed) to praise or condemn the definitions of and attitudes towards England that their texts supposedly embody.

The present study arises in part from a dissatisfaction with the terms in which the debate is being conducted, and with the ways in which this debate has helped shape our perceptions of post-war poetry in the British Isles. In that sense, the title *Misreading England* is a complaint. "England" is both the subject and the object of acts of "misreading": object in so far as I suggest that much English poetry is being misread; subject in the sense that misreadings are created and/or perpetuated by English poets themselves, although prominent writers of other nationalities have also played a significant part. One of the ambitions of the present work is to expose the flaws in influential accounts of modern English poetry. Part of its originality is that it does not purport to play off one poet's version of England against another's in order to test their validity or value. Rather than adding to the proliferating attempts at (re)defining Englishness, this book proposes to shift the terms of the debate. Its aim is not to adjudicate between different poetic definitions of England. Instead, it will analyse the ways in which poetic and critical interrelationships have been affected by changing perceptions of nationhood in the British Isles since the Second World War. It will regard all poetic versions of Englishness as *misreadings* of other definitions of England. In this, it follows a methodology adapted from Harold Bloom's

[3] David Gervais, *Literary Englands*, Cambridge, 1993, 16.
[4] Benedict Anderson, *Imagined Communities*, London, 1983, 14-15.

theory of poetic influence and based on the idea that poems can often best be analysed as misreadings, that is as productive distortions of or reactions to other texts. Each chapter will analyse how a particular poet's idiom was shaped by his response to the idea of nationhood developed by earlier or contemporary writers. The main poets under discussion will be Philip Larkin, Ted Hughes, Geoffrey Hill and Seamus Heaney; much of the analysis will focus on their responses to one another or to poetic predecessors like T.S. Eliot, Edward Thomas, D. H. Lawrence, Gerard Manley Hopkins, John Clare and William Wordsworth. The term "misreading" will apply not only to poems, but also to critical readings – both because I intend to perform a metacritical analysis of the current debate on Englishness, and because many of the poets considered are also critics, and sometimes wield considerable influence as such.

The main reason for that methodological choice is not that I wholeheartedly subscribe to Bloom's theory of poetry. The Freudian model and the overly Romantic assumptions that underpin works like *The Anxiety of Influence* and *A Map of Misreading* often seem rather questionable to me. But my analyses rapidly convinced me that, when interpreted with a certain flexibility, the concept of misreading had a considerable heuristic force in a study of this type. Indeed, it has allowed me to concentrate on the textual effects that the question of England has had on a particular moment of English poetic history. In their eagerness to identify writers with certain ideas of England and Englishness, some commentators have been insensitive to the aesthetic complexity of many a poem. The pressures of their various political agendas have combined with the thematic bias of much cultural and postcolonial criticism to produce such responses. Although I recognize that some degree of thematic emphasis is inevitable, and indeed desirable in discussions of Englishness in literature, I hope to demonstrate that more strictly poetic considerations can also play a prominent role. While it partly shares the thematic bias of many other works on the topic, the present study proposes to pay greater attention to the aesthetic process that such approaches simplify or devalue. By making poetic difference central, a study based on the concept of poetic misreading avoids a view of poetry as an unmediated reflection of ideological messages, as well as the commonplaces of a popular psychology of Englishness. Instead, it foregrounds the textual productivity of the questions surrounding national identity, and the ways in which aesthetic processes can complicate the articulation of those questions.

This methodological difference, however, is not the result of a formalist or aestheticist defence of literary texts to which a criticism based on questions of identity has failed to do justice. Misreadings can also bear the marks of specific ideological pressures. The misreadings analysed in this book have taken place in particular historical contexts: the Second World War and its aftermath, the end of Empire, Welfare State culture, the British consensus and its breakdown with the rise of Thatcherism, Northern Irish nationalism, the drive towards devolution. My method here differs from Bloom's Freudian aestheticism: my focus on poetic interrelationships is not an alternative to a historical understanding of poetry; the poets I discuss are social and historical beings as well as participants in the history of English poetry. My main purpose is to explore the ways in which poetic texts have been affected *as poems* by a series of historical determinants: it is chiefly through their difference from other poems that I propose to analyse how those texts engaged with the particular historical moment in which they emerged. Poems, according to Bloom, deviate from other poems. But deviations always follow specific directions. In my view, the misreadings I am concerned with are more often determined by a range of historical factors than by a Freudian anxiety to assert one's difference from poetic forefathers.

Similarly, each new England of the mind deviates from the poetic Englands it draws on or reacts against, but the difference can be the result of many different factors. This study will indeed stress the plurality of the historical determinants that have shaped poetic responses to the question of England. By doing so, it will take issue with accounts that have focused all too exclusively on the cultural politics of national identity. The rise and impact of postcolonial criticism and the importance of cultural identity in current critical discourse have not only displaced more formalist approaches; another consequence is that less attention is being paid to some dimensions of historical experience. Thus, the end of Empire and devolution have featured prominently in recent discussions of contemporary English poetry, but the conclusions reached in analyses inspired by postcolonial or cultural models often fail to account for the role played by other determinants, ranging from individuals' biographies to considerations of class and intellectual responses to the Welfare State.

This book intends to redress that critical imbalance by restoring the texts under discussion to the broader historical and ideological configuration in which they arose. It will thus expose the limitations of a criticism too narrowly focused on questions of identity. Indeed, my metacritical analyses will also bring out the contradictions and hidden assumptions of a dominant form of contemporary criticism. My intention is not only to correct what I take to be misguided interpretations of certain poems. My exploration of their theoretical flaws will also allow me to question the ideological framework of identity thinking by showing how it suppresses the tensions inherent in post-war English poetry and evades some issues raised by other approaches (biographical, sociological, feminist, formalist and deconstructive). In that sense, the present study will be normative: not because it proposes more valuable readings of what constitutes or should constitute Englishness than the misreadings it criticizes, but because it argues that analyses informed by identity thinking and partisan attitudes towards Englishness often fail where a more flexible approach can succeed. My own bias against identity thinking will emerge clearly enough in various places, and there is no doubt that it is ideologically motivated. Nevertheless, my main purpose will be to expose the shortcomings of identity thinking as a form of literary criticism. Its ideological contradictions could lend themselves to theoretical deconstruction, but in the following discussions they will show primarily through the critical short-circuits it has produced.

My methodological choices also explain why I decided to focus almost exclusively on poets. The concept of misreading is primarily part of a theory of poetry; and although Harold Bloom himself has also used the term when discussing prose, poetry still seems to be the genre that most reveals its explanatory power. There is little space here to discuss why it should be so, but I hope that my analyses will constitute some form of confirmation. My decision to make a flexible use of Bloom's concept means that I have sometimes included prose texts in my discussions, either because certain prose writers loomed too large behind some poets to be left out, or because those poets themselves also wrote novels or essays which it would have been foolish to ignore in a discussion of their treatment of England. There are also moments when the connections which I trace between different writers may seem a case of loose intertextual resemblance rather than ascertainable influence and poetic misreading. I have endeavoured to convey that distinction whenever possible, but a measure of uncertainty is inevitable in discussions of literary influence. The extent to which some of my comparisons are underpinned by actual processes of misreading remains speculative, but the critical insights that those comparisons yielded were too enlightening to limit myself to a rigid definition of poetic misreading. However, there were also many cases where the textual evidence pointing to actual misreadings was considerable, so that I decided to keep the concept of misreading as a guiding methodological principle. I hope that my discussions themselves will provide enough justification for what may seem a rather bold move.

My focus on poets has also narrowed the scope of what could otherwise have become a survey of unmanageable proportions. It undeniably has its drawbacks in that the writing of Englishness may precisely seem to call for a discussion that crosses generic boundaries. Monographs like David Gervais's *Literary Englands* show the potential benefits of such an approach, and also acknowledge its limitations: Gervais's study "is meant to be a flame-thrower, not a compendium or a literary history".[5] My ambition is not to try and trace the shifting concept of Englishness through a wide range of texts. But my focus on a limited number of poets has other reasons than purely practical ones.

First, poetry more than other genres has tended to be discussed in the light of Englishness. English critics are prone to look for candidates for the post of Poet Laureate, whether official or not – and whether to praise or attack him/her. English poets themselves are certainly not always loath to contend for the title. John Lucas's *England and Englishness* is devoted to poetry from 1688 to 1900; but while it ends with a suggestion that in more recent times, authority has shifted to the novel, the right to speak for England remained one of the key themes of his *Modern British Poetry from Hardy to Hughes*. As the subtitle of Tom Paulin's *Minotaur: Poetry and the Nation State* confirms, critical discussions of Englishness often draw on poetry.[6] While one may deplore the comparative lack of explorations of Englishness in other genres (particularly drama), my purpose here is not to broaden the debate, but to interrogate its terms. English poetry and its critical reception therefore offer a richer field than other areas. This inevitably brings certain limitations: on the whole, the Englishness of poetry tends to be an idea or image rather than a psychology, which means that my study will deal with definitions of or responses to the essence or the "matter" of England, rather than with Englishness understood as "national character". The latter will obviously be given a role too, but by and large considerations will be more "topographical" than psychological. For a consideration of "Anglo-Saxon attitudes" in the same period, it would probably be more fruitful to consider English fiction, especially since the aftermath of the war was marked by a return to social realism in the English novel.[7] More recently, postmodern novelists like Julian Barnes, Peter Ackroyd and Graham Swift have written fiction that also engages with Englishness in ways that deserve attention.

---

[5] *Literary Englands*, 274.
[6] John Lucas, *England and Englishness: Ideas of Nationhood in English Poetry 1688-1900*, London, 1990 and *Modern British Poetry from Hardy to Hughes*, London, 1986, Tom Paulin, *Minotaur: Poetry and the Nation State*, London, 1992.
[7] See for instance M. Spiering's *Englishness: Foreigners and Images of National Identity in Postwar Literature*, Amsterdam, 1992.

My decision to focus on bodies of work that were written between the Second World War and the last decade of the twentieth century also needs some justification. Of course, there is a sense in which the war and its aftermath can be regarded as a watershed in England's perception of itself: Britain holding out alone, the loss of Empire, the waning of British influence on the international stage, the gradual "failure of economic nerve" make up the well-known (and sometimes simplified) background against which post-war English poetry is often discussed; the conclusion to Seamus Heaney's influential essay "Englands of the Mind" is perhaps the best illustration.[8] These developments undeniably created a need for a redefinition of England, as did the more recent rise of competing nationalisms that have separated England from Britain. But it may be easy to overestimate the extent to which the poetic Englands of the period differ from previous ones as a consequence. The poetic debate on England has an older history, and the First World War is at least as important a landmark as the Second.[9]

Significantly, this is a view with which all three English poets whom I will discuss seem to confirm: for Ted Hughes, the First World War was the "number one national ghost"; Geoffrey Hill is similarly haunted by the sense that "there has been an elegiac tinge to the air of this country since the end of the Great War"; Philip Larkin designed a poetic tombstone for a certain England, inscribed "MCMXIV".[10] If new poetic Englands emerged after the Second World War, they sometimes bore more than a faint resemblance to the Englands that previous writers had imagined round or after the First. In that sense, political developments that occurred after 1945 only reinforced an earlier desire to redefine England. If, as chapters 3 and 4 will show, Ted Hughes seemed concerned to define a primitive Englishness unblemished by a now defunct British Imperialism, his anti-Imperialist politics and pro-Irish sympathies can already be found in the writings of Edward Thomas. Thomas already felt that he had been "robbed ... of the small intelligible

---

[8] Seamus Heaney, *Preoccupations: Selected Prose 1968-1978*, London, 1980, 169.

[9] See for instance Jeremy Hooker, "Seeing Place", in *In Black and Gold: Contiguous Traditions in Post-War British and Irish Poetry*, ed. C.C. Barfoot, Amsterdam, 1994, 27-44. Hooker writes that "Heaney's argument is, in certain respects, limited. For one thing, it does not acknowledge the larger historical context of the subject, or the extent to which English poets of the First World War ... had experienced a painful tension between their love of England and their knowledge of the British State" (37).

[10] Ted Hughes, *Winter Pollen: Occasional Prose*, ed. William Scammell, London, 1994, 70; Hill's words appear in an interview with John Haffenden – see *Viewpoints: Poets in Conversation with John Haffenden*, London, 1981, 93; "MCMXIV" is a poem to which I will return.

England of Elizabeth and given the word Imperialism instead", and wrote eloquently about his response to hearing "Rule Britannia" intoned with pride: "This raised my gorge; I could not help shouting 'Home Rule for Ireland.'"[11] Hughes's hatred of militarism, his fascination with the Viking and Anglo-Saxon past and his attraction to Catholicism all seem to be foreshadowed in D.H. Lawrence's powerful story about the First World War, "England, my England." Unlike Henley's, Lawrence's England was emphatically not British or Imperial: like Hughes's later, it was a "savage England" where "the spirit of the place linger[ed] on primeval, as when the Saxons came". The eyes of Lawrence's protagonist "had a touch of the Viking in them"; his wife belongs to an old English family where "the old dark, Catholic blood-authority" still rules.[12] But Lawrence's England was not purely a product of the Great War any more than Hughes's is of more recent history; rather, it drew on Romantic traditions which Lawrence's reaction against militarism, Puritanism and industrialism reactivated. The roots of Thomas's and Lawrence's alternative Englands in the English Romanticism of Blake or Coleridge opens even longer historical perspectives, which would themselves require a separate study.[13]

Nevertheless, I will also show that Hughes does introduce new poetic accents which can be explained by his response to more recent English history, such as precisely the Second World War. Hughes's numerous poems about the First World War should not obscure his treatment of the Second World War in poems like "A Motorbike" (*Moortown*, 104). Similarly, Hill's numerous references and allusions to the Great War do not take away the fact that his most personal poems about England, *Mercian Hymns*, draw on his recollections of a childhood marked by the Second World War. The 1940s also formed the background against which Philip Larkin struggled to find a literary voice; his jokey comment that his "mind has stopped in 1945, like some cheap wartime clock"[14] is typical of his self-deprecatory mood and is belied by many poems, but it also confirms the importance of what was undoubtedly a formative period for him. Larkin, Hughes and Hill seem to belong to the same generation (being born in 1922, 1930 and 1932 respectively), and rose to prominence in the same years: Larkin's *The Less Deceived* appeared in 1955,

---

[11] Edward Thomas, *A Language Not to Be Betrayed: Selected Prose of Edward Thomas*, ed. Edna Longley, Manchester, 1981, 199, 221.
[12] Lawrence, *England, My England*, 138, 150.
[13] As we will see, Coleridge's contrast between the "spiritual, Platonic old England" and "commercial Great Britain" is one which still surfaces regularly in post-war poetry. See *Anima Poetae*, ed. Ernest Hartley Coleridge. Boston and New York, 1895.
[14] Philip Larkin, *Selected Letters*, ed. Anthony Thwaite, London, 1991, 604.

Hughes's *The Hawk in the Rain* in 1957, Hill's *For the Unfallen* in 1959. They also belong to a generation which is now becoming part of history, as was sadly confirmed by the death of Ted Hughes during the completion of this project. Perhaps we are now acquiring a measure of necessary distance from which to assess them. They also largely responded, in their different ways, to similar historical changes, although I will have occasion to stress that the decade separating Larkin from Hughes and Hill did matter more than is sometimes suggested.

My choice of poets within the chosen period is not, on the whole, particularly original. Larkin, Hughes and Hill are often regarded as the dominant English poetic talents who emerged in the 1950s and went on to dominate the following decades. Their canonical status is confirmed by the regularity with which they are discussed together in many accounts: several studies discuss them as the contrasting English voices of a generation;[15] critics as diverse as John Lucas, Tom Paulin, Neil Corcoran and David Gervais have all written substantially on this trio of usual suspects. I have decided to leave that state of affairs unchallenged, for a variety of reasons. First, it was never my aim to substitute an alternative canon which would include other, neglected versions of Englishness, for reasons set out above. Second, the relative abundance of critical material on those three names has provided one of the very objects of my inquiry. Third, the concept of misreading seems to work best when applied to canonical poets: it could indeed be argued that the work of less canonical figures is not as significantly informed by processes of poetic influence. Fourth, I readily admit that my own tastes are generally canonical. The last reason is not the least important, and is connected with the perhaps more surprising decision to discuss Seamus Heaney in a book on English nationhood.

Another of my aims is indeed to stress the extent to which Heaney has engaged, in many different ways, with the poetry of Larkin, Hughes and Hill. In fact, Heaney is perhaps their most regular and interesting misreader, both through his critical treatments of their works and through the influence that they have had on his own poetic output. More intriguingly still, Heaney's critical and poetic misreadings of English poetry have often had a direct, though largely unrecognized bearing on his formulations of his own sense of Irish nationhood. This study will therefore challenge tendencies to consider modern Irish poetry separately

---

[15] See Heaney's "Englands of the Mind" (*Preoccupations*), Sean O'Brien's chapter "The Ends of England" in *The Deregulated Muse,* Newcastle, 1998, and David Kennedy's introductory remarks in *New Relations: The Refashioning of British Poetry 1980-1994*, Bridgend, 1996.

from its English counterpart: if anything, Heaney's work shows that there is still considerable poetic interaction between two traditions which some would regard as distinct, and that this interaction can affect – of all things – national self-perceptions and attitudes to nationhood. Heaney's relation to his English contemporaries will also raise important theoretical questions. Indeed, his poetry has often been discussed in a postcolonial theoretical framework. That this same terminology is increasingly being applied to English poetry is partly due to Heaney himself, who used the term "colonial" in "Englands of the Mind".[16] But the theoretical implications of that move have not been properly thought through. Indeed, while Heaney's work has been hailed by critics for whom postcolonialism offers a politically radical notion of culture and national identity, the nature of his debt to distinctly English brands of cultural and political conservatism is insufficiently recognized. Articulations of English nationhood therefore constitute one of the sites in which the political contradictions of postcolonialism and identity thinking become apparent.

The importance of Heaney's misreading of post-war English poetry confirmed my focus on the three near-contemporaries to whom he responded most. A study of the same subject based on a different methodology would have tried to do justice to other English poets of Larkin, Hughes and Hill's generation whose works also grappled stimulatingly with a problematic sense of English identity. Donald Davie, Roy Fisher and Tony Harrison come to mind, as does U. A. Fanthorpe, although her comparatively late arrival on the scene means that she may more fruitfully be discussed alongside younger talents who have explored the question of England: Carol Ann Duffy, Andrew Motion, Sean O'Brien, Simon Armitage, Glyn Maxwell are only the more obvious names. Such poets, however, belong to a newer generation; their Englands and their poetics are still in some respects similar to those of their predecessors, but they have been shaped by other experiences.[17] I have also excluded other poets who were active in England in the years when Larkin, Hughes and Hill were writing, but who started their careers before the Second World War: explorers of England and Englishness as diverse as John Betjeman, Stevie Smith, Basil Bunting and David Jones, although some of them have a minor role in various discussions.

---

[16] *Preoccupations*, 151.

[17] David Kennedy thus argues that, unlike Larkin, Hughes and Hill, Armitage and Maxwell no longer have a unified sense of England; their Englands are rather a series of irreconcilable fragments. See *New Relations*, 55-78.

No doubt the list of those whose treatments of England influenced the poets I focus on could also have been longer. There was little space to discuss Ted Hughes's relation to such a key English Romantic as William Blake (or to the Anglo-Irish Romantic Yeats). The absence of Kipling may also strike one as a gap. Thomas Hardy and W.H. Auden might at times have featured more prominently than they eventually do. In the end, I focused on the misreadings and textual traces which seemed most relevant, but once again I lay no claim to exhaustiveness. The starting point I have chosen needs little chronological justification, since T.S. Eliot's *Four Quartets* is the most considerable poem written in England during the Second World War. However, some may still find it odd to start a discussion of post-war English poetry with the last major work of T.S. Eliot. Eliot's name is still too often equated with a cosmopolitan modernist poetics which suppressed the native tradition of English poetry and hence somehow displaced Englishness as a theme, even though England is a central element in the high symbolism of *Four Quartets*. Philip Larkin is one of the commentators to whom we owe that clear-cut opposition, and his rise to prominence in the 1950s is commonly thought to have paralleled the decline of the Eliotic modernism with which he had no truck. Larkin's poetry, however, suggests that this simple story hides the complexity of his own misreading of Eliot. One of the ambitions of this book is to modify entrenched commonplaces about poetic affinities and antagonisms; the following analysis of Larkin's poetic relation to Eliot will provide an example that also sheds light on a shift in wartime and post-war ideas of England.

CHAPTER ONE
THE USES OF SYMBOLISM: LARKIN AND ELIOT

When Larkin established his reputation in the 1950s, his poetry was linked with the down-to-earth, empirical, accessible and definitely English qualities of what quickly came to be known as the Movement.[1] Larkin's own advocacy of sanity and accessibility, his interest in a native tradition, as well as his condemnations of modernist difficulty, were all confirmed when his *Oxford Book of Twentieth Century English Verse* appeared in 1973: Larkin's anthology was immediately attacked for favouring a parochial and unambitious kind of poetry. But his own work was often too complex and shot through with too many influences to be contained within the safe and convenient categories that defined the Movement. From the 1970s onwards, some critics started drawing attention to the presence of symbolist elements in Larkin's poetry. Those symbolist aspects – most prominent in his 1974 collection *High Windows* – gave the lie to the view that Larkin simply dismissed the symbolist/modernist experiments of the first half of the century and reverted to a home-grown English empiricism. Larkin's moments of symbolist transcendence have been explained in different ways. On the one hand, they have been linked to symbolist or modernist examples whose influence was only imperfectly repressed when the young Larkin took Hardy as his model. Andrew Motion argues that Yeats remained an influence on Larkin beyond the derivative early poems of *The North Ship* and that this influence is still perceptible even in Larkin's most Hardyesque poems. Seamus Heaney also mentions Yeats and draws a parallel between Larkin's visionary moments and Joycean epiphanies. In her more detailed analyses of several poems from *High Windows*, Barbara Everett points to sources in the work of the French symbolists whom Larkin pretended not to read. She reads Larkin's poems as parodies of the symbolists' rarefied aesthetic idealism – an idealism which nevertheless retained its appeal for him too. The preposition in Everett's title ("Philip Larkin: After Symbolism") thus remains ambivalent, denoting a debt which also implies a rejection.[2]

Tom Paulin, on the other hand, has suggested that the closing images of "The Whitsun Weddings", "Money" and "High Windows" could be

---

[1] Robert Conquest's introduction to *New Lines*, in which several poems by Larkin appeared, remains the best known summary of Movement attitudes. See *New Lines*, ed. Robert Conquest, London, 1956.

[2] Andrew Motion, *Philip Larkin*, London, 1982, 82; Seamus Heaney, *The Government of the Tongue*, London, 1988, 16, 19; Barbara Everett, "Philip Larkin: After Symbolism", in *Poets in Their Time*, London, 1986, 230-44.

related to certain moments in poems by Hardy, whose empiricism did not preclude a more visionary strain.[3] But one could object that Larkin's visions, unlike Hardy's arresting moments, actually introduce elements which are quite unrelated to the scenes of the poems (the "arrow-shower" that concludes the train journey of "The Whitsun Weddings" is one example). Although Paulin makes out a strong case for the imagist quality of some of Hardy's poems, Larkin's moments of vision are on the whole more reminiscent of the symbolist predecessors mentioned by Motion, Heaney and Everett. Stephen Regan, however, has taken issue with the a-historical bias of those analyses, which never explain why the poems should yearn for transcendence in the first place. In his reading of "Here", Regan interprets Larkin's yearning as "a socially generated impulse: the response of the alienated intellectual to a changing post-war culture".[4]

Larkin's symbolism has thus been analysed in terms of either literary history or social history, as if the two approaches were mutually exclusive. Regan's account implies that Larkin would have lost himself in transcendental visions even if symbolism had never existed, while the analyses he challenges show Larkin struggling and coming to terms with his symbolist predecessors on the Olympian battlefield of poetry, far removed from historical contingencies. This critical divide ironically confirms the divorce between art and society in which symbolism originated. But as it developed, symbolism sometimes acquired a particular relevance in the social sphere, particularly in English literature. Barbara Everett hints at this when she points out that Eliot, in *Four Quartets*, tried to fit the aesthetics of his French models into an ethical framework. But although she writes that a poem like "Sympathy in White Major" performs a similar critique of aesthetic purism, her analysis tends to identify Eliot with the sort of symbolist modernism which had become unavailable for Larkin:

> [Larkin's] poems appear to have benefited from a kind of heroic struggle not to be modernistic, not to be mere derivative footnotes to a Symbolism as much disapproved of as admired; they have wished to be, not merely after, but well after Eliot.[5]

On the whole, Larkin's relation to Eliot seems to have met with a critical resistance which is not without its own obvious justifications.

---

[3] Tom Paulin, *Thomas Hardy: The Poetry of Perception* (2nd edition), London, 1986, 32.
[4] Stephen Regan, *Philip Larkin*, London, 1992, 52-59, 105.
[5] Everett, "After Symbolism", 237, 232.

Larkin's attacks on modernism have long encouraged critics to think that he simply dismissed Eliot's work instead of engaging in a productive dialogue with it. Yet, in the very letter in which he criticized the "American-continental properties" of Eliot, Larkin also acknowledged that, like Yeats, Eliot had "had a demonstrable effect on the course of English poetry".[6] Larkin's *Oxford Book of Twentieth Century English Verse* is rightly regarded as a drastic revision of Eliot's canon, but it is a strange piece of Eliot-bashing that gives Eliot thirty pages – more than anyone else gets, including Hardy and Yeats.

Yet, despite these ambiguities in Larkin's view of Eliot, sustained comparisons between the two poets are lacking. Most of the parallels that have been drawn between Larkin and Eliot concern the resemblance that Larkin's self-deprecating speakers (notably that of "Church Going") bear to Eliot's anti-hero Prufrock, himself modelled on the personae of the French poet Jules Laforgue. Larkin certainly would not have disowned that ancestry, since he once described himself as "bald, deaf, bicycle-clipped Larkin, the Laforgue of Pearson Park".[7] But even this seems to have been regarded as little more than a psychological coincidence, a fortuitous similarity that does not undermine the distinction between the modernist *émigré* and the standard-bearer of literary Little-Englandism. Thus, Blake Morrison concedes that the speaker of "Church Going" is vaguely Laforguean, but he is essentially concerned to show that Larkin's poem continues a tradition of native verse embodied by Hardy, Graves, Cameron, Betjeman and Auden, and apparently forgets that Eliot too contributed to the English tradition of poetic churchgoing – not least in "Little Gidding", where he had wrapped himself in the borrowed robes of Englishness.[8]

This omission alerts us to another flaw in the dominant critical view of Larkin's relation to Eliot, namely its generalizations about the "symbolist modernism" represented by Eliot, and its disregard for the evolution of symbolism within Eliot's work. While a certain vagueness in the definition of symbolism has allowed some critics to link Larkin with figures as diverse as Yeats, Joyce and Mallarmé, it has made it possible for others to use symbolism as a by-word for a foreign hermeticism against which Larkin defined his own idea of a staunchly English, empirical poetry. What is needed is a new assessment of specific

---

[6] Philip Larkin, *Selected Letters*, 380-81.
[7] *Ibid.*, 460.
[8] Blake Morrison, *The Movement*, London, 1986, 230-37. Morrison's omission of Eliot is all the more surprising since he mentions that Eliot's *Four Quartets* were regarded as a major text in Oxford while Larkin was studying there (228).

transcendental moments in Larkin's work in the light of a historical analysis of symbolism and of its transformations within English literature – transformations for which Eliot was largely responsible.

In the last three *Quartets*, Eliot put symbolism in the service of his Christian faith and of his English patriotism. The poems partly revolved round the symbol of a rose which was simultaneously sensuous, socio-political and spiritual,[9] and thus provided a fusion of religious and patriotic visions during the darkest hours of the Second World War. The pure symbolism of Eliot's beginnings was complemented by a discursive dimension which emphasized the poet's commitment to his Christian patriotism. As Neil Corcoran comments,

> the poem's patriotism is therefore the enemy of Eliot's early
> symbolist manner: it insists on acknowledgements and
> recognitions, on decorums of public tact and accountability,
> which the *symboliste* hermeticisms and fragmentations [of earlier
> poems] were ... almost designed to avoid.[10]

Eliot's transformation into a self-styled Christian patriot appeared to be such a complete reversal that it became all too easy to stress the gap that lay between *Four Quartets* and *The Waste Land*. Yet, as Barbara Everett has shown, *Four Quartets* is a text that still engages extensively with French symbolist models.[11] Eliot's new patriotic fervour was also striking, but the English patriotism of the *Quartets* was ultimately much more complex than many of his readers perceived. Neil Corcoran, for instance, expresses a failry widespread view when he writes that, in *Four Quartets* "the deracination of a waste land is supplanted by the chthonic rootedness that is now and England, beginning and end, nourishing the corn".[12] But such a reading goes against the grain of Eliot's own dismissal of "daemonic, chthonic/powers" in favour of a more austere mysticism (*ECP*, 213); it also remains silent about Eliot's final consignment of the rustic dancers of "East Coker" to "dung and death" (*ECP*, 197).

---

[9] See Eliot's comments quoted in Helen Gardner's *The Composition of Four Quartets*, London, 1978, 137.
[10] Neil Corcoran, *English Poetry since 1940*. Harlow, 1993, 5-6. Corcoran is one of the few critics to suggest that "Church Going" may be read as a response to "Little Gidding" (13).
[11] Barbara Everett, "Eliot's *Four Quartets* and French Symbolism", *English* XXIX/133 (1980), 1-37.
[12] Corcoran, *English Poetry since 1940*, 5.

The patriotic vision of *Four Quartets* was not in fact rooted, but almost defiantly spiritual. As Steve Ellis has shown, it challenged other expressions of English patriotism which were developing as Eliot was writing the poems, and which rested on pastoralist and/or primitivist exaltations of the English landscape. Eliot's mysticism and the depopulated landscapes of *Four Quartets* can consequently be seen as "an attempt to preserve a notion of England that will elude any jingoistic appropriation in the 1930s and 1940s"; indeed, the England of the *Quartets* "has a decidedly odd air compared with the enthusiatic home-front, neo-Georgian or Churchillian modes with which we generally associate wartime England". The patriotism of the *Quartets* "takes the form of putting the brakes on the more effervescent patriotism of others; of insisting on England as a relative rather than an absolute value".[13] Misreadings that stressed Eliot's embrace of more established forms of Englishness simplified the idiosyncratic patriotism of *Four Quartets*. Ellis thus finds it ironical that "the *Quartets* have appealed, and still do appeal, to readers for whom the very mention of England – as in 'History is now and England' – is an immediate trigger for nostalgian reverie".[14] This enthusiastic misreading of the *Quartets* also had its flipside; the patriotism of the poems has in fact more often been debunked than praised. A widespread scepticism about Eliot's right to speak for England was accompanied by aesthetic objections: many considered that *Four Quartets* amounted to a selling short of the forbidding aesthetic integrity that characterized Eliot's early work.

In the *Quartets*, high symbolism became aware of its responsibilities to an audience it addressed in an almost didactic tone, and the complexities of Eliot's poetics did not prevent a poem like "East Coker" from selling remarkably well.[15] The most recent complaint about the aesthetic compromise that Eliot's new stance entailed comes from Geoffrey Hill, who argues that the tone of the *Quartets* was calculated to "assuage and console" the readers who had been alienated by Eliot's earlier poetry. Hill points out that the "you" of the *Quartets* no longer refers to the secret sharer whom Prufrock addressed in his mysterious love song; rather, it betrays Eliot's surrender to the poetic flatness of

---

[13] Steve Ellis, *The English Eliot: Design, Language and Landscape in Four Quartets*, London, 1991, 24-25, 27, 91.

[14] *Ibid.*, 165.

[15] As Lyndall Gordon points out, the poem sold nearly 12,000 copies within a year. Gordon also stresses the fact that, "with the disappearance of other writers, ... the recent death of Yeats, and the success of 'East Coker', Eliot became from this time pre-eminent in England". See *Eliot's New Life*, Oxford, 1988, 110.

didacticism. Hill adds that the "residual beneficiaries" of Eliot's new tone have been Anglican liturgy and, of all people, Larkin.[16]

Larkin's mode of address and his use of the pronouns "we" and "you" have usually been analysed as rhetorical strategies through which he and other Movement poets established a sense of intimacy with their readers,[17] but Hill's criticism shows that Eliot may have provided an example to some of them. While Auden's addresses to the reader could also have inspired Larkin, Auden's legacy may have been mediated by Eliot, who understood that he could learn from Auden in his own attempt to write a classical, impersonal poetry which laid claim to a special relevance in an English context.[18] But the readers whom the revolutionary-minded Auden of the 1930s wanted to shake out of their ideological complacencies had become the audience for whom a naturalized convert wrote his patriotic poems in the middle of the Second World War. The "we" and "you" of the *Quartets* do not really buttonhole the reader; rather, they are spoken by a voice which oscillates between a genial didacticism and the more pontificating manner that stems from Eliot's lofty conservatism. Larkin's own use of the pronouns "we" and "you" may not be underpinned by a similar ideology, but it has also been described as a "paternal dictatorship": "beneath the sociable tone of Movement writing is a strong determination to inform, instruct, even manipulate."[19]

Moreover, of all poets associated with the Movement, Larkin was the only one with pronounced, if occasional, symbolist yearnings. This means that his work may be an ideal place to study the effects that the *Quartets* had on English poetry. I therefore propose to analyse Larkin's use of symbolism in some key poems as a response to the kind of symbolism which Eliot had developed in *Four Quartets*: a symbolism which was both poetic and discursive, and which came to embody a Christian and patriotic vision of England. This analysis will simultaneously place Larkin in the literary history of symbolism and in his socio-historical context; it will thus narrow the gap between these two narratives by emphasizing the complex meshing of symbolism with perceptions of England.

Although Larkin's intellectual life was always dominated by the agnosticism and the scepticism that culminated in the uncompromising

---

[16] Geoffrey Hill, "Dividing Legacies", *Agenda*, XXXIV/2 (1996), 22-24.
[17] See Morrison's chapter "The Sense of an Audience" in *The Movement* (99-144).
[18] See Ellis, *The English Eliot*, 144.
[19] Morrison, *The Movement*, 144.

vision of the death-haunted poem "Aubade", modernist quests for transcendence and spirituality had a certain appeal for his youthful self. His infatuation with Yeats pervades his early collection *The North Ship*, while his letters of the 1940s reveal a substantial interest in the philosophy of D. H. Lawrence. Eliot's presence does not stand out as much, and yet it cannot be ignored. The young Larkin did at some stage write some brilliant pastiches of Eliot's early "Sweeney" poems, which remain unpublished. But the Eliot of *Four Quartets* makes his way more subtly into the poems that Larkin wrote during and immediately after the war. Thus, the first stanza of "Come then to prayers" (*LCP*, 5) rehearses one of the themes of Eliot's *Murder in the Cathedral* – a play that Larkin claimed to admire.[20] Eliot's concern with the difficulty of achieving authentic humility was also a question that preoccupied Larkin here: "[we] are required lastly to give up pride,/and the last difficult pride in being humble." The injunction "kneel upon the stone" echoes Eliot's "you are here to kneel/Where prayer has been valid". Eliot's pilgrim kneels down to be illuminated in the church at Little Gidding, since "there are other places ... /But this is the nearest" where revelation can occur (*ECP*, 215). Larkin similarly explored the location and duration of transcendental moments in the following lines of "Many famous feet have trod": "And in many differing times and places/Truth was attained (a moment's harmony)" (*LCP*, 15).

Larkin's lines both echo Eliot's religious poetry and move away from its Christian specificity; elsewhere, his transcendental leanings are also held in check by his sceptical temperament. When Larkin discovered spiritual yearnings in himself, he adopted the same diffident and ironic tone with which he lambasted his modernist predecessors. He once wrote to his friend Jim Sutton: "I am delving into my soul with the hope of finding something. It'll probably be an old tin kettle". The last phrase recalls the way in which Yeats rebuked his own transcendental pretensions in "The Circus Animals' Desertion" ("old kettles, old bottles, and a broken can"), but also Larkin's dismissal of Eliot as "an old tin can" in a previous letter to Sutton.[21] In the context of the 1940s, however, spirituality and transcendence had public as well as private meanings for emerging poets like Larkin. His early "A Stone Church Damaged by a Bomb" shows the sort of significance that they could acquire. The poem was a contribution to Ian Davie's anthology *Oxford Poetry 1942-1943*. Like many other poems in the anthology, Larkin's piece has its Yeatsian

---

[20] Philip Larkin, *Required Writing*, London, 1983, 66.
[21] Larkin, *Selected Letters*, 53; W.B. Yeats, *The Poems*, ed. Daniel Albright, London, 1990, 235; Andrew Motion, *Philip Larkin: A Writer's Life*, London, 1993, 173.

overtones. But other aspects of "A Stone Church Damaged by a Bomb" recall Eliot's "Little Gidding", which had been published in 1942 and whose influence is also felt in the Oxford anthology. It was in a secluded chapel that Eliot had finally apprehended the timeless moment. "History is now and England" (*ECP*, 222): the church of "Little Gidding" was the repository of the values which Eliot wanted to defend, the rallying symbol round which all could be "folded in single party" (*ECP* 220). It was also a place where Eliot's spiritual yearnings could mingle with his desire for a "significant soil", thus offering a sense of rootedness which did not imply any surrender to the "daemonic, chthonic/powers" (*ECP*, 213) which Eliot wanted to keep at bay.

Larkin's poem (*LCP*, 269) starts with a similar vision, conveyed through the kind of symbolist paradoxes that characterize the *Quartets*. The church is "Planted deeper than roots", but it also "leaps up against the sky"; it is "A prayer killed into stone/Among the always-dying trees". However, a first sceptical note is introduced when Larkin writes that "where they lie/The dead are shapeless in the shapeless earth". Larkin's spiritual vision is further undercut in the last stanza of the poem: his focus there is on "the wound/This petrified heart has taken". The poem ends by asking whether any mind can possibly restore an experience as frail as "coral ... budding under seas": "none sees what patterns it is making." As later in the final vision of "Here", which is "unnoticed" and "hidden", the only transcendence that remains is "out of reach" (*The Whitsun Weddings*, 9).

By insisting on the damage done to the church, the poem subverts Eliot's Christian vision of wartime England. Eliot's reassertion of the strength of Christianity is clearly being questioned in the poem, but Larkin is not only playing off his agnosticism against Eliot's belief. He also challenged the conservative patriotism for which the *Quartets* had become a central text, not least at Oxford.[22] This is suggested by the bantering tone of the following remarks to Amis:

> Out of ... fourteen reviews of *Oxford Poetry* ... five mention "A Stone Church Damaged by a Bum" [*sic*] and one quotes it in full, so you can take me, young Amis, as the organ voice of Old England. The genital organ voice.[23]

---

[22] In that sense, Larkin participated in the misreading that simplified the patriotism of the *Quartets*.

[23] Larkin, *Selected Letters*, 80.

In the increasingly secular climate of the postwar years, Eliot's transcendental vision of a Christian England rapidly became obsolete. Not only did his mystical patriotism appear incongruous, but the poetic achievement of *Four Quartets* became a huge memorial to English symbolism, which an emerging generation of English poet-critics were keen to displace. Yet, the demise of Eliot's patriotic and religious symbolism did not take place overnight. It was a process which can be traced, among other places, in certain moments in Larkin's poetry: on the one hand, moments where Eliot's discursive suggestions of transcendence are evoked and then subverted (as in "Church Going"); on the other hand, visionary moments where the kind of symbols that Eliot had invested with patriotic and religious meanings resurface only to confirm the loss of their power (as in "The Whitsun Weddings").

Thematically, "A Stone Church Damaged by a Bomb" looks forward to "Church Going". But the Eliotic symbolism of the early poem has now been replaced by English poetic conventions: rhyme, metre, a descriptive empiricism grounded on the presence of an observer in specific surroundings – the speaker of the *Quartets*, by contrast, was a disembodied voice hovering above a rather abstract landscape.[24] But like Eliot's imaginary pilgrim, (and unlike many of his English predecessors), the speaker of "Church Going" has no personal association with the church he is visiting.[25] When he admits that he is generally "at a loss", "Wondering what to look for" (*The Less Deceived*, 28), he reveals himself as one of the visitors to whom Eliot says: "If you came by day not knowing what you came for" (*ECP*, 215). Eliot's sense of having "no purpose" or a purpose "beyond the end you figured" (*ECP*, 215) is contrasted in "Church Going" with the more obvious and debatable aims of other visitors: the "dubious women" who seek miracles and visions, the "ruin-bibber", the "Christmas addict" and the "crew" who "know what rood-lofts were" (*The Less Deceived*, 28-29).

Whereas the first stanzas of "Church Going" are representative of the sceptical, debunking empiricism of the Movement, the stately language of the last two stanzas isradically different. While it is not unusual for Larkin to end a poem with abstract reflections, he hardly ever strikes as lofty a note as in the last stanza of "Church Going". The poem's bicycle-

---

[24] For a contrast between "Little Gidding" and English landscape poems, see Alan Marshall, "England and Nowhere", in *The Cambridge Companion to T.S. Eliot*, ed. A. David Moody, Cambridge, 1994, 101-2.

[25] Christopher Clausen provides an interesting account of how both Eliot and Larkin dispensed with the personal nostalgia that pervaded earlier poems about churches in "Tintern Abbey to Little Gidding: The Past Recaptured", *Sewanee Review*, XCIV/3 (1976), 419-24.

clipped observer has often been referred to as the typical Movement figure, the average Welfare State Englishman.[26] But his last remarks reveal surprisingly high aspirations. The self-ironic Laforguean figure suddenly decides to yield to his impossible yearning for spirituality and belonging. In fact, the shift almost reads like a summary of Eliot's shift from the ironic decadence of Prufrock to the Christian poet of *Four Quartets*, were it not for the fact that "Church Going" eventually confirms the unavailability of the values that Eliot embraced.

Eliot's church symbolizes a faith that connects the speaker with the history of the nation. The mystic's reflections mingle with a celebration of historical continuity and national community. Larkin's agnostic is also a solitary visitor who ends up meditating on communal history. And although Larkin claimed in an interview that the inspiration for the poem first came from a visit to a dilapidated church in Northern Ireland, other elements indicate that the church is closely bound up with England in Larkin's imagination.[27] The fact that the speaker donates an "Irish sixpence" can be interpreted as a confirmation that this is an English church which "was not worth stopping for" (*The Less Deceived*, 28). Moreover, the church is only one among many, and Larkin's drafts reveal that the bicycle-clipped persona's numerous visits are made to English churches: "What brings me time and time again into your silences/up and down England?"[28] Moreover, the fact that the "I" of the poem slips into "we" in the third stanza indicates that, when Larkin's visitor is reflecting on the future of churches, he is, to paraphrase "The Importance of Elsewhere" (*The Whitsun Weddings*, 34) meditating on communal "customs and establishments" that are his own, namely English and not Irish. This, however, does not mean that "Church Going" is a straightforward assertion of national belonging and patriotic fellow-feeling. Indeed, Larkin's attitude to his Englishness is as problematic in "Church Going" as it will be in "The Importance of Elsewhere".[29]

The sense of community embodied by the church initially appears to be undermined: "it held unspilt" "what since is found/Only in separation ..." (*The Less Deceived*, 98). Yet, in the last stanza, the speaker pulls himself and the community together in a surprisingly upbeat passage:

---

[26] See particularly Al Alvarez's introduction to *The New Poetry*, London, 1962, 20.

[27] See John Haffenden, *Viewpoints*, 124. Larkin's biographical note is qualified by his attraction to a similar theme in the earlier poem "A Stone Church Damaged by a Bomb".

[28] See A.T. Tolley, *Larkin at Work: A Study of Larkin's Mode of Composition as Seen in his Notebooks*. Hull, 1997, 75.

[29] "The Importance of Elsewhere" is analysed at length in chapter 6.

A serious house on serious earth it is
In whose blent air all our compulsions meet
Are recognised, and robed as destinies.
And that much never can be obsolete ...

(*The Less Deceived*, 29)

"Serious earth" could easily turn into Eliot's "significant soil" (*ECP*, 213). The drafts of the poem confirm that Larkin was using a rhetoric that echoed Eliot's concerns: discarded passages include phrases like "thoughts on time", "being born indigenous to earth".[30] The first person plural, which is so central to Eliot's tone in the *Quartets*, resurfaces as "*our* compulsions meet" (emphasis mine) and are "robed as destinies": once again, the church stands for a community rooted in its country and institutions.

But that "never obsolete" sense of community is regained through a rhetoric which, in the context of Larkin's new poetics, looks suspiciously obsolete. The inversion of the first line, the rare "blent" and the hackneyed "robe of destiny" image all seem to contradict the judgement on their present and future relevance. Moreover, the poem eventually lapses back into the singular: Larkin's successor will always be a "someone" who will "gravitate towards this *ground*" (*The Less Deceived*, 29. Emphasis mine) – a word which lacks the mystical overtones of "earth" and "soil". Church going becomes a confirmation of solitude and separation. In this poem, Larkin uses a "we" which would probably remind Geoffrey Hill of the "we" of the *Quartets*, but he never feels confident enough to use the "you" which comes up so naturally in other poems. The absence of the second person, and the fact that the first person plural is eventually abandoned, show that "Church Going" dramatizes the loss of any transcendental sense of community. *The Less Deceived* has often been considered as an expression of the post-war consensus, and yet "Church Going" eventually stresses isolation. When read carefully, the poem actually reveals that Larkin's churchgoer consciously fails to speak for any sense of national community. Whereas Eliot idealized wartime England through symbols of community and continuity, Larkin could find no way of encompassing post-war England in a coherent poetic vision. Eliot had hoped that the war would enhance a sense of continuity beyond "now and England" (*ECP*, 222), but for Larkin "Church Going" was one of the stages that would lead to the "England gone" of "Going, Going" (*High Windows*, 22).

---

[30] Tolley, *Larkin at Work*, 82.

The only community in the poem is that of the many dead who "lie round". Those final words, rhyming as they do with "ground" (*The Less Deceived*, 29), move down from the "blent air" in which "our compulsions meet" and usher in intimations of mortality. The positive transcendence held out at the beginning of the stanza is undercut by a final vision of nothingness, in the same way that the mention of the shapeless dead undermined the initial spiritual *élan* of "A Stone Church Damaged by a Bomb" (*LCP*, 269). The poem's religiosity dissolves at the thought of the "many dead", as it does in Stevie Smith's poem "Edmonton, thy cemetery ...":

> ... Doubt returns with dreary face
> And fills my heart with dread
> . . . .
> And I begin to sing with him
> As if Belief had never been
> Ah me, the countless dead, ah me
> The countless countless dead.

Commenting on those lines, Larkin significantly wrote that "the language and history of the Church of England and its liturgy are in [Smith's] blood, but so is doubt".[31] The "wisdom" which is gained through the contemplation of death is a purely stoical one, and is quite remote from the significance with which Eliot invested his eschatological explorations. The dead will lie among "grass, weedy pavement, brambles, buttress, sky" (*The Less Deceived*, 28): Larkin's description takes us back from the Christian patriotism of "Little Gidding" to the solitude and the desolation of *The Waste Land*, where "the grass is singing/Over the tumbled graves" around an "empty chapel, only the wind's home" (*ECP*, 78).

Larkin also explores ritual and community in "The Whitsun Weddings" (*The Whitsun Weddings*, 21-23), and although the poem does not echo Eliot in the same way that "A Stone Church Damaged by a Bomb" and "Church Going" do, a comparison of Eliot's and Larkin's methods still proves quite instructive. "The Whitsun Weddings" ends on one of the most memorable symbolist moments in Larkin, namely the intriguing vision of an "arrow-shower" becoming rain. Tom Paulin speaks of a "Yeatsian big-bang effect of magisterial visionary power". He adds that "The Whitsun Weddings" is a poem

---

[31] Larkin, *Required Writing*, 157.

imbued with the communal solidarity of Britain in the 1940s and 1950s … it draws a moving frame across a landscape of cinemas, cooling towers, scrap-yards and county cricket matches in order to reveal an altered country that is also timeless.[32]

Given the terms he uses, it is surprising that Paulin should think of Yeats rather than Eliot. "Little Gidding" was the major poem of the 1940s, and wartime solidarity was one of its central themes. And if anyone had explicitly formulated the idea that England was "timeless", it was Eliot. Moreover, the image of the arrow-shower was inspired by Laurence Olivier's version of *Henry V*, which, like the last three *Quartets*, was a cultural product of wartime patriotism.[33] Like "Little Gidding", "The Whitsun Weddings" thus attempts to fuse symbolism and patriotism by drawing on historical iconography. Besides, both poems deal with religious rituals: Larkin's weddings at Whitsun are a more democratic version of Eliot's Latinate Pentecost (*ECP*, 214). In both poems, time seems to be transfigured: Eliot's England is "the intersection of the timeless moment" (*ECP*, 215); Larkin's journey includes fifty minutes that "in time would seem/Just long enough to settle hats and say/*I nearly died*" (*The Whitsun Weddings*, 22). Beyond their obvious differences, "Little Gidding" and "The Whitsun Weddings" also exhibit similarity of purpose. But Larkin's patriotic outburst turns out to be much more problematic than Eliot's.

The metaphor of the arrow-shower is tentatively introduced at the end of the penultimate stanza. As the train nears its destination, Larkin's travellers imagines London, "Its postal districts packed like squares of wheat:/There we were aimed". While "wheat" may call for the shower that will fall in the end, "aimed" prepares for "arrow". But the optimistic momentum that builds up in the last stanza is constantly qualified by the awareness that the "frail travelling coincidence" is nearly over, and that "what it held/Stood ready to be loosed" (*The Whitsun Weddings*, 23). "Loosed" is rather positive in the context of "aimed" and "arrow", but it also points to dissolution, like the description of death in "Ambulances": "what cohered" in each life "at last begins to loosen" (*The Whitsun Weddings*, 33). "The Whitsun Weddings" too is haunted by death: "a

---

[32] Tom Paulin, *Minotaur*, 285-86.

[33] Larkin himself pointed to the source of the image in Olivier's film – see Andrew Motion, *Philip Larkin: A Writer's Life*, 288. Although both *Henry V* and *Four Quartets* originate in the same circumstances, one should still distinguish between Olivier's recycling of a vocal Shakespearean nationalism and Eliot's complex patriotism.

happy funeral", "*I nearly died*" (*The Whitsun Weddings*, 22); the poem plays upon the sexual sense of "dying" but never manages to suppress its literal meaning. Many lines end on suggestions of a positive climax that is undercut by the beginning of the next line: "held" is followed by "ready to be loosed", "swelled" by "a sense of falling",[34] and "arrow-shower" by "sent out of sight": like other forms of fulfilment, this one remains "out of reach" for the speaker (*The Whitsun Weddings*, 9). The weddings only cohere in the mind of an observer whose sense of exclusion is painfully felt at the end. As in "Church Going", Larkin's attempt at celebrating communal rituals is followed by a sense of solitude mingled with apprehensions of death, compounded here by a difference in social class and confirmed by a poetic short-circuit.

Indeed, when the speaker tries to sum up the significance of the journey, he abandons the metonymic mode which had underpinned his descriptions of the English landscape and his gradual inclusion of the newlyweds in his vision. After a tentative excursion into a more discursive mode, the poem ends on the surprising symbolist vision of the arrow-shower. The "sense of falling" which the speaker experiences when the brakes take hold is paralleled by the jolt caused by his sudden lapse into a metaphoric mode.[35] His vision is introduced by a tentative "like"; the transition shows that Larkin was much less confident in his vision than Eliot, who could move smoothly between the discursive and symbolist strands of the *Quartets*. Moreover, Larkin's metaphor ultimately fails to convey its patriotic meaning. As Tom Paulin has pointed out, the reference is oblique, and only readers with a certain background could grasp its significance.[36] This was no problem for Eliot, who relied on the subconscious resonance of his symbols, but it engenders major complications for Larkin. Unlike Eliot, Larkin has included the poet's presence in a communal scene which he describes with scrupulous attention to detail, even though he himself remains an outsider. His lapse into symbolist vision confirms his separation from the lower-class couples who would not understand it. If the metonymic mode of "The Whitsun Weddings" seems to embody a democratic poetics that

---

[34] This also recalls the evocation of post-coital gloom in "Dry-Point" (*The Less Deceived*, 19).
[35] David Lodge underlines the "mythical, magical and archaic resonances" of the metaphor (a figure of speech which he associates with modernism), and relates it to the "dignity and grandeur of diction" that characterizes the last stanza of "Church Going". See "Philip Larkin: The Metonymic Muse" in *The Modes of Modern Writing: Metaphor and Metonymy and the Typology of Modern Literature*, London, 1977, 218.
[36] Paulin, *Minotaur*, 235-36.

reflects the post-war consensus, the final metaphor simultaneously breaks that consensus and fails to elevate it to the status of historical myth.

Whereas Eliot's transcendence was affirmative and resonated with religious and patriotic meanings, Larkin's is an inverted transcendence which only affords glimpses into lack and absence. Unlike Eliot, Larkin can describe rather than name England, but this should not be taken as a sign of patriotic confidence. Indeed, the transcendental ambitions of Eliot still lingered in Larkin, but he explicitly failed to find a poetically convincing way of endowing England with transcendental significance, so that his empirical English landscape eventually falls into an abyss of non-meaning. His England disappears into the void of his unattainable visions, in the same way that the word "England" was crossed out from the drafts of both "Church Going" and "The Whitsun Weddings".[37] By the time he wrote *High Windows*, his English patriotism only re-emerged in the embittered lament of "Going, Going" in the strained celebration of community in "Show Saturday" or in the defensive Little-Englandism of his letters. In other poems, England had vanished into the dazzling visions of a full-fledged symbolism, where churches go "mad/In the evening sun" and high windows opened onto blue, empty skies (*High Windows*, 40, 17). In his moments of failed or negative transcendence, Larkin subverted the symbolism that Eliot had put in the service of religious patriotism, and was left with visions of absence which are perhaps the nearest English equivalent to the purity of Mallarméan azure and to the first symbolists' fascination with nothingness.

---

[37] See Tolley, *Larkin at Work*, 75, 91.

CHAPTER TWO
THE SOUND AND THE FURY: GEOFFREY HILL

Larkin's inversion of Eliot's symbolist patriotism shows how unavailable the vision of *Four Quartets* became in the years that followed the war. Eliot had celebrated the cohesion of a nation that had become the sole repository of the European values which had always been one of his central concerns. Beyond the apocalyptic vision of the timeless moment that was "now and England" (*ECP*, 222), he had suggested the possibility that its regeneration as a Christian society would mark the beginning of a new era. Instead of that, Britain was about to be demoted to the status of a peripheral nation, and the decline of religious feeling accelerated. *Four Quartets* became a cult text for an embattled conservative elite who sometimes used Eliot's poem to denounce the bureaucratic secularism of the Welfare State. Eliot himself may have followed the consensual politics of the *Quartets* so far as to vote Labour in 1945,[1] but his supporters found other uses for his last major work. Dame Helen Gardner thus breaks into a jibe at Clement Attlee in the midst of her introduction to *The Art of T.S. Eliot*. Commenting on Eliot's struggle with words "under conditions/That seem unpropitious" (*ECP*, 203) she writes that "our age, with its undigested technical vocabulary, its misuse of metaphor ... cannot be regarded as propitious for a poet", and adds by way of illustration:

> It is odd that nobody seems to have asked the Prime Minister, who in 1948 decided to exhort the nation on a thousand hoardings to "that extra ten percent of effort that will turn the tide", whether he had ever heard of Canute. The public receives this and similar absurdities about "targets" and "ceilings" with absolute calm.[2]

For Gardner, the "unpropitious" circumstances (by which Eliot partly meant the war) describe a peacetime that belied Eliot's hopes for a cultural revival.

---

[1] See Jeffrey Perl, *Skepticism and Modern Enmity*, Baltimore, 1989. Perl writes that "the lessons of the war ... moved Eliot to vote Labour" (127). He also notes that whereas "Eliot's metaphors for consensus had been absolutistic" in the early part of his career, "his post-war metaphors were benign, even democratic" (120).
[2] Helen Gardner, *The Art of T.S. Eliot*, London, 1948, 8.

Gardner's sarcasm is of course rather untypical of her magisterial scholarship, which pioneered a critical tradition that would regard *Four Quartets* as a timeless, metaphysical poem and would rarely condescend to comment on secular issues.[3] However, the extent to which the historical specificity of the poem was suppressed in critical commentaries stands as a measure of the obsolescence in which Eliot's patriotic vision had fallen in the post-war years.

Eliot himself was turned into a living monument, consecrated by the Nobel Prize. But his poetic voice had gone silent, and the awe that his figure inspired among younger poets (not least because of the influence he wielded in the publishing world) was not matched by attempts to perpetuate his poetics. Among most of the British poets who came to prominence after the war, Eliot's last great achievement was either dismissed or, in cases like Larkin's, subtly subverted.

Yet Eliot has had a clear and acknowledged impact on a poet who has been expressly concerned to redefine England. In his sophistication, his erudition, his concern with Christian themes, Geoffrey Hill has often seemed to tread a path opened by Eliot. Eliot's influence on Hill goes far beyond such obvious similarities as their religious inspiration and a shared dislike of liberalism;[4] it has clearly infiltrated Hill's aesthetics. Not only does Hill broadly subscribe to Eliot's poetics of impersonality,[5] but his verse echoes Eliot's poetry (especially *Ash Wednesday* and *Four Quartets*) in its very details. Eliot's penchant for paradox and wordplay looms large behind some of Hill's phrases:

> And you my spent heart's treasure
> my yet unspent desire
> measurer past all measure
> cold paradox of fire
>
> (*HCP*, 141)

---

[3] See the chapter "Representing *Four Quartets*: The Canonizers at Work" in John X. Cooper's *T.S. Eliot and the Ideology of Four Quartets*, Cambridge, 1995.

[4] Hill contrasts the radical Toryism of Oastler with modern conservatism, which he dismisses as "whiggery rampant". See John Haffenden, *Viewpoints*, 86. Eliot's aversion to liberalism or "whiggery" is evident in essays like "The Function of Criticism", in *Selected Prose of T.S. Eliot*, ed. Frank Kermode, New York, 1975.

[5] Hill sees "no reason to quarrel with the celebrated passage from Eliot's 'Tradition and the Individual Talent' which does not deny personality but enters caveats against the false equation of poetry with a certain kind of luxuriating in personality" (Haffenden, *Viewpoints*, 86).

music's creation of the moveless dance
the decreation to which we all must move.

(*HCP*, 149)

... wild and objectless
longing incarnate in the carnal child.

(*HCP*, 150)

At this dark solstice filled with frost and fire

(*HCP*, 151)

The derivative character of such lines has prompted adverse critics like Tom Paulin to claim that "Hill is a parasite on Eliot's imagination, and any account of his work must face this frankly in order to argue the ultimate authenticity of the style". A debt to Eliot is not likely to endear a poet to British critics of a radical persuasion: the virulence of Paulin's attack is matched by John Lucas, who takes issue with Eliot's conservative view of England and consequently argues that Hill is "feeding cadaverously on a cadaver".[6] Yet Hill's attitude towards Eliot is much less reverential than Paulin's and Lucas's accounts suggest.

Hill actually differs from Eliot in several key respects, not least in his representation of England and English history. Hill does not recognize England in the patriotic idiom of Four *Quartets* any more than Larkin did. As discussed in the preceding chapter, he has recently attacked that poem with a vehemence that may have surprised those who regard him as Eliot's heir.[7] The paradox is that, whereas his most obvious debt to Eliot shows in passages that recall *Four Quartets*, Hill's admiration for Eliot is largely limited to the latter's early poetry. The patriotic, Anglican aspects of later Eliot, on the other hand, fill him with dissatisfaction. Hill's exploration of England, like Larkin's, is informed by the changes that occurred in the aftermath of the Second World War; his poetry responds to the loss of Empire and the rise of a Welfare State ideology that resisted aestheticization. Hill's response, however, is as opposed to Larkin's outlook as it is critical of Eliot's patriotism; indeed his hostility to Larkin can be measured by his comparisons between Larkin's tone and the didactic tone evident in some parts of *Four Quartets*. This hostility is such that, although Hill rightly perceives some similarities, he never

---

[6] Tom Paulin, *Minotaur*, 281; John Lucas, *Modern British Poetry form Hardy to Hughes*, 149.
[7] See Hill's essay "Dividing Legacies", 9-28.

considers that Larkin may be subverting Eliot's poetics. I therefore
propose to analyse Hill's poetry in the light of his double opposition to
Larkin and later Eliot. In the following analyses, I will show how Hill's
misreading of Eliot also allowed him to develop a poetic vision of
England that would differ radically from Larkin's.

Unlike Eliot, Hill can claim to be more directly acquainted with
native traditions than the American expatriate who sometimes simplified
and idealized English history in his eager attempt at identification. Hill's
recreation of Offa's early mediaeval kingdom in *Mercian Hymns*
apparently conveys a stronger, more effortless sense of personal
involvement than Eliot's uses of English history. Those prose poems
collapse the distinction between ontogenetic and phylogenetic accounts
by identifying his childhood self with the elusive figure of Offa, the first
king of all England. Eliot's childhood memories, by contrast, are all
American, which is why his claim to Englishness rests on the
eschatological perspective of his "reversion" to the "significant soil"
where his English ancestors lie buried (*ECP*, 213). The landscapes of
Mercian Hymns also appear more substantial than the rarefied landscapes
of Four *Quartets*. Hill also borrows the title of his sonnet sequence *An
Apology for the Revival of Christian Architecture in England* from the
neo-Gothic architect Pugin, which shows that his forays into the English
past are not hindered by anti-Romantic prejudices that bar access to such
significant English cultural traditions as the Gothic revival.[8] Eliot's
obsessively classical taste made him prefer Wren's London churches (St
Magnus Martyr in *The Waste Land* is the best example); as for the church
in "Little Gidding", the poem leaves its architectural qualities completely
indeterminate. Hill is also more genuinely populist in his political
sympathies (though obviously not in his poetics). His sequence *Hymns to
Our Lady of Chartres* deals with the French poet Charles Péguy and
explores his blend of religious nationalism and idiosyncratic socialism;
when Eliot turned to France for his politics, he felt more drawn to the
reactionary thought of Maurras. Hill's insistence that Péguy "was
certainly not anti-semitic" (*HCP*, 206) might even be read as an implicit
indictment of Eliot and his models.

---

[8] Alastair Fowler notes that Hill's tradition "is more gothic than T.S. Eliot's – not the
tradition of Dante and Lancelot Andrewes, but of the more emotional pities of St
Francis and of Robert Southwell and the Spanish Baroque. Whereas the modernists
reacted against Romantic survivals and remained involved with them, Hill is freer to
return to Victorian mediaevalism". "Geoffrey Hill: Furious, Refined – and Great?"
Times Literary Supplement, 4 April 1986, 363.

Hill's brand of populism, rooted in the Tory tradition of Oastler, nevertheless set him at odds with the social democratic model of post-war Welfare State England. Both Larkin and Hill, in their different ways, show an ambiguous response towards Welfare State materialism, democratization and more particularly urbanization. Larkin's faithful and meticulous attention to English townscapes, which adverse critics mistook for the poetic manifesto of a "suburban mental ratio",[9] was later offset by the angry outbursts of "Going, Going", where Larkin denounced policies that turned Britain into the "first slum of Europe" (*High Windows*, 22). Likewise, Hill can half-ironically describe Offa as a "contractor to the desirable new estates" (*HCP*, 105) in *Mercian Hymns*, and produce a more sophisticated version of "Going, Going" in the significantly entitled *An Apology for the Revival of Christian Architecture in England*.[10] The eleventh sonnet of the sequence describes how "the wood has gone .... /Cement recesses smell of fur and bone", and the poem eventually focuses on the vision of "this long-sought and forsaken ground,/the half-built ruins of the new estate" (*HCP*, 162).

But the solution implicitly proposed by the title of the sequence is hardly a credible one, indeed the title almost apologizes for sounding so deliberately old-fashioned. One cannot help suspecting that Hill is fully aware that Pugin's Christian programme is no longer a possibility, if it ever was. Here too, Hill differs from the Eliot who wrote, in tones that were already not too self-assured, *The Idea of a Christian Society*. Eliot's vision of a Christian England was receding as Hill wrote, and so was the Imperial role which Britain was still playing as Eliot wrote. The Second World War had prompted Eliot to assert a patriotism that could still encompass the idea of Imperial dominance. Thus in "Defence of the Islands", he paid homage to the sailors who "contribut[ed] their share to the ages' pavement/of British bone on the sea floor" (*ECP*, 227). Even though he may have been "attached to the idea ... and only incidentally to the realities of Empire", "Imperial ambition lingers warily" in Eliot's version of England,[11] and it comes boldly to the surface when he is writing to order. Eliot's England was still the home base of the British race who had "assumed a mission" through Imperial expansion (*ECP*, 167).

---

[9] See Charles Tomlinson, "The Middlebrow Muse", *Essays in Criticism*, VII/2 (1957), 208-17.

[10] The sequence will be referred to as *An Apology* ... in the rest of this chapter.

[11] See Alan Marshall, "England and Nowhere", in *The Cambridge Companion to T.S. Eliot*, ed. A. David Moody, 103.

The Englands of Hill and Larkin, by contrast, have been shorn of that dimension. For some, the loss was also a gain: as John Fowles argued, the "agonizing reappraisal that English-Britons have had to make of [their] status as a world power since 1945 has allowed them to be much more English again".[12] But although Larkin and Hill both write about an England which is no longer Imperial, their explorations could hardly be more different. Larkin's England is both obsessively modern and occasionally suffused with what Fowles called the "afterglow" of Empire.[13] Hill's England, on the other hand, is a landscape which is fraught with the traces of a history that stretches so far back that it relativizes the Empire and its aftermath.

The word "afterglow" has a peculiar relevance to Larkin's work. It has not been hard for critics to relate Larkin's predilection for autumnal moods to their perception of the slow decline that Britain was undergoing. Although the Suez crisis is sometimes regarded as a landmark, Britain's loss of power is generally considered to have been gradual: in the public life of the nation as well as in Larkin's private life, failure was not dramatic, but rather installed itself at one's elbow "like a bore" (*LCP*, 28). "Summer is fading:/The leaves fall in ones and twos" (*The Whitsun Weddings*, 44): when Tom Paulin analyses the opening lines of "Afternoons" as a metaphor for the process that led to the dismantling of the Empire, one might object to what sounds like a rather crude equation that smacks of vulgar Marxism and makes no allowances for the personal origins of Larkin's melancholy.[14] Another important question is whether Larkin's supposed interest in Imperial betrays a longing for past greatness. Larkin is sometimes wrongly regarded as a poet who wallows in nostalgia. But if one applies Paulin's analysis of "Afternoons" to other autumnal poems, one would actually have to conclude that Larkin sometimes shared Fowles's lack of nostalgia for Britain's past glory. If, as Paulin rather simplistically argues, summer corresponds to the heyday of Imperial domination, Larkin actually feels "easier when the leaves are gone": for him, "autumn" is "more appropriate" (*LCP*, 68). "The March Past" contains a residual nostalgia for past splendour, a remorse "for things now ended/That of themselves were also rich and splendid". Yet one should beware of concluding, as

---

[12] John Fowles, "On Being English But Not British", *Texas Quarterly*, VII/3 (1964), 156.
[13] *Ibid.*, 157.
[14] Paulin, *Minotaur*, 233. See Booth's rejoinder to Paulin in "Philip Larkin: Lyricism, Englishness and Postcoloniality", in *Larkin with Poetry*, ed. Michael Baron, Leicester, 1997, 18.

Paulin does, that the poem is an unashamed post-Imperial elegy. Larkin significantly finds such remorse "astonishing, for such things should be deep,/Rarely exhumable" (*LCP*, 55). Some form of nostalgia subsists in Larkin's poetry, but it is almost experienced as embarrassing.

Larkin's poem "At Grass" (*The Less Deceived*, 45) has been analysed as a post-Imperial poem that "taps and expresses feelings of loss and regret" that were prevalent in the Fifties.[15] But it conveys that regret through a metaphor that associates nostalgia with the irritation felt in "The March Past": the old racehorses whose glory is past "shake their heads" as if to answer the question "Do memories plague their ears like flies?". The ambiguity is revealing: the horses' behaviour may be taken either as a way of answering the question in the negative (by shaking their heads) or as a confirmation (they shake their heads to chase the flies off). The last stanza suggests that the horses now "stand at ease/or gallop for what must be joy". They are resigned to their loss of glory, although "ease" is asserted with more confidence than "joy". England may put a brave face on its diminished status, but the new realities still do not make for positive cheerfulness.

Hill's England too is often autumnal. As "Autumn reshuffles the land", England "rests in its laurels and its injured stone,/replete with complex fortunes that are gone", it "stands, as though at ease with its own world" (*HCP*, 160). From the "fortunes that are gone" to the "ease" that England now affects, the sonnet seems to rehearse the themes of Larkin's "At Grass". Both poems suggest the introspective mood of a nation that must forget its past glory. It must rest "in" rather than "on" its laurels: Hill's wordplay forces us to move from the abstraction of Imperial success to the reality of his native landscape. But if, in the last poem of *An Apology* ..., the "truth" of England "shows disrepair", the kingdom that Hill invites us to "celebrate" also "grows/greener in winter" (*HCP*, 164). If there is a faint afterglow in Hill's picture of England, it is not the kind of afterglow which Fowles claims "obscures the Green England".[16] For Hill as for Fowles, the insistence on greenness is part of the recovery of native traditions which, by virtue of their sheer remoteness in time and of their rootedness in the English landscape, allow both writers to dissociate their Englands from the British Imperial idea. At the centre of Fowles's Green England stands the figure of Robin Hood, whose "legend is the only national one of which it can be said that it has been known to every man and woman since at least 1400". It is important for Fowles that

---

[15] Blake Morrison, *The Movement*, 82-84.
[16] Fowles, "On Being English But Not British", 157.

Robin Hood should be part of "*folk* history" rather than official history.[17] Fowles's Robin Hood is an English substitute for the Imperial, British figure of John Bull. Hill's rewriting of English history may be more complex, but it does not differ from Fowles's in that respect. When Hill takes his subjects in the War of the Roses, the Plantagenet kings or, even more significantly, in the emergence of an English political identity under King Offa in the eighth century, he too is proposing to fathom parts of the national psyche that have long lain dormant.

Imperial British history is given short shrift in *An Apology* ... : the sequence is essentially concerned with the English people's interaction with their own landscape throughout history, so that the three sonnets constituting "A Short History of British India" relate what looks like an anomalous excrescence that must be severed from English history proper (the tongue-in-cheek irony of the title is itself dismissive). Admittedly, Hill's condemnation of Imperialism is also qualified by his readiness to allow for more positive aspects of British rule. On the one hand, Hill can denounce the "fantasies of true destiny that kills 'under the sanction of the English name'" (*HCP*, 155); his inverted commas suggest the violence done to English values by their use in an Imperial context. On the other hand, he is not quite insensitive to "the life of empire" "attuned/to the clear theme of justice and order" (*HCP*, 157). In this too, Hill shares Fowles's ambiguities. Although Fowles condemns the "desire to spread and maintain Imperialistic and master-race ideals", he is more lenient to "the spreading and maintaining of our [English] concept of justice".[18] Taken as a whole, however, "A Short History of British India" still presents the Imperial venture as an aberration. As Calvin Bedient writes, its "heroic folly" was to try and "reroot [a] slow growing system, with its all but literal roots in the cultivated and uncultivated soil of England" in a foreign context.[19] The three sonnets are followed by the significantly entitled "Loss and Gain": "Pitched high above the shallows of the sea", England's bells "coil a far and inward echoing" (*HCP*, 158). Instead of looking outward beyond the seas, England now turns inward. For Hill, the loss of its Imperial dimension means that England is restored to its proper past and can now rediscover the native, ancestral history that has shaped its landscape and character.

---

[17] *Ibid.*, 157.

[18] *Ibid.*, 157. This belief in the positive contribution of the British to their Empire also underlies Larkin's "Homage to a Government" (*High Windows*, 29), where Larkin bemoans a retreat form Empire based solely on financial considerations.

[19] "The Pastures of Wilderness: Geoffrey Hill's 'An Apology for the Revival of Christian Architecture in England'", *Yearbook of English Studies*, XVII (1987), 152.

To call this a new patriotism, however, would not do justice to the complexity of Hill's attitude. That complexity can notably be gauged by Hill's comment on the central figure of *Mercian Hymns*:

> Offa seems to have been on the whole a rather hateful man who nonetheless created forms of government and coinage which compel one's admiration; this image of a tyrannical creator of order and beauty is, if you like, an objective correlative for the inevitable feelings of love and hate which any man and woman must feel for the patria. [20]

What distinguishes Hill most sharply from Eliot is his refusal to idealize English history. As David Gervais has pointed out, Hill's England is quite unlike Eliot's in that it "has not been ironed out or simplified by time". [21] This analysis is confirmed by the gap that lies between Eliot's decision not to "summon the spectre of a Rose" or "revive old factions" (*ECP*, 220) and Hill's compulsive surveying of the battlefield in *Funeral Music*. Moreover, that poem contains parodic passages that show Hill explicitly repudiating the version of history embodied in *Four Quartets*:

> ... we are dying
> To satisfy fat Caritas, those
> Wiped jaws of stone (Suppose all reconciled
> By silent music; imagine the future
> Flashed back at us, like steel against sun,
> Ultimate recompense). Recall the cold
> Of Towton on Palm Sunday before dawn,
> Wakefield, Tewkesbury: fastidious trumpets
> Shrilling into the ruck, some trampled
> Acres, parched, sodden or blanched by sleet
> Stuck with strange-postured dead. Recall the wind's
> Flurrying, darkness over the human mire.
>
> (*HCP*, 71)

Hill's parenthesis might have been lifted from "Little Gidding", where the enemies that fought over England "accept the constitution of silence" and are "folded in a single party" (*ECP*, 220). But the imperative "suppose" in Hill's line only invites us to consider Eliot's pacified version of

---

[20] Haffenden, *Viewpoints*, 94.

[21] Gervais, *Literary Englands*, 253.

English history, not to subscribe to it. Hill's funeral music is ultimately very different from the silent music of Eliot's *Four Quartets*. In a discussion of Eliot's later style, Hill wrote that

> in certain contexts the expansive, outward gesture towards the condition of music is a helpless gesture of surrender, oddly analogous to that stylish aesthetic of despair, that desire for the ultimate integrity of silence, to which so much eloquence has so frequently and indefatigably been devoted.[22]

After its Eliotic parenthesis, Hill's poem goes on to remind us of the blood that drenched the soil of England. Hill deliberately opposes the tendency to "play down the violence of the Wars of the Roses and to present them as dynastic skirmishes" (*HCP*, 200). But his challenge to Eliot does not stop here. His description of the battlefield and the phrase "strange-postured dead" point back to Keith Douglas's poem "Landscape with Figures":

> ... vehicles
> squashed dead or still entire, stunned
> like beetles: scattered wingcases and
> legs, heads, appear when the dust settles.
> ....
> On sand and scrub the dead men wriggle
> in their dowdy clothes. They are mimes
> who express silence and futile aims
> enacting this prone and motionless struggle
> at a queer angle to the scenery,
> crawling on the boards of the stage like walls,
> deaf to the one who opens his mouth and calls silently.[23]

English poetry has notoriously been less responsive to the Second World War than to the First, and Eliot is traditionally seen as the calm voice that reassured a beleaguered England with his patriotic *Quartets*. It is no coincidence that Hill chooses to question the authority that Eliot gained in wartime England by turning to the more marginal figure of Douglas, whose war poems provided a English soldier's account of the conflict. Hill reviewed Ted Hughes's selection of Douglas's poetry two

---

[22] Geoffrey Hill, *The Lords of Limit*, London, 1984, 9.
[23] Keith Douglas, *Selected Poems*, ed. Ted Hughes, London, 1964, 54.

years before *Funeral Music* first appeared, and commented that "Douglas's achievement is to be found in those poems whose subject is war and the environment of war": "the virtù of his art arose from the necessity of his life as a soldier."[24] In *Funeral Music*, Hill projects Douglas's visions of modern warfare onto the mediaeval landscape of England. By adapting Douglas's wartime idiom to his own exploration of English battlefields, Hill reinforces his critique of the visions of a pacified England that Eliot had provided in his own wartime poems.

Funeral Music ends with yet another rejection of Eliot's view of history:

> Not as we are but as we must appear,
> Contractual ghosts of pity, not as we
> Desire life but as they would have us live
> Set apart in timeless colloquy
> .... Then tell me, love
> How that should comfort us – or anyone
> Dragged half-unnerved out of this worldly place,
> Crying to the end "I have not finished"
>
> (*HCP*, 77)

The "timeless colloquy" is the place to which Eliot would confine his dead in *Four Quartets*. This is what Hill questions by reintroducing the human element in an almost Audenesque fashion ("Then tell me, love ...") and by calling attention to the rending pain involved in the renunciation of earthly life.

Similarly, *An Apology* ... does not replace the violence of Imperial history by the more peaceful vision of a pastoral or Platonic England: in "Loss and Gain", "Platonic England grasps its tenantry" (*HCP*, 158). As Hugh Haughton writes, the "physical pressure of the verb 'grasps' comments on the treacherous idealism of the epithet. In such ways Hill resist the glamorization of the English past that is his starting point and inspiration".[25] If Hill does not renounce the sense that England was an organic culture, his organicism is not the abstraction that Eliot offered in "East Coker": his lines still resound with "The Distant Fury of Battle".

---

[24] Geoffrey Hill, "'I in Another Place.' Homage to Keith Douglas", *Stand*, VI/4 (1964), 8. *Funeral Music* was first read on BBC Radio 3 in 1966.

[25] Hugh Haughton, "How Fit a Title ... : Title and Authority in the Work of Geoffrey Hill", in *Geoffrey Hill: Essays on His Work*, ed. Peter Robinson, Milton Keynes, 1985, 158.

His dead do not go quietly "under the hill" (*ECP*, 199) to nourish the soil
on which they danced, they "maintain their ground –

> That there's no getting round –
> Who in places vitally rest
> Named, anonymous; who test
> Alike the endurance of yews
> Laurels, moonshine, stone, all tissues

(*HCP*, 26)

Hill sees it as the task of his poetry to "prod dead men from their stone" ,
to free them from the "fatted marble" of the monuments in which their
experience may become "unbelievable" (*HCP*, 49). His poetry would,
with an extreme awareness of the ambiguities inherent in representing the
past, "unearth from among the speechless dead/ Lazarus mystified,
common man of death" (*HCP*, 84). Indeed, it is not only the Plantagenet
kings, but also and especially the common people whose blood was shed
on the soil of England – "the trodden bone" (*HCP*, 84) – that Hill
commemorates.

Hill's Toryism draws on more radical and populist traditions than
Eliot's; his mediaevalism is also at odds with Eliot's own focus on the
sixteenth and seventeenth centuries. Until recently, Eliot's revaluation of
Jacobean poetry was regarded as an original attempt to make the
Metaphysicals central to English poetry. In fact, Eliot had been preceded
in this by the decadent poets who admired Cavalier poetry for its
aristocratic character, its intricacy, its interest in mysticism and occultism,
or the morbidity of Donne.[26] Eliot's original contribution to that
rediscovery, I suggest, lay in his focus on the religious and political
aspects of Jacobean poetry. Whereas the decadents turned to
Metaphysical poetry as a way of criticizing and escaping from the
dominant ideology of Victorian England, Eliot's more political outlook
allowed him to reconcile his admiration for Jacobean poetry with some
aspects of a discourse which he encountered in England: the idealization
of Imperialism which underpinned a whole section of British historical
writing.

Eliot's idealizing accounts of the Elizabethan and Jacobean periods
are indeed on a par with the historiographic mode that prevailed in the
English culture with which he was trying to identify. They are
symptomatic of a shift from early Victorian mediaevalism to a renewed

---

[26] See Murray Pittock, *Spectrum of Decadence*, London, 1990, 90-96.

focus on the Tudor period – a shift which was initiated by later Victorian historians like the Imperialist Froude, and which became dominant after the latter's death. That shift represented

> a move from the community of the mediaeval village based on the Church and the Latinate culture, internationalist in some sense and often associated with radicalism, to the more aggressive expansionist, sophisticated and, above all, English world of Elizabeth.[27]

Although Christian and Latinate culture remained centrally important to Eliot, it is not too difficult to translate this opposition into a contrast between Eliot's and Hill's versions of English history. Significantly, Eliot refers to Froude's *Elizabeth* in the notes to *The Waste Land* (*ECP*, 83). The scene which shows Elizabeth and Leicester on the Thames is one of the few passages in the poem that convey an unambiguous sense of past greatness.

The basis of Eliot's lasting attraction to the Elizabethan period was in fact mostly ideological, as is made clear by his repudiation of Metaphysical poetics and his move towards classicism in the 1920s. For although Donne and others were now being compared unfavourably with classical models like Dante and Lancelot Andrewes, Eliot remained awed by the emergence of the Church of England, that "masterpiece of ecclesiastical statesmanship", under Elizabeth.[28] And while the austere classicism of *Four Quartets* was partly a critique of the neo-Tudor revivalism that shaped middle-class taste in the inter-war period,[29] Eliot still praised the political virtues of the Tudor monarchy. Despite his relative dismissal of Tudor art and literary forms, the politics of Tudorism remained an essential part of the ideology which Eliot now expressed in a classical form. In *Four Quartets*, his explorations of the English past led him back to his Tudor ancestor Thomas Elyot ("East Coker") and to the early seventeenth-century community of "Little Gidding". The ideology of Tudorism allowed Eliot to combine organicist politics with the belief

---

[27] Alun Howkins, "The Discovery of Rural England", in *Englishness: Politics and Culture 1880-1920*, eds Robert Colls and Philip Dodd, London, 1986, 70. The "Tudor period" must be interpreted in a broad sense. As Howkins makes clear, "it was a construction based on the later years of the reign of Elizabeth, lasting until the 1680s but with gaps, especially in the 1650s" (70). Eliot's negative view of the Puritan revolution is perfectly consistent with that aspect of Tudorism.

[28] *Selected Prose of T.S. Eliot*, 180.

[29] See Steve Ellis *The English Eliot*, 101, 150.

in Britain's Imperial mission expressed in "The Rock" and "Defence of the Islands": on the one hand, Tudorism glorified adventurers like Drake, but it also depicted an England which remained "firmly rural". Indeed, "Froude himself made the connection between industry, urbanization and racial degeneration which characterized Rome".[30] It is precisely this kind of thinking which informs Eliot's nightmarish visions of mechanical urban life and sterility in *The Waste Land*. Eliot tried to escape from the waste land by embarking on a quest for spiritual regeneration. But Eliot's journey is also literal in that it takes him from the urban nightmare of London into foreign landscapes.[31] In this respect, *The Waste Land* is not dissimilar from other texts which extolled the moral and spiritual values of geographical exploration, such as Kipling's Imperial fictions or Froude's portraits of Elizabethan explorers. Eliot was certainly no simple apologist for the Empire as such, but he might have learnt from Conrad how to sublimate Imperialism and admire its spiritual form: "the idea only."[32]

Tudorism and Imperialism became more difficult to maintain after the Second World War, and Hill's poetry bears witness to a reversion to the mediaevalism of the early Victorians.[33] Victorian historiography was compatible with radical populist traditions and did not look for justifications of British Imperialism in the English past. As we have seen, Hill's organicism sits uneasily with the idea of Imperial expansion, and is less abstract than Eliot's: it only has its place within a specific topography. His explorations of the English landscape are pervaded by a sense that it still bears the marks of a history that has its claims upon him. This is the view of English history that informs the archaeological poetics of *Mercian Hymns*.

Mercian Hymns is undoubtedly the work in which Hill has gone furthest in exploring the matter of England. The emotional charge of that project

---

[30] Howkins, "The Discovery of Rural England", 71.

[31] See David Trotter, "Modernism and Empire: Reading *The Waste Land*", *Critical Quarterly*, XXVIII/1-2 (1986), 143-53.

[32] Joseph Conrad, *Heart of Darkness* (1902), Penguin, 1983, 32. In his introduction to *A Choice of Kipling's Verse*, Eliot also points out that Kipling "wished to set before his readers an ideal of what [the Empire] should be" (*On Poetry and Poets*, London, 1957, 243, 247). Eliot treats Kipling's Imperialism with much more moderation than other contemporary critics, and takes the unfashionable view that "for too many people, an Empire has become something to apologize for" (243).

[33] Victorian mediaevalists had an aesthetic counterpart in the figure of Pugin, who looms large in Hill's imagination: he features in *An Apology ...* and in *Canaan* (72).

is apparent from a high degree of personal involvement which remains unmatched in other works. In *Mercian Hymns*, Hill is fusing the history of the nation with childhood memories, and the result is a form which seems to depart from his impersonal aesthetics: "I was invested in mother-earth, the crypt of roots and endings" (*HCP*, 108). This does not mean that Hill repudiated Eliot's example and switched allegiance to the English lyricism that evocations of childhood would traditionally call for. The form of *Mercian Hymns* is apparently as foreign to English poetry as that of the *Quartets*. To some, it seems to have come to Hill via Eliot; Anthony Thwaite thus writes that "if *Mercian Hymns* has any stylistic source ..., it may be ... Saint-John Perse's *Anabasis*, which Eliot translated in 1931".[34] But here too, Hill's apparent debt to Eliot is filled with ambiguity.

Like *Mercian Hymns*, Perse's poem deals with the creation of new settlements, and pays much attention to landscape and physical detail. It is similarly concerned with the persistence of history through poetry: at the end of the sequence, Perse's city-builder addresses a genealogist: "Ô généalogiste sur la place! combien d'histoires de familles et de filiations?" ("O genealogist upon the market place! How many chronicles of family and connexions?"). His last words refer to his brother, who is significantly a poet: "... de mon frère le poète on a eu des nouvelles. Il a écrit encore une chose très douce. Et quelques-uns en eurent connaissance ..." ("... tidings there are of my brother the poet: once more he has written a song of great sweetness. And some there are who have knowledge thereof ...").[35] Hill's *Hymns* are told by such a poet/genealogist, who stands in close relationship to his "outclassed forefathers": "I am your staggeringly-gifted child" (*HCP*, 133). Perse, however, was exploring a landscape which was foreign and mysterious. Some features suggest the Middle East, but it remains geographically and historically indeterminate. The poem at times revels in an exoticism which reminds us that Perse, as a prominent diplomat, could draw on his experiences in French colonies for his inspiration. But by and large, the poem discourages ideological interpretation and presents itself as a metaphysical quest. In that respect, Eliot's interest in Perse points to a kinship between two essentially Platonic minds. Eliot consciously attempted to blend the political and religious dimensions of *Four Quartets*: the rose of "Little Gidding" was

---

[34] Anthony Thwaite, *Poetry Today*, London, 1996, 67.
[35] Saint-John Perse, *Collected Poems*, Princeton, 1971, 138, 142. The translations are Eliot's.

simultaneously sensuous, socio-political and spiritual.[36] However, Eliot's fascination with Perse's mixture of sensuousness and metaphysical brooding may suggest that the political link was often the weakest one in Eliot's symbolist chain. Hill, on the other hand, is both a religious and a political writer like Eliot, but *Mercian Hymns* is most clearly concerned with English history; if Hill adapts Perse's idiom, it is in order to produce a meditation which is culturally specific.

In this respect, the idiom of *Mercian Hymns* may also owe much to the prose sections of David Jones's meditations on the history of Britain in *The Anathemata*. The Latinate sophistication of *Mercian Hymns* is prefigured in the following passage:

> The cult-man stands alone in Pellam's land: more precariously than he knows he guards the signa: the pontifex among his house-treasures, (the twin-*urbes* his house is) he can fetch things new and old: the tokens, the matrices, the institutes, the ancilia, the fertile ashes – the palladic foreshadowings: the things come down from heaven together with the kept memorials, the things lifted up and the venerable trinkets.[37]

But whereas this poem set another precedent for Hill, Jones himself remained aesthetically and philosophically close to Eliot as well as Perse. Jones's poem is indeed an "anabasis" which draws on the same historical sources that influenced Eliot: in his preface, Jones pays acknowledgement to Dawson, Spengler, Maritain, Frazer, Weston.[38] Like *The Anathemata*, *Mercian Hymns* is part of a tradition of English prose poetry which is indebted to Eliot's translation of Perse. But Hill also goes beyond Jones and gestures back to an earlier poem which already stood in a more critical relation to its Eliotic model. Indeed, *Mercian Hymns* also recalls Auden's parody of Eliot's translation of Perse in some of the prose sections of *The Orators*. While the starkness of Auden's physical descriptions matches Perse's, his focus on violence is a more likely source of inspiration for Hill than anything to be found in either Perse or Jones:

> Clatter of nails on the inn's flagged floor. The hare-lipped girl sent with as far as the second turning. Talk of generals in a

---

[36] Helen Gardner, *The Composition of Four Quartets*, 137.
[37] David Jones, *The Anathemata* (1952), London, 1955, 50.
[38] *Ibid.*, 85, 36.

panelled room translated into a bayonet thrust at a sunbrowed throat, wounds among wheat fields.[39]

The alliterations and the syntax of Auden's lines also adumbrate the poetics of *Mercian Hymns*,[40] indeed Auden's Anglo-Saxon techniques may have helped Hill to counterbalance the Eliotic Latinity of *The Anathemata*. Hill also shares with Auden a sort of macabre humour which Eliot himself had abandoned by the 1930s. In all these respects, Hill is again subverting rather than following Eliot's later poetics.

Eliot's translation of Perse had already left its marks on English poetry before *Mercian Hymns* appeared, so that Hill's use of a French model is less of a paradox than it may seem at first sight in a poem concerned with the emergence of an English national identity. Moreover, the poem also bears some resemblance to Anglo-Saxon chronicles. This double poetic ancestry corresponds to the complex nature of the England that Hill describes. Offa was *"Rex Totius Anglorum Patriae"*, but this is of course proclaimed in Latin. The sequence constantly stresses Offa's European connections: he is "the friend of Charlemagne" (*HCP*, 105), receives ambassadors, travels to Rome etc. Hill, who regards etymology as a form of history,[41] constantly alternates Anglo-Saxon archaisms ("burh", "darg", "moldywarp", *HCP*, 124, 129, 116) with elaborate Latinisms or quotations from French and Latin. In his attempt to substitute a native history for an Imperial one, Hill unearths the mixed roots of mediaeval England, its interactions with continental Europe. His foreign erudition is perfectly consistent with his visceral Englishness; his insistence on the European dimension of England is of a piece with his rejection of a more recent British Imperial identity. *Mercian Hymns* was published three years before Britain's entry into the EEC, which revealed an England split between a sense of itself as one of Europe's main regions and a cultivation of post-Imperial links through the Commonwealth. Hill's poetry, with its numerous European references, can also be read as an intervention in that debate.

Hill's cosmopolitanism is a quality he shares with Eliot. But Hill reveals his debt to a European heritage which, unlike Eliot's, is now incompatible with the idea of Great Britain. Eliot believed that, regional

---

[39] *The English Auden*, London, 1986, 65.
[40] One example from *Mercian Hymns*: "Drunk, they defy battle-axes, bellow of whalebone and dung" (*HCP*, 130). Hill's use of alliteration will be discussed below. Hill's English concerns in *Mercian Hymns* also echo the subtitle Auden gave to *The Orators*: "An English Study".
[41] Haffenden, *Viewpoints*, 88.

specificities notwithstanding, "the parts of Britain must have in one sense a common culture".[42] This common culture was reflected in the work of David Jones, whom Eliot described as "decidedly a Briton" in his introduction to Jones's *In Parenthesis*. In his own preface, Jones himself writes of his Welsh and English fellow soldiers that "together they bore in their bodies the genuine tradition of the island of Britain, from Bendigeid Vran to Jingle and Marie Lloyd" – the music-hall artist whom Eliot thought embodied the best of English lower-class culture.[43] Hill, on the other hand, distinguishes between the Englishness which is his main concern and a British identity for which he has little time: he has made it clear that he was concerned with "English history, English culture, the English people. And I use the word 'England' deliberately, not as some solecism for Great Britain".[44] Jones was also stressing the importance of a British common ground when he agreed that "the middle ages were not far wrong in choosing Arthur, rather than Alfred or Edmund or Harold, as the central figure of the national heroic legend".[45] Whereas ancient Britain was central to the imagination of the Anglo-Welsh Jones, Hill constructs his *Mercian Hymns* around the emphatically Anglo-Saxon figure of Offa, who was "guardian of the Welsh Bridge" (*HCP*, 105).

However much he may owe to Jones, Hill is at pains to proclaim his difference. *Mercian Hymns* similarly invites comparison and contrast with *Four Quartets*. I have already pointed out how Hill's treatment of childhood makes his exploration of England less problematic than Eliot's. It is also significant that Hill's childhood memories mostly stem from the historical background against which the *Quartets* were written, namely the Second World War. In Hymn XXII, Hill remembers how

> At home the curtains were drawn. The wireless boomed
> its commands. I loved the battle-anthems and the
> gregarious news.
>
> (*HCP*, 126)

---

[42] T.S. Eliot, *Notes Towards the Definition of Culture*, London, 1948, 62. Eliot's sympathy towards regionalism did not extend to nationalism: "For Ireland, Scotland and Wales to cut themselves off completely from England would be to cut themselves off from Europe and the world" (55); "if the nationalistic motive in regionalism were pushed very far, it certainly would lead to absurdity" (58).

[43] David Jones, *In Parenthesis* (1937), introduced by T.S. Eliot, London, 1953, vii, x. For Eliot's comments on Marie Lloyd, see *Selected Prose of T.S. Eliot*, 172-74.

[44] Geoffrey Hill, Interview with Blake Morrison, *New Statesman*, 8 February 1980, 213.

[45] *In Parenthesis*, 13.

This is taken from one of the two hymns entitled "Offa's Defence of the English People"; the other one refers to a "coiled, entrenched England" (*HCP*, 124). Hill's deliberately anachronistic method blurs the distinction between his childhood and Offa's reign, and thus also establishes a kinship between Offa's kingdom and wartime England. In Hymn XIV, Hill reports that Offa "threatened malefactors with his noon cigar" (*HCP*, 118), which rather comically identifies Offa with the cigar-smoking figure of Winston Churchill. This blend of English history and of topical references to the war also characterized Eliot's *Four Quartets*, but once again Hill's account of the English past and of the war's significance is radically at odds with Eliot's. Hill's version of the defence of an isolated island becomes a way of reaching back to an ancestral Englishness that re-emerges as the war is dispelling more recent national myths.

Instead of a pattern of timeless moments that seemed to originate in the period Eliot most admired (the sixteenth and seventeenth centuries) Hill weaves a more complex tapestry, the texture of which incorporates not only a longer period, but also a wider variety of landscapes and experiences. Hill's English history has been rid not only of the delusions of Empire, but also of the abstract transcendence of the timeless moment. His treatment of transcendence in Hymn XXIII is very different from Eliot's:

> In tapestries, in dreams, they gathered, as it was en-
> acted, the return, the re-entry of transcendence
> into this sublunary world. *Opus Anglicanum*, their
> stringent mystery riddled by needles: the silver
> veining, the gold leaf, voluted grape-vine, master-
> works of treacherous thread.
>
> (*HCP*, 127)

This hymn can be read as a subversion of the arresting symbolist bareness that characterizes Eliot's England: "Here, the intersection of the timeless moment/ Is England and nowhere. Never and always." (*ECP*, 215). The transcendence that visits the English experience in the *Quartets* is strikingly abstract; it refines England into an immaterial essence and creates a void around a sudden revelation conveyed in terse paradoxes. Hill's transcendence, by contrast, is caught up in the stylistic, lexical and alliterative intricacies that are the equivalent of the tapestry Hill is describing. Hill further cautions us against its artificial nature: it is a piece of cunning craftsmanship, a "masterwork of treacherous thread". And, as Heather Glen has noted, the section that immediately follows charts, "in its plain Anglo-Saxon, ... an opposite progression"; no longer "the aestheticized attenuation of a mystery in treacherous masterworks, but an increasingly straightforward assertion of a basic human life":[46]

> They trudged out of the dark, scraping their boots
> free from lime-splodges and phlegm. They munched
> cold bacon. The lamps grew plump with oily re-
> liable light.

(HCP, 127)

Whereas the first section of Hymn XXIII was characterized by the alternation between Latinate and Anglo-Saxon words, the latter clearly predominate in the second section. Hill wants to expose the Latinate, Eliotic abstractions that embody "transcendence" as "treacherous", and whereas the latter word is still essentially Latinate, the alliterative movement of the hymn subsumes it in the Anglo-Saxon quality of the words that follow: "masterworks of *treach*erous *thread*./ They *trudg*ed ..." (emphasis mine).

What also distinguishes Hill from Eliot is a far greater sensitivity to physical detail. When Hill writes of "wine, urine and ashes" (*HCP*, 120), one is reminded of Eliot's "flesh, fur and faeces" (*ECP*, 196). However, Eliot's revulsion from physicality has given way in Hill to a fascination that endows the scenes and landscapes of *Mercian Hymns* with a remarkable physical immediacy. In Eliot's "dung and death" (*ECP*, 197), dung is only part of a cycle that ends in death; but when Hill's working men "piss amid splendour; their latrine seeth[ing] its estuary through nettles", they add to the layers that make up the English landscape:

> ... telluric
> cultures enriched with shards, corns, nodules, the
> sunk solids of gravity. I have raked up a golden
> and stinking blaze.

(HCP, 116)

The English soil and the human traces it bears form a continuum for Hill: artefacts and nature flow into one another to produce such phrases as "crypt of roots" (*HCP*, 108), "scrollwork of fern" (*HCP*, 109), "shields of fungus" (*HCP*, 123). The landscapes of *Mercian Hymns* have been so

---

[46] Heather Glen, "Geoffrey Hill's 'England of the Mind'", *The Critical Review*, XXVII (1985), 102.

deeply marked by human activity that they invite decoding: Whereas Eliot's English dead left us "a symbol perfected in death" (*ECP*, 220), Offa "left behind coins, for his lodging, and traces of red mud" (*HCP*, 134). The essence of England must then be reached through archaeological meditation rather than glimpsed through mystical apprehensions of the timeless moment. The method is best illustrated by Hymn XIII:

> Trim the lamp; polish the lens; draw, one by one, rare coins to the light. Ringed by its own lustre, the masterful head emerges, kempt and jutting, out of England's well.
>
> (*HCP*, 117)

The extreme care which Hill takes to make English history palpable, however, suggests that considerable efforts are needed to retrieve it. For if the Second World War and its aftermath sent Hill looking for his poetic England, it also seems to have constituted a watershed that badly damaged the continuities that he is retracing. The paradox that makes those years both inspiring and inhibiting for Hill is clear in his comment that Offa's dominion "endur[ed] from the middle of the eighth century to the middle of the twentieth century (and possibly beyond)" (*HCP*, 200). Calvin Bedient has written that

> for Hill, history effectively ended with the aftermath of the Second World War, the catastrophe of his own young post-war conscience. Always he writes back from there, his sensibility spreading back like a stain (Where Larkin is chockful of contemporary England, Hill might never have left his wartime wireless.[47]

As I have shown, contemporary England can make its way into Hill's poetry, although his rare responses to it definitely betray some unease. There is nevertheless an effort, as Heaney put it, to "make contemporary landscape live in the shadows of a rich tradition".[48] This is indeed what Hymn I by calling Offa as "overlord of the M5" (*HCP*, 105). Hill's search for the persistence of the past also gives rise to his subtle lexical weaving of archaic elements into a twentieth-century scene, as in Hymn XXI:

---

[47] Calvin Bedient, "On Geoffrey Hill", *Critical Quarterly*, XXIII/2 (1981), 18.
[48] Heaney, *Preoccupations*, 160.

"Cohorts of charabancs fanfared Offa's province and his concern ... Their windshields dripped butterflies" (*HCP*, 125). The use of mediaeval terms like "cohort" and "fanfare" to describe a bus trip to Wales might seem forced, but by the time the poem gets to "windshields" Hill has achieved a certain success. The use of the word "shield" resurrects the origin of the metaphor in a way that fuses past and present with near-natural ease.

"Charabancs" suggests that the scene may be taking place in the inter-war period – a period poised on the verge of Hill's great historical divide. But when more contemporary elements blend with the past, Hill's anachronisms sometimes become all too obviously strained. "Overlord of the M5" is already rather dubious, but when in Hymn XVII Offa drives through France in a maroon GT while listening to the car radio (*HCP*, 121), one suspects that Hill himself is perfectly aware of an insurmountable tension. The problems implicit in his method have been accurately described by Hugh Haughton:

> the fraught anachronism of Hill's poetry represents the imaginative pull of the past for a poet obsessed above all by the persistence of what has been lost, and the impossibility of reappropriating it: the idea of continuity – and the stark fact of distance.[49]

Larkin's suggestion that "the past is past" (*The Less Deceived*, 42) is the possibility that Hill's poetry must refute, even though some of his words seem at times to confirm it. Most of all Hill wants to avoid a wholesale rejection of the past. Whether or not a decisive break occurred around 1945, Hill's poetry will reassert the claims of memory. Whereas Larkin's poetry shows a fascination with change and oblivion, Hill's is riddled with marks of a struggle to ward them off.

Larkin rarely wrote about history, but "An Arundel Tomb" can be instructively contrasted with Hill's treatment of similar historical subjects. The comparison will also shed light on the poets' formal and linguistic strategies. Hill's "Requiem for the Plantagenet Kings" (*HCP*, 29) provides an interesting starting point:

> At home, under caved chantries, set in trust

---

[49] Haughton, "How Fit a Title ... : Title and Authority in the Work of Geoffrey Hill", 131.

With well-dressed alabaster and proved spurs
They lie; they lie; secure in the decay
Of blood, blood-marks, crowns hacked and coveted
Before the scouring fires of trial-day
Alight on men; before sleeked groin, gored head,
Budge through the clay and gravel, and the sea
Across daubed rock evacuates its dead.

Although the poem ends on a vision of loss and disappearance, it
paradoxically dwells on the features of the dissolving corpses. The
insistence on "they lie", reinforced by the semi-colons, first seems to
point to a permanence which is then belied by the transformations
heralded by "before". "They lie" is exposed as ambiguous: the
Plantagenet kings are not only supine, their pose is also spurious. The
syntax of the poem progressively loosens, the heavy punctuation gives
way to a more flowing style which suggests the action of the sea that
"evacuates its dead". But the very process of decay is described with such
a careful attention to physical detail that the vanished corpses are made
vividly real; indeed Hill manages to lend a baroque dimension to the
tomb, which may otherwise retain the "plainness of the pre-baroque" of
its equivalent in Larkin's poem (*The Whitsun Weddings*, 45). Moreover,
the corpses themselves come alive in the process of their evacuation,
since they "budge through clay and gravel". Hence the paradox of "secure
in their decay": the elegant pose of the tomb is a lie that Hill exposes by
exploring the reality of what goes on beneath it.

"An Arundel Tomb" similarly moves from the enshrined permanence
of the mediaeval couple in the first stanza to an account of the ravages
performed by time. In the first stanza, Larkin shows how "the earl and
countess lie in stone/Their proper habits vaguely shown/As jointed
armour, stiffened pleat" (*The Whitsun Weddings*, 45). The stanza consists
of one sentence whose main verb suggests the same static quality as Hill's
"they lie", but Larkin similarly puns on that verb, since the poem
eventually suggests that they "hardly meant" their "stone fidelity" (*The
Whitsun Weddings*, 46). The first stanza is self-contained, consisting as it
does of a single sentence; its rhymes are also perfectly regular, which
gives an impression of stateliness which Larkin later exposes as false. As
the poem develops, sentences begin to run across stanzas (most strikingly
in the enjambement leading from stanza 4 to stanza 5), and the change
coincides with the description of the "soundless damage" of time.
Moreover, the full rhymes of the first stanza are eventually replaced by
the systematic half-rhymes of the last stanza. Such formal changes are, as
Paul Foster observes, "mode[s] by which [Larkin] can lead us from the

visual certainties and securities of the initial description to the hesitancies of the final stanza".[50] Larkin, however, does not develop any compensating strategy that would make it possible to restore the dead's concreteness. The tomb is turned from a physical reality into an abstraction which Larkin does not even believe in: an "attitude" which is only an "untruth" (*The Whitsun Weddings*, 46). Unlike Hill, Larkin does not substitute a more authentic reality for the lie that the tomb embodies.

In "An Arundel Tomb", Larkin allows syntax to override the tight formal patterns which he can otherwise so obviously control. In this respect, the poem seems to illustrate what Davie analysed as a return to the syntax of prose in English poetry. Modernism had done away with syntax and cultivated the single word, and Davie argued that such poetics were the aesthetic corollary of a rejection of democracy and an admiration for authoritarianism. Syntax, on the other hand, denies any privilege to the individual word and corresponds to a democratic politics, the "rule of law in the civilized community".[51] Those were the values round which the post-war consensus were established. Davie's interpretation of the uses of syntax in terms of political allegiances has its appeal, but it ultimately fails to account for what turned out to be Larkin's real attitudes towards the Welfare State. Neither does it do justice to Hill's brand of reactionary politics. Hill's poetry distorts syntax, but it is simultaneously haunted by the horrors of fascism; and if Hill is obviously suspicious of present democratic arrangements, he nevertheless remains concerned with the idea of the English people as a community.

In the cases of Larkin and Hill, syntax bears a more indirect relation to ideology than Davie's model suggests. Their respective uses of syntax in "An Arundel Tomb" and "Requiem for the Plantagenet Kings" reflect the differences between their historical imaginations, which may in turn be traced back to different ideological premises. While Davie stresses the levelling effect of syntax, one can also regard syntax as first and foremost a process of change. Syntactic interdependence (in which Davie sees an analogy for democracy) is a synchronic phenomenon, but in the diachronic act of reading, the effect of the flow of syntax is to prevent the reader from dwelling on particular words. As each word is read, it automatically vanishes to make way for what follows. The increasing importance of syntax over formal patterns in "An Arundel Tomb" thus dramatizes the action of time as it questions the ontological stability of the scene.

---

[50] Paul Foster, *An Arundel Tomb*, Chichester, 1987, 30.
[51] Donald Davie, *Purity of Diction in English Verse*, London, 1967, 99.

Hill's use of syntax in "Requiem" could be analysed along similar lines, although his fascination with physical detail provides a thematic compensation. But Hill's poetry (particularly in *Mercian Hymns*) is mostly noted for its tortuous syntax, its arresting lexical curiosities, its alliterative logic and other linguistic extravagances. It often looks as if Hill were distorting syntax so as to break up the horizontal flow of reading and encourage us to read his words vertically. Each word or phrase is a potential well of meanings that must be fathomed through etymological readings, patient hermeneutic brooding or sensuous enjoyment:

> Coiled entrenched England: brickwork and paintwork stalwart above hacked marl. The clashing primary colours – 'Ethandune', Catraeth', 'Maldon', Pengwern'. Steel against yew and privet. Fresh dynasties of smiths.
>
> (*HCP*, 124)

Hill's words long to be compared to Offa's coins: the reader is invited to "draw, one by one, rare coins to the light" (*HCP*, 117). The analogy is also suggested by Hill's description of Offa's coins as "*resonant* in silver" (*HCP*, 115. Emphasis mine). Hill is as it were one of Offa's minters; his hymns, like the coins, are produced at the king's request: "'I liked that,' said Offa, 'sing it again'" (*HCP*, 105).

Hill's words call attention to their ontological status, their rootedness in the reality that they mediate and whose sensuousness they must evoke and embody. Hill's style is often described as chiselled or marmoreal, and has invited comparison with sculpture.[52] The metaphor may also go a long way towards explaining Hill's use of colons and his propensity for appositions. Hymn I is one of the best examples of this strategy, since it consists entirely of noun phrases joined by colons: Offa is "King of the perennial holly-groves, the riven sand-stone: overlord of the M5: ... guardian of the Welsh Bridge and the Iron Bridge: contractor to the desirable new estates: saltmaster: money-changer ... " (*HCP*, 105). This is Hill's first attempt at making Offa emerge from the recesses of English history. Each apposition uncovers a facet of the King's figure; like so many chisel blows on the surface of history they define his many contours.

---

[52] Seamus Heaney has likened Hill to the mason carving a stone in Hymn XXIV, and has offered a sensitive reading of Hill's etymological method (*Preoccupations*, 161).

Larkin's poetry does not always conform to Davie's idea of "syntactical" verse. "MCMXIV" (*The Whitsun Weddings*, 28) is an interesting illustration, since its subject matter is also historical: it summarizes the idealized version of England that supposedly vanished with the Great War. The poem notoriously lacks a main verb, and its static character is reinforced by the title "MCMXIV", which suggests the immobility of a tombstone. But Larkin's series of noun phrases has a radically different effect from the proliferation of appositions that characterize Hill's poems. They constitute an enumerative litany which is more like a series of slides projected in rapid succession than a prolonged meditation upon a single object. The poem ends with an apposition (introduced by a colon) which sums up a past England and declares it to be irretrievable: "Never such innocence again." Whereas Hill ponders gravely on the continuity of English history beyond 1945, Larkin situates an irreparable break at the beginning of the other major shock that was the First World War. The almost casual mention of "fields/Shadowing Domesday lines" parallels Hill's speculation about the endurance of mediaeval history, but it also shows how little Larkin was interested in such long perspectives. Characteristically, his attention is focused on the disappearance of a late Victorian/Edwardian culture. Whereas Hill by-passes Imperial Britain and tries to recapture an ancestral England, Larkin makes no such distinctions: the past, whether British or English, late Victorian or mediaeval, is one in its pastness, and if Larkin explores an England that has been deprived of its British dimension, he does so by focusing on its contemporary aspects. His attention to contemporary detail is such that it can produce lines where syntax is levelled into pure enumeration, but the aim here is not really to underscore the transience of what is described (as in "MCMXIV"), but rather to create a recognizable reality effect: "(Knitwears, Summer Casuals, Hose/In browns and greys, maroon and navy)" (*The Whitsun Weddings*, 30); "Cheap suits, red kitchen-ware, sharp shoes, iced clothes,/Electric mixers, toasters, washers, driers" (*The Whitsun Weddings*, 9).

When one compares Larkin's treatment of history with Hill's, the two-dimensionality of Larkin's past becomes striking. "MCMXIV" seems to be made up of snapshots, and indeed one often gets the impression that Larkin's approach to the past is photographic – as in his reflections on "*the past*" in "Lines on a Young Lady's Photograph Album" (*The Less Deceived*, 13) – or at any rate visual. What matters about the Arundel tomb is whether or not it "involves the eye", and the rest of the poem constantly emphasizes visual impressions: "one *sees*, with a sharp tender shock"; "just a detail friends would *see*"; "succeeding *eyes* begin/ to *look*, not read" (*The Whitsun Weddings*, 45. Emphases mine). Larkin's is essentially a poetry of visual perception, and never more so than when it deals with history. The scene in "An Arundel Tomb" could be recorded by a floating eye. Sight being the most immaterial of the senses, Larkin's past loses much of its substance: nothing opposes the process through which the mind turns its perceptions into pretexts for meditation. Hence the ease with which poems like "An Arundel Tomb" or "Church Going" veer off into abstraction.

Hill's approach, by contrast, calls upon the full range of the senses. No sense organ is left unused in his efforts to convey the English past in all its overwhelming sensuous concreteness: "I have raked up a golden and stinking blaze," "Metal effusing its fragrance, a variety of balm", "He lavished on the high valley its *haleine*", "We ran across the meadow scabbed with cow-dung" (*HCP*, 116, 120, 121, 126),

> ... Crepitant   oak   forest where the boar
> furrowed black mould,   his snout intimate with
> worms and leaves.
>
> (*HCP*, 115)

The difference also lies in the fact that Hill's poems do not include references to a possible observer. The *Hymns* are so steeped in the sensuous ecstasy of their vision that the locus of perception and enunciation is often elusive. Hill suppresses subjectivity so as to allow the landscape to speak for itself. Only in fleeting moments does one get the sense of an underlying voice, though the suggestions are all oblique. The presence of the hymnodist can only be inferred from imperatives that could either be directed at an implied reader or be self-referential: "Trim the lamp" (*HCP*, 117). Moreover, the constant blurring between the identities of King Offa, Hill's childhood self and his poetic persona makes for uncertainty in pronominal reference in many of the *Hymns*. Larkin either uses the figure of an observer (as in "Church Going") or allows the reader to identify with a point of view which, although not clearly mentioned, hovers above the scene that the poem describes. Larkin's perceptions and meditations require the very subjectivity that Hill needs to dissolve in his endeavour to make the past come alive.

Although his poetry has earned him a reputation for forbidding cerebrality, Hill's dissolution of subjectivity sometimes challenges the very instrument that could make sense of any arcane complexity. The sheer sensuousness of *Mercian Hymns* justifies the compliment paid by Al Alvarez on the blurb of Hill's *Collected Poems*: "[he] leaves you not so much with statements to be understood intellectually as with physical states." This is also partly true of *Funeral Music*, of which J. F. Lloyd observes that "even when the language is symbolically motivated, there is a sensuality which remains unincorporated into the symbolic system".[53] The complexity of Hill's poetry should not blind us to the existence of more irrational undercurrents. In this too, Hill is reminiscent of Eliot, whose intellectualism and insistence on impersonality coexisted with an interest in the poetic possibilities of the "depths of feeling into which we cannot peer".[54] Like Eliot, Hill can combine intellectualizing poetics with more irrational obsessions which go beyond such established forms of irrationalism as Christian dogma. Indeed, Hill's imagination sometimes shows signs of a morbid fascination with physical decay that recalls early Eliot, although its object and significance are quite different. The following analyses will show that Hill is as it were fusing some of the features of Eliot's early idiom with the later patriotic ambitions of *Four Quartets*. Eliot acknowledged that "Little Gidding", although the most accomplished of the *Quartets* in his eyes, was different from much of his earlier work in its "lack of some acute personal reminiscence never to be explicated, of course, but to give power from well below the surface".[55] *Mercian Hymns*, on the other hand, shows Hill both at his most patriotic and at his most personal. It is now time to investigate what kind of irrational motivation may be associated with the more sensuous aspects of Hill's writings, and what implications it may have for Hill's re-definition of England.

Mercian Hymns has been seen as a poetic release; Seamus Heaney hailed it as a departure from the somewhat "stiff and corbelled rhetoric" of Hill's previous collections.[56] Its sensuous scenes sometimes thematize release, though in a rather disturbing way:

> Eel-swarms. Coagulations of frogs: once, with branches and half-bricks, he battered a ditchful: then sidled away from the stillness and silence.
>
> (*HCP*, 111)

---

[53] J. F. Lloyd, *Geoffrey Hill and British Poetry, 1956-1986*, unpublished D.Phil thesis, University of Oxford, 1991, 182.

[54] *Selected Prose of T.S. Eliot*, 91.

[55] Quoted in Helen Gardner's *The Composition of Four Quartets*, 67.

[56] Heaney, *Preoccupations*, 163.

The blurring of identities in the collection makes it difficult to determine whether Hill is here evoking his own violent tendencies as a child or the sadistic figure of Offa.[57] Later in the same hymn, Hill describes how a child "flayed" a schoolmate named Ceolred and then "journeyed for hours, calm and alone, in his private derelict sandlorry named *Albion*" (*HCP*, 111). Such violence is not rare in *Mercian Hymns*, and it is conveyed in a language where the harsh concreteness of Anglo-Saxon lexis dominates: "Iron buckles gagged; flesh leaked rennet over them; the men stooped, disentangled the body" (*HCP*, 122). Hill's rhetoric even turns the very soil of England into a metaphor for its ruler's violence:

> Earth lay for a while, the ghost-bride of livid
> Thor, butcher of strawberries, and the shire-tree
> dripped red in the arena of its uprooting.
>
> (*HCP*, 131)

The "traces of red mud" (*HCP*, 134) left by Offa may well have taken their colour from the bloodshed on which Hill dwells in the *Hymns*.

Hill's previous collections were certainly not devoid of a similar fascination with blood and violence; Hill's "connoisseur of blood" could sometimes be applied to himself (*HCP*, 49). Of course, blood has a particular significance within the Christian framework that Hill is using. It is, after all, "Christ's blood" which underlies Hill's declaration that

> By blood we live, the hot, the cold,
> To ravage and redeem the world:
> There is no bloodless myth will hold.
>
> (*HCP*, 16)

Other instances of goriness appear in contexts that are, if only vaguely, religious:

> ... Choicest beasts
> Suffuse the gutters with their colourful blood.
> Our God scatters corruption.
>
> (*HCP*, 63)

---

[57] If the former, one may also wonder what personal charge may have been associated with the eerie descriptions of fields after battle in *Funeral Music* (*HCP*, 72).

Yet Hill's predilection for religious themes only partly accounts for the recurrence of bloody imagery in his poetry. By the time he wrote *Mercian Hymns*, the fastidious restraint that was typical of much of his early verse gave way to an exultation in the possibilities offered by his poetic material, as the passages quoted above have shown. Moreover, the religious framework which gave meaning to Hill's penchant for bloody imagery is no longer available, as the Christian theme recedes into the background. Offa's visit to Rome is motivated by essentially political considerations, and certain hymns endow him with a pagan dimension:

> Tutting, he wrenched at a snarled root of dead crab-
> apple. It rose against him. In brief cavort he was
> Cernunnos, the branched god, lightly concussed.
>
> (*HCP*, 119)

Hill seems in fact to indulge the violent side of his imagination with greater licence when he is writing about English history. His exploration of the violence of the English past in *Mercian Hymns* was already adumbrated in earlier poems. The analysis of "Requiem for the Plantagenet Kings" has already shown how Hill dwelt on the "blood, blood marks, crowns hacked and coveted" and the "gored head" of the dead (*HCP*, 29). *Funeral Music* was characterized by a similar goriness. Bloodletting there is sometimes given a religious dimension, although the rituality of executions is implicitly mocked by the bluntness of Hill's description: "... Crash. The head/Struck down into a meaty conduit of blood", "Spattering block-straw with mortal residue" (*HCP*, 70). In the rest of the sequence, however, Hill's exploration of battlefields has the more secular value of a purely historical record, as he lingers on "the strange-postured dead" beaten into a "human mire" (*HCP*, 71), "Reddish ice [that] tinged the reeds" and the "carrion birds/Strut[ting] upon the armour of the dead" (*HCP*, 76), those who "among carnage" "tup in their marriage-blood, gasping 'Jesus'" (*HCP*, 72). This gasp is an expression of sheer physical excess that thoroughly secularizes its religious origin; the first lines of that poem achieve a similar effect by splitting another religious oath across the enjambement: "They bespoke doomsday and they meant it by/God" (*HCP*, 72). Hill's notes to the poem are even more revealing. Commenting on the beheadings of noblemen that are alluded to in the first poems, he remarks that "in the case of Suffolk the word 'beheaded' is a retrospective aggrandizement; he was in fact butchered across the gunwale of a skiff". Hill further makes it clear that he wanted his sequence to run counter to the tendency to "play down the violence of the Wars of the Roses and to present them as dynastic skirmishes", and points out that "in the accounts of the contemporary chroniclers it was a holocaust" (*HCP*, 200). This seems to be consistent with the historiographic revision that Hill performs from his Tory radical point of view, and which emphasizes the sufferings of the common people. Nevertheless, by the end of Hill's note, one begins to wonder whether his focus does not betray a certain voyeurism:

> one finds the chronicler of Croyland Abbey writing that the blood of the slain lay caked with the snow which covered the ground and that, when the snow melted, the blood flowed along the furrows and ditches for a distance of two or three miles (*HCP*, 201).

If the violence that pervades Hill's poetry has been noted by several critics, it has been analysed in rather broad terms that do not account for crucial differences in his treatment of pain and death. Gervais comments that Hill "studies power with an appalled fascination for the price it extorts from its victims, whether in the Middle Ages or in the Third Reich". Haughton's diagnosis is no different:

> Hill's is undoubtedly an extreme historical imagination, drawn to situations of maximum moral and civil conflict – the fate of the Jews in Europe, the armies of the Plantagenet kings, the 'holocaust' of the battle of Towton, the endurance of poets, prisoners and martyrs, the Crucifixion ...[58]

Such analyses overlook the gradations between Hill's aesthetic treatments of these various extreme situations. Hill himself may not make qualitative distinctions between the catastrophes of human history when he describes Towton as a "holocaust". But there is a marked difference between the almost inhibiting tentativeness of Hill's poems about the concentration camps on the one hand, and the morbid fascination that makes him dwell on the goriness of the English past on the other. Hill is one of the poets who have been most plagued by doubts about the possibility of there being any poetry after Auschwitz, or any poetry that could deal satisfactorily with Auschwitz. His "Two Formal Elegies" for the Jews in Europe hardly dare to touch the "abused/Bodies" of the Holocaust victims (*HCP*, 30). And when Hill alludes to them, he does so with a restraint that

---

[58] Gervais, *Literary Englands*, 253; Haughton, "How Fit a Title ... : Title and Authority in the Work of Geoffrey Hill", 131.

contrasts with the hyperbolic morbidity of the descriptions found in *Mercian Hymns* and *Funeral Music*: "Arrogant acceptance from which song derives/ Is bedded with their blood" (*HCP*, 30).

Hill's interrogation of poetry's claims to encompass the Holocaust reaches its height in "September Song". The poem is also an elegy for the Jews, but as Hill confesses: "(I have made/an elegy for myself it/is true)" (*HCP*, 67). The self-reproaching parenthesis may be another sign that Hill wishes to remain on his guard against any "luxuriating in personality".[59] But this raises the question of how far he has stuck to his critical stance in his explorations of English history. For if the strategy he pursues in *Mercian Hymns* dissolves subjectivity and traditional structures of understanding, it may paradoxically allow him to indulge in what has been termed a form of "morbid fantasizing"[60] through which some darker side of personality comes to the surface (a paradox which was also Eliot's). Thus, while many critics emphasize that Hill brings out the otherness of the English past and makes us aware of an alienation from a deeper England,[61] Hill's blurring of identities between his childhood self and the figure of Offa can also suggest the contrary: "Not strangeness, but strange likeness" (*HCP*, 133). Elsewhere, Hill's recollection of "the omens of childhood" shows that the spell of his early years is an extremely potent one: "So, with an ease/That is dreadful, I summon all back" (*HCP*, 85). Given the strong urge to identify with Offa in *Mercian Hymns*, one may also query whether what results is a fusion of identities or a case of self-projection. One then comes to suspect that Hill's hymns to Offa, instead of bringing a forgotten England to the surface, could be a series of "selfless raptures that are all his own", to borrow the phrase that Hill tantalizingly uses in *An Apology* ... (*HCP*, 153).

Similarly, the language of *Mercian Hymns* may reflect Hill's view that etymology is a form of history, but there are moments when his alliterations and wordplays no longer partake of, but rather compete with his linguistic archaeology. Thus, in Hymn II, Offa's name becomes the basis for a series of variations that link it to contemporary England: "Best-selling brand, curt graffito. A laugh, a cough. A syndicate. A specious gift. Scoffed-at horned phonograph" (*HCP*, 106). Whereas on other occasions Hill is fathoming the diachronic depths of English words,

---

[59] Haffenden, *Viewpoints*, 86.
[60] Fowler, "Geoffrey Hill: Furious, Refined – and Great?", 363.
[61] Gervais thus writes: "to come to terms with history as human experience the poet has to recognize its otherness. The last thing Hill offers us is an opportunity to believe that we are medieval" (*Literary Englands*, 223).

this hymn is a game played within the synchronic system of contemporary English. Such games emphasize the playful aspect of Hill's method, which reminds us that the poem partly finds its roots in a child's imagination. The following phrases from Hymn XXVII are a fine example: "Merovingian car-dealers, Welsh mercenaries; a shuffle of house-carls" (*HCP*, 131). As Vincent Sherry has noted, "car-dealers" and "shuffle of house-carls" combine to create the impression that Hill is shuffling and dealing his own words like playing-cards. In such moments, "anarchy intrudes ... as he enters the alternate order of play".[62]

This has important implications for Hill's archaeological method; indeed, the poet is here trading the rigours of etymology for the liberties afforded by the arbitrariness of synchronic *différance*. It is not a coincidence that the style he devised for *Mercian Hymns* echoes not only Eliot's translation of Perse, David Jones's *The Anathemata* and Auden's *The Orators*, but also the work of another playful literary linguist: James Joyce.[63] The following passages from *Ulysses* display a preference for apposition and lexical sophistication which clearly points forward to *Mercian Hymns*:

> Ineluctable modality of the visible: at least that if no more, thought through my eyes. Signature of all things I am here to read, seaspawn and seawrack, the nearing tide, that rusty boot. Snotgreen, bluesilver, rust: coloured signs. Limits of the diaphane.

> Enter the antechamber of birth where the studious are assembled and note their faces. Nothing, as it seems, there of rash or violent. Quietude of custody rather, befitting their station in that house, the vigilant watch of shepherds and of angels about a crib in Bethlehem of Juda long ago.[64]

The Joycean quality of *Mercian Hymns* raises further questions about Hill's archaeological ambitions; indeed, the most striking aspect of Joyce's historical parallels between Dublin and ancient history is their

---

[62] Vincent Sherry, *The Uncommon Tongue*, Ann Arbor, 1987, 139.

[63] Seamus Heaney hints at a possible debt when he writes that Hill "follows the Joycean precedent set in *Ulysses* of confounding autobiographical material with literary and historic matter drawn from the past (*Preoccupations*, 160). Heaney's comment, however, suppresses the tensions inherent in such a method, for reasons to which we will return in chapter 5.

[64] James Joyce, *Ulysses* (1922), Penguin, 1992, 45, 553.

blatant arbitrariness. The basis of Hill's efforts to blend Mercia and present-day England may after all turn out to be equally fragile. Hill's linguistic methods and the Joycean aspect of *Mercian Hymns* thus reinforce the impression that his exploration of the English past is split between the impersonal claims of archaeology and the temptations of subjective arbitrariness.

The sense of alterity conveyed by Hill's poetry thus seems to have its roots not so much in historical distance (though this is undeniably a factor) as in the nature of Hill's imagination – an imagination which is radically at odds with the historical circumstances it inhabits. Tom Paulin has argued that Hill's sophistication has blinded many critics to the *"Blut und Boden* nature of Hill's imagination".[65] This is not an unreasonable diagnosis, but only if *"Blut und Boden"* are taken in their very literal sense, and are divested of the political implications that Paulin sees in them. In view of Hill's traumatized reaction to Nazi atrocities, charges of fascism would hardly seem fair. It is not difficult to see how Hill's interest in reactionary thinking can have elicited certain hasty parallels between his Tory radicalism and more sinister forms of right-wing extremism. But Paulin pays too little attention to the way in which Hill's politics actually inform – or do not inform – his poetry. Indeed, it would take some effort to read Hill's poems as an endorsement of a particular ideology. This is not only due to its obscurity: Hill's poetry is no coded propaganda either. Rather, the complexity of his verse reflects a general, almost inhibiting scepticism that may well extend to the political tradition for which Hill has openly professed his admiration. To take but one example, the epigraphs which open *An Apology* ... are borrowed from Coleridge ("the spiritual, Platonic old England") and another one-nation Tory, namely the Disraeli who wrote *Coningsby* (*HCP*, 152). But, as I have already pointed out, Hill later exposes "Platonic England" as less than Platonic; as for Disraeli, Hill knows perfectly well that the young novelist who had affinities with Tory radicalism also became the politician who extolled the Imperial vision that Hill criticizes. Moreover, it is hard to believe that Hill could take his own archaic title too seriously.

This is not to deny the reactionary nature of a poetry that is clearly dissatified with post-war English democracy; but the nature of that reaction may be more oblique than Paulin supposes. I would suggest that Hill's poetic explorations of English history are an aesthetic, rather than political, reaction to the dominant post-war mood. Its oppositional character does not lie in a coherently articulated politics, but in its

---

[65] Paulin, *Minotaur*, 281.

baroque and Gothic fascination with a violence that was so lacking in the period in which Hill was writing. Alastair Fowler's comments on Hill's taste for bloody imagery are quite revealing: "It is hard not to relate [Hill's] goriness to that of Hughes's *Crow* (1970) and to see both poets as having succumbed to the 1960's lust for violent emotion."[66] The next chapter will analyse how Hughes's poetry was itself a critical way of engaging with its post-war context. In the meantime, the parallel between both poets can be taken further, as *Mercian Hymns* invites comparison with Hughes in other ways. When Hill writes that "the princes of Mercia were badger and raven" (*HCP*, 110), he identifies England with the sort of wild animals which Hughes turned into his own totems of Englishness.[67] Likewise, in *Funeral Music*, Hill describes armies waiting for battle "with England crouched beastwise beneath it all" (*HCP*, 72). He also referred to his sequence as "a florid grim music broken by grunts and shrieks" (*HCP*, 199), which proves than he can occasionally relinquish the stately formalities of his verse to allow more barbaric strains to come to the fore.

What should be emphasized is that this tends to happen when Hill is most concerned with defining England. If he indeed "correct[s] the bloodlessness of Eliot and Larkin"[68] the correction is not simply a swing of the pendulum against a dominant poetic idiom: it takes place within a specific cultural context. Unlike the England of Eliot (which was indeed Platonic in its abstraction), and unlike the England that vanishes in Larkin's nihilistic moments, Hill's England must cling to a sense of itself as vividly substantial. If Hill insists on the blood shed in the course of English history, it is not only because he wants to revise Eliot's aristocratic chronicle by substituting a more populist version. One may query whether Tory radicalism can accommodate the voyeurism of Hill's descriptions of suffering in *Funeral Music* or *Mercian Hymns*. For all Hill's rationalizations of violence and martyrdom in Elizabethan literature,[69] the main reason behind his own emphasis on the violence of the English past may be that it provides an aesthetic gratification to an imagination that cannot rest content with Larkin's neutral landscapes.

---

[66] Fowler, "Geoffrey Hill: Furious, Refined – and Great?", 364.
[67] Hughes finds the body of a badger during the "high moment of driving through England" in 'Coming Down through Somerset' (*Moortown*, 48). Hill's raven can be compared with Hughes's crow, although the latter is a problematic emblem (see chapter 4).
[68] Fowler, "Geoffrey Hill: Furious, Refined – and Great?", 364.
[69] See "The Absolute Reasonableness of Robert Southwell" in *The Lords of Limit*.

Hill's historical poetry ultimately turns out to be a complex blend of political meditation and aesthetic recreation (in both senses of the word), which makes his position unique within the context in which his poetry appeared. Hill was admittedly not alone in wishing to divert attention from the delusions of British Imperialism and revert to native English roots: as we have seen, John Fowles also sought to rediscover a remote, Green England (to which Hill adds a dark red tinge). Moreover, the revival of interest in the native past was far from uncommon among post-war English historians. But Hill's agenda differs from theirs in one key respect. Indeed, Fowles and the post-war historians were essentially concerned to provide a historical justification for the new political values that had come to dominate English culture. The focus on the *"English* national past" in post-war historical studies was part of a "Whig interpretation of history" which regarded the Welfare State as the *telos* of the history of the nation.[70] As David Cannadine has pointed out, English history was depicted as "a great and unique drama in which, century after century, revolution followed revolution so inexorably that no self-respecting period of the British past seemed complete without one". And yet,

> the succession of revolutions was presented as being simultaneously dramatic yet benign: in the sixteenth century because the Tudor revolution came from above and was carried out by due process of law; in the seventeenth because the long-term effects of the Civil War were minimal and of 1688, beneficial; in the eighteenth because the industrial revolution was generally held to be a good thing; and in the nineteenth because revolution was avoided and reform and improvement triumphed instead .... We can now see more clearly that the end-product was essentially the old Whig history of Britain's privileged yet pioneering past dressed up in Butskellite guise.[71]

Fowles's mythologizing account illustrates a similar view of England's past: the Green England of Robin Hood was interpreted as a precedent for the introspective mood and the striving for social justice within a liberal framework that characterized Welfare State culture. The "subversive

---

[70] Peter Ghosh, "How We Got Where We Are", *London Review of Books*, 28 November 1996, 18.
[71] David Cannadine, "The State of British History", *Times Literary Supplement*, 10 October 1986, 1139.

ideal" of the true Englishman is "to live in the justest country in the world", Fowles saw this ideal as underpinning the creation of the Welfare State. The "Green England" was thus te source of the Whig/Labour/Democrat movement that initiated social reform.[72]

Hill's politics, incompatible as they are with any form of "Whiggery", do not accord with such a version of English history. Whereas the Welfare State historians offered rather sanitized versions of crises in English history and sometimes came close to dismissing the Wars of the Roses as an inflated myth,[73] Hill re-emphasizes the violence of mediaeval conflicts, stresses the "mannerly extortions" that lay behind the eighteenth-century vision of a Platonic England (*HCP*, 160) and the physical sufferings of the lower classes during the industrial revolution.[74] At the centre and origin of it all lies the reign of Offa, "martyrologist" (*HCP*, 105) and violent ruler. But if Hill's imagination is drawn to Offa rather than Robin Hood, the reason is not that the former's reign has direct political implications for the present. Rather, Offa gives Hill the opportunity to voice an aesthetic protest which is not really directed against the political content, but chiefly against the cultural forms produced by the English Welfare State.[75] Offa is not a political model (except in so far as he contributed to the unification of England), he is a figure of sensuous excess through which Hill can perform an oblique critique of post-war blandness and English decency, qualities which he explicitly associates with late Eliot and Larkin.[76]

In the collections that followed *Mercian Hymns*, Hill reverted to quieter modes and the more elaborate forms that he had given up in favour of prose poetry. His taste for bloody scenes has not disappeared altogether, as is made clear by the morbid feast of his "Pre-Raphaelite Notebook" (*HCP*, 167), but it now manifests itself more rarely. In *An Apology* ... Hill's baroque imagination abandoned mediaeval battlefields and settled

---

[72] Fowles, "On Being English But Not British", 154-55, 160.

[73] See Hill's note to *Funeral Music*, see also A.J. Pollard's *The Wars of the Roses*, London, 1988, 14-15.

[74] "It is one thing to celebrate the 'quick forge', another to cradle a face hare-lipped by the searing wire" (*HCP*, 129).

[75] Hill's dissatisfaction with the post-war cultural scene becomes quite explicit when he complains that, as a playwright, Eliot "could genuinely mistake 'the fashionable requirements' of Shaftesbury avenue or the Edinburgh Festival for the needs of a 'wider audience'" (*The Lords of Limit*, 135-36). In the light of that remark, Hill's forbidding obscurity can also be seen as an expression of cultural dissent.

[76] See "Dividing Legacies", 22-24.

instead on the sublimations of Gothic architecture and on the "quaint
mazes" (*HCP*, 152) of an intricate style that complies with the exigencies
of the sonnet form. Its landscapes are on the whole more civilized, and
Hill's attention to detail now focuses on more peaceful images that are
almost brittle in their refinement:

> The twittering pipistrelle, so strange and so close,
>
> plucks its curt flight through the moist eventide;
> the children thread among old avenues
> of snowberries, clear-calling as they fade.
>
> (*HCP*, 159)

The violence of civil and religious conflicts and of sensual excesses is
now hinted at rather than indulged in: "it is the rood blazing upon the
green", "tremulous boudoirs where the crystals kissed" (*HCP*, 152, 160);
ultimately that violence is subsumed in a vision that achieves a synthesis
of nature, culture and religion: "Touched by the cry of the iconoclast/
how the rose-window blossoms with the sun!" (*HCP*, 164). This is a
vision of fullness that reasserts the unity of English culture and landscape
while simultaneously recalling the conflicts that have marked its history.
Hill's own exposure of violent oppression may be a form of iconoclasm
too, but it paradoxically becomes another contribution to the persistence
of England expressed in the final image. Hill's blossoming rose-window
can also be pitted against the vision of emptiness that Larkin had offered
a few years earlier:

> ... the thought of high windows:
> The sun-comprehending glass,
> And beyond it, the deep blue air, that shows
> Nothing, and is nowhere, and is endless.[77]
>
> (*High Windows*, 17)

The exquisite, though never quite naive images of England in *An
Apology* ... might suggest that Hill had made concessions to more
traditional forms of nostalgia for "Old England". But Hill has vigorously
defended himself against such charges, agreeing with John Haffenden's

---

[77] The "sun-comprehending glass" recalls the light that "thronged the glass" in the
church of "An Arundel Tomb" (*The Whitsun Weddings*, 45). The intensity of Larkin's
nihilism also introduces a sort of inverted religious quality in the poem.

suggestion that "to celebrate a thing is not necessarily to endorse it".[78]
Hill's call to "celebrate that kingdom" (*HCP*, 164) is not one from which
political implications are easily drawn; instead, it directs our attention
towards the sensuous background against which conflicts are played out.
Just how much that background provides a lasting English substratum,
however, is less and less certain. Another of Hill's defences against the
charge of nostalgia sheds a different light on the matter:

> I'm accused of being nostalgic when in fact I'm trying to draw
> the graph of nostalgia. The painter Francis Bacon said
> somewhere that he was 'trying to paint the track left by human
> beings like the slime left by a snail', and it seems to me that in
> poetry also one is trying to trace the track left by human beings.[79]

The parallel with Bacon is instructive: "traces of red mud" are the last
glimpse of Offa that Hill can catch (*HCP*, 134), and the goriness of
Bacon's paintings matches that of *Mercian Hymns*. Bacon's work was
part of a reaction against "the Platonic purity of forms beloved of 1930s
modernists" – artists like Nash, whose visual classicism found a poetic
correlative in Eliot's *Four Quartets*.[80] Turning away from the simplified,
depopulated landscapes of Nash, Bacon focused instead on the suffering
of human figures: in a similar move, Hill rejects the appeal of Eliot's
silent music and draws attention to the butchered victims of mediaeval
battles and the shouts of martyrs. But Bacon's words concerning the
"tracks left by human beings" also remind us of Hill's doubts about the
endurance of Offa's dominion. And in Hill's latest collection *Canaan*,
they find an echo that shows Hill almost adopting Larkin's sense of
England as a country drained of substance:

> England – now of genius
> the eidolon –
> unsubstantial yet voiding
> substance like quicklime
>
> (*Canaan*, 1)

---

[78] Haffenden, *Viewpoints*, 93.
[79] *Ibid.*, 89.
[80] See Bryan Appleyard, *The Pleasures of Peace*, London, 1989, 63, and Steve Ellis,
The English Eliot, 24-25, 111.

However, Larkin's fascination with nothingness remains the enemy: when Hill dissociates himself from "enthusiasts of sublime emptiness/ mountaineering into old age" (*Canaan*, 70), he is alluding to "Extinction's alp" in Larkin's "The Old Fools" (*High Windows*, 20). Hill's England must remain substantial: whether mud, quicklime or blood, this substance must ward off the sense of an "England gone" which would deal a fatal blow to his historical imagination. At the same time, he must also acknowledge how much that imagination depends on the possibility of final dissolution. His England is paradoxically at its most vivid when he contemplates its disappearance. Canaan inclusdes a poem about oblivion, "Sorrel", which still manages to evoke some of the sensuousness that was so central to *Mercian Hymns*:

> Memory worsening – let it go as rain
> streams on half-visible clatter of the wind
>   lapsing and rising,
> that clouds the pond's green mistletoe of spawn,
> seeps among nettlebeds and rust-brown sorrel ...
>
> (*Canaan*, 40)

Canaan also confirms the renewed importance of Christian religion in Hill's work after the pagan interlude of *Mercian Hymns*. In the last sonnet of *An Apology* ..., Hill's appeal to a religious transcendence imbued with patriotic overtones already signalled a shift away from the more purely aesthetic concerns of *Mercian Hymns*. By the time he wrote his sonnet sequence, Hill had reasons enough to abandon the oblique form of criticism that had found expression in the sensuous savagery of Offa, and to turn instead to a more direct form of public commentary. For the object of his criticism was changing: Welfare State England was already in the last stages of the collapse that led to the advent of Thatcherism. Hill had earlier denounced the bland consensuality of English culture through his apocalyptic visions of mediaeval battlefields. But, ironically enough, the tensions amid which the post-war consensus broke down earned a Shakespearean name that recalled the Wars of the Roses. The "Winter of Discontent"[81] rhetorically re-opened the sort of conflict which Hill had aestheticized in order to create a space where his imagination could take refuge. The political developments that followed also required him to adopt a more properly political stance. Not only was his aesthetic criticism of Welfare State culture losing its *raison d'être*, but his one-

---

[81] The phrase comes from the opening lines of Shakespeare's *Richard III*.

nation Tory radicalism was becoming increasingly marginalized by the rise of neo-liberalism. As a consequence, Hill turned to the ethical concerns and public themes that he explores through the politically-loaded Christian rhetoric of *Canaan*.

Hill's main complaint is now that England has become the temple of a new philistinism that he condemns from his embattled point of view. In *An Apology* ... Hill had written of the English kingdom that "its truth shows disrepair" (*HCP*, 164); now he asks:

> Keep what in repair?
> Or place what further
> toll on the cyclic
> agony of empire?

> (*Canaan*, 51)

Canaan shows a poet who is traumatized by Thatcherism. Thatcher's exploitation of Imperial nostalgia during the Falklands War proved that the British identity that Hill dismissed had more resilience than he had previously reckoned. But Hill's invective is mostly directed against the new materialism that thrived as a result of the neo-liberal revolution. Lady Thatcher – originally the daughter of a Grantham shopkeeper – is the butt of Hill's irony in "Dark-Land": "Aspiring Grantham/rises above itself" (*Canaan*, 13). The various poems entitled "To the High Court of Parliament *November 1994*" allude to the cash-for-questions affair that exposed the new materialism at the heart of British parliamentary politics: The "strutting lords" have been admitted "to the temple" (*Canaan*, 49). Hill's satire can even assume a directness that contrasts with his usual obliqueness:

> ... your right ranters,
> proud tribunes, place-men,
> shape-shifting nabobs,
> come the millennium.

> (*Canaan*, 51)

> prize apologists
> for plebeian nobleness, who would have found it hard
> telling one servitor from another, who spun
> half-crowns to enlightenment – I take this penny –
> grant inequity from afar to be in equity's covenant,
> its paradigm drawn on the fiducial stars
> its aegis anciently a divine shield

over the city.

(Canaan, 70)

Hill's increasingly archaic populist radicalism now leaves him with
little choice but to reach back to William Cobbett, whose critique of a
nascent industrial capitalism already hinted at "Commodity with uplifted
hands/awed by its own predation" *(Canaan,* 9). His emphasis on
England's European identity must now face the fact that Europe is
dominated by the "liberties of Maastricht" – a softer version of
Thatcherism *(Canaan,* 30). While Hill still clings to his radical Tory
principles, he ends his collection on a note that implicitly acknowledges
their lack of political purchase on the present. Turning his gaze to the
Westminster parliament and "Barry's and Pugin's grand/dark-lantern
above the incumbent Thames", he wonders:

> Who can now speak for despoiled merit,
>   the fouled catchments of Demos,
> as 'thy' high lamp presides with sovereign
> equity, over against us, across this
> densely reflective, long-drawn, procession of waters?

(Canaan, 72)

The interrogative mode implies that Hill's own critique does not emanate
from a standpoint which can lay claim to poetic, discursive or political
representativity. Hill must eventually seek refuge in the densely self-
reflective mood of his brooding on lost traditions which married the
aesthetic with the political and the religious. It is the latter dimension that
now provides a correlative for Hill's essential England, as the barbaric
sensuousness of Offa's Mercia makes way for the Christian concept of
"Mercy" – a word that recurs throughout *Canaan* (8, 13, 25, 36, 42, 48,
60, 63). Mercy is now made central to a vanishing England which only
survives in the homespun religious heritage to which Hill is clinging.
Reflecting on "a track of peculiar virtue – English – which so
often/deceives us by the way", he writes:

> Exhaustion is of the essence, though in the meantime
> what song has befallen those who were laggard
> pilgrims, or none. It is as you see. I would not
> trouble greatly to proclaim this.
>   But shelve it under Mercies.

(Canaan, 42)

Another interesting word in these lines is "you". Hill has attacked Eliot's use of the pronoun in "Little Gidding", complaining that Eliot had chosen to communicate by didactic "tone" rather than by aesthetic "pitch".[82] Whether Hill's own use of the second person in *Canaan* partakes of tone or pitch may be hard to decide. What is certain is that it sometimes betrays an exasperation which results from the isolation of Hill's complex talent, but also tends to lend it the cantankerousness of a frustrated erudite:

> There was a time, any Methodist could have told you
> Ebenezer means stone of help.
>   As for the rest,
> ruunt in servitium, crammed vacancy's rabble –
> this also is admitted: *introit turba.*
>
> (*Canaan*, 71)

Welfare State England had provided the context against which Hill devised some of his most original poetic idioms. But the realities of neo-liberalism have now taken over, and Hill's response to the change is a collection which appears divided in ways that are more aesthetically damaging than the tensions which informed volumes like *Mercian Hymns*. Muttered prayers and occasional flashes of sensuous music alternate with a political diatribe which cannot but doubt its own relevance. One is not sure whether the formal diversity and the dislocated typography of *Canaan* are meant to reflect the dissolution of England or whether they betray the fact that England as a subject is slipping from Hill's poetic grasp.

Hill's next collection *The Triumph of Love* rehearses the grievances of *Canaan* in an even more embittered mode. "Britannia's own narrow/miracle of survival", the "British walking-wounded" continue to weigh on Hill's England and to thwart what he sees as a genuine self-understanding, so that what is left is "a nation/with so many memorials but no memory" (*The Triumph of Love*, 7, 47, 40). The sensuous England of *Mercian Hymns* has now receded even further than in *Canaan*, its evocation is now both desolate and acerbic: Hill's "exasperated ears" still occasionally catch

> archaic burrings like a small, high-fenced
> electricity sub-station of uncertain age

---

[82] "Dividing Legacies", 22-23.

in a field corner where the flies
gather and old horses shake their sides

(The Triumph of Love, 26)

Once again, Hill is as it were rewriting Larkin's "At Grass", but the complex ironies of *An Apology...* have been replaced by a cantankerousness that invites comparison with another Larkin – the Larkin of the infamous, self-loathing letters. Hill can wrest poetic brilliance from that pose, as in his self-description as an "incontinent/fury wetting the air" *(The Triumph of Love,* 19), but his self-reproach too often seems to be a way of pre-empting criticism.

Hill still remains closer to the sensuous felicities of his earlier style when he evokes a landscape which he orders himself to renounce:

Leave it now, leave it; give it over
to that all-gathering general English light,
in which each separate bead
of drizzle at its own thorn-tip stands
as revelation.

(The Triumph of Love, 26-27)

This, of course, is also "England at once too weepy and too cold" *(The Triumph of Love,* 74); Hill's lingering fascination with the minutiae of England remains shot through with a criticism that has become increasingly shrill. His latest poem still attests to the "inevitable feelings of love and hate which any man and woman must feel for the patria".[83] But despite its title, one cannot help but suspect that *The Triumph of Love* has tipped the balance in favour of Hill's exasperation – both at England and at his own incurable attachment to it.

---

[83] Haffenden, *Viewpoints,* 94.

CHAPTER THREE
ENGLAND AGAINST NATURE?: TED HUGHES

On the face of it, a comparison between Geoffrey Hill and Ted Hughes could amount to an exploration of one of the major faultlines that divide the landscape of contemporary English poetry.[1] Hill often appears as a highly cerebral poet of culture, Hughes as a daemonic poet of nature whose exaltation of instinct clashes with Hill's intellectualism. But the preceding chapter has shown that when Hill relaxes his formal and ironic controls, currents emerge that are similar to those that run on the surface of Hughes's poetry. On the other hand, one should not underestimate the extent to which Hughes has attempted to give formal and intellectual consistency to the play of primitive energies on which his imagination thrives. It does not therefore come as a surprise that the opening poems of their respective first collections (published in 1957 and 1959) reveal a remarkable degree of convergence, while simultaneously pointing forward to the different paths their authors would take and to the points where those paths would cross again.

Both "The Hawk in the Rain" (*The Hawk in the Rain*, 11) and "Genesis" (*HCP*, 15-16) describe struggles with the elements: Hughes's speaker faces a "banging wind" that "thumbs [his] eyes, throws [his] breath, tackles [his] heart", and the violence in the opening sentence of Hill's poem is as vigorous: "Against the burly air I strode" (*HCP*, 14). The "dead weight" of the land of "Genesis" conveys the same sense of inertia as Hughes's "ploughland", the "clay that clutches … each step to the ankle". Hill's account of beginnings then turns to a bestiary which both echoes and anticipates some of Hughes's descriptions of animal violence. While the salmon "ramming the ebb in the tide's pull" (*HCP*, 15) were still waiting to unleash their power in Hughes's *River* (1983), the bird of prey with its "triggered claw/Feathering blood along the shore" was already a well-known feature of English poetry in the late 1950s: Hughes's first collection was filled with such creatures. Hughes's hawk in the rain would also reveal its murderous side in the chilling monologue "Hawk Roosting" (*Lupercal*, 26), in which many critics saw an apology for violence. In "Genesis", Hill's speaker first wants to "beware" of creatures "Forever bent upon the kill", but he eventually comes to a surprisingly Hughesian conclusion:

---

[1] See for instance Martin Dodsworth's "Ted Hughes and Geoffrey Hill: An Antithesis", in *The New Pelican Guide to English Literature: 8. The Present*, ed. Boris Ford, London, 1983, 81-93; or "The Final Contention between Geoffrey Hill and Ted Hughes" in Eric Homberger's *The Art of the Real*, London, 1977, 210-15.

By blood we live, the hot, the cold,
To ravage and redeem the world:
There is no bloodless myth will hold.

(*HCP*, 16)

Of course, the myth on which Hill is drawing here is a Christian one, and
his poetry has repeatedly found inspiration in the religion against which
Hughes built his darkest myth of violence in *Crow*. Hill remains
poetically committed to a cultural heritage with which Hughes sometimes
showed little patience in his quest for primal energies. But the second
chapter has shown that Hill's exploration of Christian themes in his first
two collections was sometimes motivated by aesthetic rather than
religious considerations. In those cases, Hill's use of religious motifs was
sometimes far from orthodox. And in *Mercian Hymns*, Hill's violent
imagery was stripped of its religious dimension as he attempted to capture
the essence of England in the sensuous, barbaric excesses.

This shift in Hill's poetic priorities could actually be summarized by
the transformation that takes place in Hughes's "The Hawk in the Rain".
Indeed, Hughes's poem is the secular misreading of a religious poem,
written by an author whose latent interest in English nationhood has been
brought out and foregrounded by Hughes. Hughes openly acknowledged
his debt to Gerard Manley Hopkins, and Hopkins's influence is nowhere
more evident than in "The Hawk in the Rain", which is clearly inspired
by Hopkins's sonnet "The Windhover". "The Hawk in the Rain" seems
so derivative at times that one may guess why Hughes chose not to
include it in his *Selected Poems*, despite the importance it clearly had
when the eponymous collection was first published. Nevertheless, the
poem constitutes a revealing development in English poetry. For if
Hopkins's strongly stressed and alliterative music had not lacked
imitators before, Hughes's poem may well be the first to be informed by a
consistent and original interpretation of Hopkins's work.

I will have various occasions to return to Hughes's use of alliteration.
What needs stressing here is that the alliterative quality of much of his
poetry cannot be dissociated from his attempt at reviving a more ancient
mode of English poetry: the mediaeval, Anglo-Saxon tradition which was
gradually supplanted by the Norman invasion, Latinization and the
introduction of regular metre. For Hughes, those two processes coincided
with the social and religious changes through which England eventually
"lost her soul".[2] The original English poetic tradition went underground

---

[2] Ted Hughes, *Winter Pollen*, 119.

and occasionally surfaced in the works of marginal figures like Hopkins, whom Hughes took as models in his own attempt to restore the poetic sensibility of an older England. Hughes's extended discussion of the rival traditions of English verse devotes several pages to an analysis of the first lines of "The Windhover".[3] In "The Hawk in the Rain", alliteration, sprung rhythm and the long succession of epithets in some lines ("and I/Bloodily grabbed dazed last-moment-counting/Morsel in the earth's mouth") are so many stylistic strategies which Hughes obviously borrowed from Hopkins. Thematic similarities with "The Windhover" hardly need mentioning, since in both poems the speakers are observing a kestrel. The originality of Hughes's poem lies in the way it resolves the ambiguity of its model and adapts Hopkins's religious idiom to its own secular concern, that is a revolution in poetic perceptions of England.

Hopkins's sonnet[4] bears the dedication "To Christ our Lord". But although "The Windhover" celebrates Christ through the figure of the kestrel, the terms of its praise are not always clear. While in the first eight lines the speaker is lost in the rapturous contemplation of the bird's mastery of the air ("the achieve of, the mastery of the thing"), the sestet introduces a complication: "Brute beauty and valour and act, oh, air, pride plume here/Buckle!" Several interpretations of the verb have been proposed, and the coherence of Hopkins's poem hinges upon the resolution of its ambiguity. In one of its more archaic meanings, "buckle" suggests a preparation for battle, which would tie in with the use of a chivalric vocabulary to describe the hawk ("King-/Dom of daylight's dauphin"). Another meaning, ("clasp, fasten together") would imply a continuity with the praise of the bird's control in the preceding lines. The third meaning ("collapse") would by contrast point to a radical change of tone.[5] Hughes for his part has firmly opted for this last interpretation of the verb in his own poem, and has amplified its effects: the speaker speculates about the sudden and violent collapse of the hawk:

> Fall from his eye, the ponderous shires crash on him,
> The horizon trap him; the round angelic eye
> Smashed, mixed his heart's blood with the mire of the land.

---

[3] *Ibid.*, 337ff.
[4] Gerard Manley Hopkins, *The Poems of Gerard Manley Hopkins*, eds W. H. Gardner and N. H. MacKenzie, Oxford, 1970, 69.
[5] The different meanings are considered in the notes to *The Poems of Gerard Manley Hopkins*, 267-68.

Hughes's last line is based on a reading of "The Windhover" which relates the sudden exclamation "Buckle!" to the images developed in the last tercet of Hopkins's poem:

> ... sheer plod makes plough down sillion
> Shine, and blue-bleak embers, ah my dear,
> Fall, gall themselves, and gash gold-vermilion.

The "gash" of the last line establishes a connection between the fall of the embers and the crucifixion of Christ. This retrospectively encourages the reader to interpret "buckle" as a sudden renunciation of strength, an act of sacrifice through which the Christ-like kestrel prefers the majesty of self-immolation to the "brute beauty" and "pride" of his mastery: "AND the fire that breaks from thee then, a billion/Times told lovelier, more dangerous, O my chevalier!"

In this reading, Hopkins implies that it is through sacrifice that Christ brings redemption. However, the imagery of the poem turns what is primarily an act of self-abnegation into a thrilling aesthetic climax: Christ's death is "lovelier, more dangerous", and the concluding image does not point to the moral and spiritual example set by Christ, but primarily conveys a strong sense of visual delight. Some critics are accordingly disturbed by the fact that "the crucifixion is being seen as beautiful".[6] This departure from Christian dogma, however, plays into the hands of Hopkins's self-styled pagan heir. Indeed, the redemption that Hughes's hawk might bring by "mix[ing] his heart's blood with the mire of the land" is a thoroughly secularized version of the ambivalent sacrifice that Hopkins describes. What Hughes has done is to carry Hopkins's lapse from a strict adherence to orthodoxy to an extreme conclusion: "The Hawk in the Rain" invests most heavily in the celebration of the sheer violence of natural life.

Considering the ease with which Hughes was to transform Hopkins's poem, one can understand why Eliot, reviewing recent developments in English poetry from the height of his dogmatic position in 1934, expressed doubts about the religious dimension of Hopkins's verse and dismissed him as "a nature poet".[7] However, "The Windhover" did not belong to the mainstream of English nature poetry. Its unusual diction and lexical extravagances combine with the sheer excess of its ecstatic vision to make it unorthodox in one more respect than in its equivocal

---

[6] See John Robinson, *In Extremity: A Study of Gerard Manley Hopkins*, Cambridge, 1978, 51.
[7] T. S. Eliot, *After Strange Gods*, London, 1934, 48.

representation of sacrifice. Indeed, its violently exalted tone breaks the bounds of the traditional English rural idyll. It was not in fact until Hughes produced his own misreading that one found Hopkins's technical, linguistic and thematic idiosyncrasies gathered and magnified in a manifesto for a radically new kind of English nature poetry.

By the late 1950s, conditions may have been propitious for such a change. In a climate marked by the waning of the Christian faith, Hughes rid Hopkins's celebration of natural processes of its already problematic religious dimension, and turned its exuberance into a protest against the quieter representations of the English landscape that were still being proposed by the heirs of Hardy's empiricism. Hughes's hawk is a missile launched against the "ponderous shires" of Southern English rural and suburban melancholy, it is set on a collision course with poets like Davie, whose collection *The Shires* embodied a residual core of traditional Englishness years after those shires had been hit by Hughes's violence. This violence was also directed against the "stubborn hedges" that run across English hills, recalling nature's submission to the social laws and human arrangements which are Davie's central concerns. In that respect, Hughes was also playing off the Hopkins who wrote "Inversnaid" ("long live the weeds and the wilderness yet") against the Hopkins who could still grow lyrical about "landscape plotted and pieced" in "Pied Beauty".[8]

Hughes's dissatisfaction with the traditional aesthetics of English scenery is matched by a desire to animate the national landscape with a redeeming violence: if the hawk is finally vanquished as "the ponderous shires crash on him/the horizon trap[s] him", his blood "mix[es] with the mire of the land". In this poem, Christian imagery, though divested of its original spirit, still provides Hughes with the raw material of his quest for a new poetic vision of England. For as Hill wrote, "there is no bloodless myth will hold" (*HCP*, 16). Interestingly, the tensions between the demands of religious orthodoxy and the temptations of aesthetic vision in Hopkins's work have not only proven fruitful ground for Hughes. They have also been related to Hill's own use of ritual in a poetry which is no longer sustained by the absolute certainties of faith. Comparing Hopkins and Hill, Christine Pagnoulle notes the lack of doctrinal coherence in Hopkins's praise of Christ in poems like "The Windhover", and adds "this incoherence is the gash or gap into which Hill's anguish of absence comes pouring in".[9] Hill may also have inherited more than an interest in

---

[8] *The Poems of Gerard Manley Hopkins*, 89, 69.

[9] Christine Pagnoulle, "Music Alone Survives? Collapsing Faith in Some Sonnets by Gerard Manley Hopkins and Geoffrey Hill", *Cahiers Victoriens et Edouardiens*, XLII (1995), 104.

the liturgical traditions on which Hopkins drew. The darker side of Hopkins's baroque imagination seems to have survived in Hill as well as Hughes. And Hopkins's idiosyncratic brand of patriotic populism, expressed in an often arcane poetry, may also have set an example for Hill.

Hill's relation to Hopkins is less crucial than Hughes's open indebtedness, but Hopkins mattered to both poets for similar reasons. The final images of "The Windhover" and "The Hawk in the Rain" provide yet another context in which to analyse the grim visions of Hill's *Funeral Music*: "Recall the wind's/Flurrying, darkness over the human mire" (*HCP*, 71); "Among carnage the most delicate souls/Tup in their marriage blood, gasping 'Jesus'" (*HCP*, 72). Hopkins's hesitation between the claims of Christian orthodoxy and the violent sensuousness of his poetry is more openly dramatized in the last line: the exclamation "Jesus" becomes an expression of sheer ecstasy that is erotic and macabre all at once. As for Hughes, his poetry tips the balance decisively in favour of pagan excess and violence. Those transformations of Hopkinsian excess have particular implications for Hughes's and Hill's views of England. *Funeral Music* and similar passages from *Mercian Hymns* showed an attempt to reopen the wounds of a national history which had been rarefied into abstraction by Eliot and was threatened by the dazzling absences of Larkin's forgetting. Whereas Hill's equation of a residual England with violence assumes the form of an imperative addressed to memory ("Recall", *HCP*, 71), Hughes pursues a similar objective mostly through incantations to elemental and natural forces – the very forces that Eliot had dismissed as "daemonic, chthonic/Powers" (*ECP*, 213). However, some of Hughes's forays into English history do resemble Hill's, the difference being that Hughes's poems are predictably less encumbered by the historical decorum which retains its attractions for Hill. Hughes's "The Martyrdom of Bishop Farrar" can easily be compared with *Funeral Music*. Whereas Hill described his sequence about the victims of mediaeval conflicts as "florid grim music interrupted by shrieks and grunts" (*HCP*, 199), Hughes's vivid and phonetically suggestive rendering of Farrar's death by burning on the stake tries to render the martyred bishop's half-human cries, the "black oozing twist of stuff" that he has become (*The Hawk in the Rain*, 58).

The contrast between the complexity of Hill's historical imagination and Hughes's reliance on more immediate forms of excess is also reflected in their responses to Hopkins's linguistic innovation. Hughes is mostly interested in the ways in which the sensuous surfaces of Hopkins's verse (his strong stresses and consonants) revive an original tradition of English verse. Hill, on the other hand, has inherited Hopkins's passion for etymology and his taste for daring lexical coinages.[10] He praises Hopkins for his ability to fathom the "etymological stratum" of English in a poetry laden with the "hereditary accruals of the vernacular". When Hill describes Hopkins's use of a "native and natural rhythm of speech" as "ideological", he hastens to add that "this is not said in reproof": ultimately, Hopkins's "vocation was to redeem the time".[11] Hill's definition of etymology as history parallels Hughes's view of phonetics as a battlefield on which English cultural struggles have been enacted. But despite a difference in emphasis, both Hughes and Hill invest Hopkins's poetics with similar political associations.

In a sense, Hopkins was an obvious model for Hughes and Hill to turn to in their explorations of a primitive England that had been obscured by Victorian Britain. Hopkins's poetics were largely marginal in the Victorian age from which they were kept secret. The discovery of Hopkins after the First World War coincided with the emergence of modernism, which meant that his poetics would chiefly be noted for their obscurity, rather than for their Romantic English populism. It is this aspect, however, which was foregrounded by the poets who started their careers in the aftermath of the Second World War and the loss of Empire. Hughes, who is even more eager than Hill to dissociate himself from British Imperialism, connects the heyday of the Empire with the apogee of the national language's alienation from the Anglo-Saxon roots which Hopkins tried to keep alive. Hughes traces modern standard English back to the language of "the military garrison of the Empire", an "officers' mess and parade ground vocal system which we inherit as Queen's English".[12] In a comment which is clearly indebted to Hughes, Tom Paulin writes that "Hopkins's language issues from the ranks, not the officer class".[13] Hopkins's interest in sprung rhythm, dialect and etymology point to a Romantic valuation of English folklore which also underlies the populism of "Tom's Garland" or "Harry Ploughman" – poems that point forward to Hughes's idealized portraits of English rural types like Dick Straightup (*Lupercal*, 17).

---

[10] For instance, Hill's "wiry heath-fern" in *An Apology* (*HCP*, 162) condenses the "wiry heathpacks, flitches of fern" of Hopkins's "Inversnaid" (*The Poems of Gerard Manley*, 89). The echo was noted by Tom Paulin in *Minotaur*, 281.

[11] Geoffrey Hill, *The Lords of Limit*, 151, 97, 103.

[12] *Winter Pollen*, 119. Hill used a similar vocabulary when he praised the poet Ivor Gurney for his "bid to wrest the 'English manner' from the hands of the officer class and to bestow it upon comrades in 'heavy servitude'". See "Gurney's Hobby", *Essays in Criticism*, XXXIV/2 (1984), 105.

[13] Tom Paulin, *Minotaur*, 91.

It can be tempting to explain Hopkins's eccentric poetics and his marginal status through Hughes's readings. But Hopkins's politics are more shifty and elusive than this account suggests. His poem "What shall I do for the land that bred me" is a jingoistic piece which wouldn't pale in comparison with Kipling, whose talent for tapping the resources of demotic English speech also reminds us that such poetics do not necessarily challenge Imperialism.[14] Although Hopkins's poetry often conveys a sense that "England [was] wife/To [his] creating thought",[15] it remains difficult to abstract a coherent national vision from his writings. "What shall I do for the land that bred me" seems to flow from the Imperialistic jingoism which also made him bemoan the fact that his country had been "shamefully beaten by the Boers". But his strong sense of Englishness was at other times compatible with support for Home Rule in Ireland. In one of his letters, he reports that "Home rule or separation is near .... I shd. be glad to see Ireland happy, even though it involved the fall of England".[16]

Hopkins's nationalism, though deeply felt, reflected tensions between different versions of Englishness which he may not have felt called upon to solve. On the other hand, the ideological configuration in which Hill and Hughes emerged as poets encouraged the kind of renewed attention to native English resources which Hopkins's untimely project had embodied decades earlier. Hughes's distaste for British Imperialism underlies the savage caricature of "The Retired Colonel", "a Mafeking stereotype" looking "As if he had Victoria rolled/In a Union Jack". This "man-eating British lion" is set beside emblems of a more authentic Englishness, like "the last English/Wolf" or "the last sturgeon of Thames" (*Lupercal*, 42). Both are kin to the ancestral pike that haunts the pond of the English unconscious: "Stilled legendary depth:/It was as deep as England" (*Lupercal*, 57). A "killer from the egg" (*Lupercal*, 56), Hughes's pike is the animal equivalent of the murderous figure of Offa. The real England is not to be found in recent history, but in a past so distant that it lays itself open to imaginative recreation. Indeed, Hughes almost seems to derive the very graphemes of the word "England" from the adjective "legendary" in the preceding line: his England, like Hill's Offa, is also "cushioned on a legend" (*HCP*, 117).

---

[14] In Hopkins's case, it may be significant that "What shall I do for the land that bred me" is a poem which does not bear the mark of his stylistic innovations. Hopkins was also unsure about his use of the word "England" in the poem, wondering whether it might not be "too exclusive" (*The Poems of Gerard Manley Hopkins*, 316. Note 156).
[15] *Ibid.*, 101.
[16] Gerard Manley Hopkins, *Selected Prose*, ed. Gerald Roberts, Oxford, 1980, 97, 150.

The denunciation of the Empire and of its psychological legacy is constant in Hughes's work, from the early caricature of "The Retired Colonel" to the ritual gesture of "The Ghost Dancer" who "puffs the stump of Empire up in smoke" (*Wolfwatching*, 53). Imperial attitudes are part of the negative characterization of most of the male characters in *Gaudete*: their mechanical sterility is recurrently emphasized and contrasted with the hyperbolic vitality of the protagonist Lumb, who releases his energies on the women of an English village and thus cuckolds all the local husbands. Among those men is Hagen, who plots revenge on his wife's lover: "Humiliation of Empire, a heraldic obligation/Must have its far-booming say" (34). Lumb's presence in the village is comparable to the music played by one of the daughters of the village: it "vandalizes the ponderous ill-illumined Victorian house" and "beat[s] at the faded ochre prints of imperial battles" (44).

Whereas the nature poems in *Lupercal* located England in the national landscape, *Gaudete* ends with Lumb re-emerging "in the West of Ireland" (9). This might seem puzzling at first, but Hughes's Englishness, unlike Hill's, does not exclude Celtic elements. Whereas Hill can at times pass for an overscrupulous historian, Hughes's bold primitivism can lead him so far back in history as to turn his quest for Englishness into a rediscovery of Celtic Roots. *The Remains of Elmet* are set in a region which was the "last British Celtic Kingdom to fall to the Angles" (9); in *Moortown Diary*, where Hughes describes a part of Devon that resists "stray infiltrations of modernity", the local farmers remind him of "that Celtic tribe the Romans had known as the Dumnoni" (viii). Whereas the adjective "British" in "The Retired Colonel" was invested with negative Imperial connotations, it becomes positive when synonymous with "Ancient Briton", a term which is central to the archaeology that Hughes practises in *Remains of Elmet*.[17] As I will have other opportunities to show, Hughes's Englishness would ideally merge with the Celtic culture of ancient Britain, rather than keep it at bay like Hill's Offa. This also explains why Hughes is quite unperturbed by the fact that Hopkins's poetic experiments drew on ancient Welsh poetry as well as on Anglo-Saxon. Hill never mentions this aspect of Hopkins, which would complicate the terms of his praise. It was after all quite fitting that Hopkins, as Hughes approvingly points out, followed his exploration of native traditions "through Wales into Ireland"[18] – a journey that Hughes and his protagonists have never been reluctant to make.

---

[17] See for instance the poem "The Ancient Briton Lay Under His Rock" (*Remains of Elmet*, 84).
[18] Hughes, *Winter Pollen*, 49.

The significance of Hopkins's art for Hughes and Hill gives the lie to Eliot's pronouncement that Hopkins's innovations were "not adaptable for many purposes".[19] Twenty years after that dismissal, English poetry was faced with realities that Eliot could not have envisaged. England's renewed attention to native roots provides the rationale for the uses to which Hughes and Hill put Hopkins's linguistic experiments. But one still has to explain why his exalted, baroque sensuousness should have been inflated into the fascination with excess and violence in which Hill's and Hughes's imaginations also meet.

Hughes, like Hill, is a declared admirer of Francis Bacon. His poem "A God" (*Moortown*, 156) is strikingly reminiscent of Bacon's crucifixions, particularly in its comparisons of Christ to slaughtered animals. Hughes's description of the crucifixion reads like a close up of the butchered, flayed or tortured figures whose cries disturb the decorum of Hill's verse. Not surprisingly, the two poets have given different reasons for their interest in Bacon: whereas Hill related Bacon's techniques to his own views on memory and the subsistence of traces, Hughes has spoken of Bacon as one of the artists who envision "something deeper than what you lose if civilization disappears".[20] Once again, Hill's imagination is inextricably bound up with historical concerns, whereas Hughes's veers off more readily in the direction of myth. But Bacon's appeal may have deeper and common roots for both Hill and Hughes.

At this stage, one should bear in mind that only two years separate the births of Hughes (1930) and Hill (1932), and that both poets started publishing in the late 1950s. By that time, the changes that had affected Britain had already sparked off a first poetic reaction that had come to be known as the Movement. However, the distinctive brand of Little Englandism with which it was associated had been turned into an orthodoxy centred round empiricism, common sense and decency, against which rebellion was swift in coming.[21] In such a cultural climate, Hughes and Hill were welcomed by critics like Al Alvarez, who were eager to overthrow the domination of Movement attitudes. But whereas Alvarez largely proposed an a-historical psychologism and cosmopolitanism inspired by American models, both Hughes and Hill were still quite

---

[19] Eliot, *After Strange Gods*, 47.
[20] For Hill's comment, see Haffenden, *Viewpoints*, 89. Hughes's words appear in an interview with Ekbert Faas: "Ted Hughes and *Crow*", in Ekbert Faas's *Ted Hughes: The Unaccommodated Universe*, Santa Barbara, 1980, 207-8.
[21] Movement orthodoxy was largely propounded by Robert Conquest in his introduction to *New Lines*. The spokesman of the rebellion was Al Alvarez in his introduction to *The New Poetry*.

willing to take part in the debate on England's identity. The need for a poetic counter-orthodoxy does not by itself completely account for the specific direction in which both poets chose to contribute to the redefining of national self-perceptions.

The fact that Hughes and Hill belong to the same generation does not only mean that both were in an ideal position to meet the demands of a shifting poetic taste at a particular time. They also share more. Indeed, both experienced the realities of wartime England as children living in provincial parts of the country. Hill comes closest to a personal account of that period in *Mercian Hymns*, XXII:

> At home the curtains were drawn. The wireless boomed
> its commands. I loved the battle-anthems and the
> gregarious news.
>
> Then, in the earthy shelter, warmed by a blue-glassed
> storm-lantern, I huddled with stories of dragon-
> tailed warships and warriors who took wing im-
> mortal as phantoms.
>
> > (*HCP*, 126)

This can be compared with the following autobiographical sketch by Hughes:

> My [youthful] writing grew mainly out of my reading. I specialized in fantastic happenings and gory adventures. I set my tales, generally, North of the Great Divide, in the Wild West, in tropical jungles, and Africa – places as far away as possible from the sooty town I lived in and the gloom of the war.[22]

This is complemented by the explanatory note to one of his Laureate poems, where Hughes explains that he wants to

> re-shuffle back into the pack of relative meanings under that word "nationalism" the British experience of the first half of this century, when both national and personal survival were threatened, everything collapsed to the basic scenario and nothing was listened to but the private crystal-set under the breastbone – the sacred tones of "the ring of the people", on the simplest human wavelength (*Rain-Charm for the Duchy*, 59-60).

---

[22] *Winter Pollen*, 4.

Those passages point to the importance of the historical background against which two similar poetic imaginations were shaped. They developed in a complex mixture of attraction to and reaction against the various national self-projections that were made available to them. On the one hand, the gloom that had descended on the country generated a youthful escapism into fantasies of a morbid or violent nature. For both Hughes and Hill, the Second World War embodied first and foremost the state of inertia into which their rural surroundings were plunged, rather than the large-scale destruction of urban centres (though Hughes obviously has that in mind too when he talks about "survival", and the drawn curtains of the family house in *Mercian Hymns* show that the danger from German aircraft was omnipresent). On the other hand, the emotional patriotism broadcast by the wireless and the crystal-set made a strong impression on both future poets.

The wartime patriotism which had fed their consciousnesses would have to be adapted in the yeard hat followed. The onus was on them to ensure its survival in a personal, retrospectively internalized form ("under the breastbone") which would constitute the bedrock on which they built new poetic versions of English patriotism. This new patriotism had to meet two requirements. First, it had to be ideologically different from the loud British patriotism of the Empire, which was now increasingly discredited. Second, it had to possess the emotional power of the "anthems" and the "ring of the people" that had been such potent wartime symbols. This meant that their attraction to excess would also provide a contrast to the bland decencies which the poetry of the early 1950s was thought to reflect too slavishly. The violent fantasizing of their youthful escapism provided both poets with a material to match, readily available, and belonging to the same strata of their development. Such a mixture could not easily be accommodated in the mainstream English poetic tradition, which explains why Hughes and Hill often turned towards marginal poets in their search for models. Not surprisingly, they were drawn to similar figures. Among these, Keith Douglas is an interesting example, since his work stresses the importance of the Second World War for both poets. Hill's use of Douglas in *Funeral Music* and his review of Hughes's selection of Douglas's poems have been discussed in the preceding chapter. In his introduction, Hughes characteristically emphasizes Douglas's marginality – "he seems to have no difficulty with the terrible, suffocating, maternal octopus of English poetic tradition" – and also writes that the war "brought his gift to maturity".[23] Hill's and Hughes's comments thus betray the importance of the conflict in their

---

[23] *Winter Pollen*, 213, 214.

own imaginations. Hill's poetry sometimes conveys a "sense of guilt about having come too late; of having been spared because he did not have to fight a war; of not being a survivor of personal, political or religious persecution".[24] Donald Davie has described Hughes's attitude in similar terms: "[Hughes] seems to regret having been excluded, by being born too late, from the carnival of violence which World War legitimized".[25] Davie's rhetoric sounds somewhat unfair, but his comment has a certain relevance to some of Hughes's writings, to which we will return.

Hopkins was another important figure, whose aesthetics now set a precedent for Hill's and Hughes's respective projects. Hopkins's propensity towards baroque excess was attractive enough, but it also found expression in a form that drew heavily on the ancestral, popular and often marginalized resources of the national language. And while their fascination with Hopkinsian excess would constantly threaten to destabilize the coherence of their visions of England, Hughes and Hill started to explore those resources in order to devise styles that would fit their concern with nationhood.

Hill and Hughes also emerged in the years when an old-fashioned English philologist rose spectacularly to the status of cult novelist. Although Tolkien's popularity (which spread world-wide) cannot be solely explained by a renewed attention to native English roots, the fact remains that *The Lord of the Rings* is not such an unlikely book to mention in the same breath as Hughes's poetry, or even *Mercian Hymns*. The parallel goes beyond an exploitation of philology: Tolkien's versions of ancestral legends fused a potent sense of adventure with an equally strong attachment to a remote, native English past.[26] Hill retrospectively identified his childhood self with the first king of England, and this violent hybrid creature was then let loose in the rich, intimate and barbaric English landscape of *Mercian Hymns*. Hughes's own strategies took a variety of forms which this chapter and the next will explore. But it will be necessary to keep in mind that Hughes and Hill differ from Tolkien in one key respect. *The Lord of the Rings* has been read as an allegorical account of England's role in the Second World War, in which the hero leaves the quiet atmosphere of the Shire to confront the dangers that lie beyond it. Hughes and Hill, on the other hand, attempt to identify

---

[24] See E. M. Knottenbelt, *Passionate Intelligence: The Poetry of Geoffrey Hill*, Amsterdam, 1990, 103.

[25] Donald Davie, *Under Briggflats*, Chicago, 1989, 220.

[26] The fact that the novel also became a cult text for the emerging ecological movement offers another interesting parallel between Tolkien and Hughes.

a marginal England with danger and violence. This seems to have clear political implications: it will hardly be possible to argue, as Donald Davie has done with regard to *The Lord of the Rings*, that their poetry could be interpreted as an allegory about the nature of power which ultimately extols the virtues of Welfare State democracy. Tolkien's trilogy, in Davie's view, celebrates the wisdom of (English) popular common sense at the expense of authoritarianism, so that if "the book answers to a hunger for the heroic", "the driving force of the book is unheroic, even antiheroic".[27]

But the fact that Hughes and Hill were reacting against the "civic" poetry of which Davie was the main spokesman does not necessarily imply that their works can be read as apologies for the authoritarianism which Davie denounced. The main reason is not really that they favour a kind of right-wing English populism that steers clear of totalitarianism, although such politics can have an appeal for them. The contrast between Hill and Fowles developed in the preceding chapter showed that Hill's difference does not ultimately reside in his admiration for radical Toryism, but in a cultivation of aesthetic excess. Similarly, I would suggest that Hughes's vision of England is indeed, to adapt Davie's terms, an aesthetic reaction against the "unheroic", but that it is also too complex to be identified with ideological forms of hero-worship.

Hughes's need to recapture an authentic England is reflected in his poems about nature and English history as well as in his use of techniques that hark back to the very sources of English poetry. It has also informed a substantial part of his critical writings over the years. But one should be wary of drawing hasty parallels between the poetry and what looks like its discursive rationalization in the hope of arriving at a stable definition of Hughesian Englishness. Both poetry and theory exhibit contradictions which thwart the emergence of a coherent idea of nationhood. Consequently, the critical relation in which Hughes's work stands to post-war England comes to consist in an essentially aesthetic gesture – one which is hard to reconcile with the political interpretations which it may invite or propose. Hughes's quest, perhaps more than Hill's, paradoxically attests to the growing impossibility of fusing aesthetic and ideological envisionings of England. Indeed, Hughes's work is perhaps one of the places in which some of the fusions that were attempted in the history of English poetry and criticism are finally undone.

In a sense, it is hardly surprising an accomplished nature poet should have become Poet Laureate. Ever since Wordsworth turned away from London

---

[27] Donald Davie, *Thomas Hardy and British Poetry*, London, 1973, 94, 98.

and withdrew in the Lake District to explore his roots, there has been a tendency in English poetry to identify England with nature, a tendency which was reinforced by the ruralism whose sources Martin J. Wiener has analysed: "having pioneered urbanization, the English ignored or disparaged cities"; after the industrial revolution England "became ill at ease enough with its prodigal progeny to deny its legitimacy by adopting a conception of Englishness that virtually excluded industrialism".[28] As John Lucas has pointed out, the movement of the *Prelude* "becomes increasingly familiar throughout the following two centuries: the heart of England is to be found in rural circumstance". This trope "will gather different political meanings": whereas Wordsworth's ruralism underpinned an essentially conservative vision of England, John Clare has been championed as a poet whose contribution to English nature poetry reflected a challenge to the existing political order.[29] What both share with most other nature poets, however, is the view that nature is a locus of wholeness, a healing spring of life, a refuge from the spread of a mechanical civilization which increasingly threatens to blot it out. The poetic longing for the organic unity of nature can either ratify a pastoral version of Burkean conservatism or prompt a revolt against the class who branded the landscape of England with signs of their oppressive ownership. But in both cases, the nostalgic gesture remains the same.

By the time the Georgians produced their own version of that theme, the idealizing nostalgia that pervades English nature poetry had become a means of expressing patriotic feeling on the eve of the First World War, as was shown by the smooth transition from Rupert Brooke's celebration of the beauties of England to his bellicose poems.[30] Georgian nature poetry would not recover from the slaughter: as Hughes himself has observed, "apart from Owen and Sassoon, the poets lost that war. Perhaps Georgian language wouldn't look half nearly so bad if it hadn't been put to such a test".[31] Since then, growing urbanization reached a stage where

---

[28] Martin J. Wiener, *English Culture and the Decline of the Industrial Spirit 1850-1980*, London, 1985, 1, 3.

[29] John Lucas, *England and Englishness*, 74. For Lucas's advocacy of Clare, see 148-51.

[30] Nature poetry was sometimes characterized by a love of England which, as in the case of Edward Thomas, seems hard to reconcile with the jingoism of War propaganda. But the example of Rupert Brooke shows that "as forms of nationalistic patriotism these positions and tones were not incompatible .... the militaristic beast would have had difficulty existing without the aesthetic beauty, just as the kitbag would have sagged without the body of literary tradition to stiffen it". See Peter Brooker and Peter Widdowson, "A Literature for England", in *Englishness: Politics and Culture 1880-1920*, eds Robert Colls and Philip Dodd, 122.

[31] *Winter Pollen*, 71.

it became possible for Donald Davie to declare that "nature poetry is a world well lost". Davie accordingly dismissed Hughes's poetry as outdated or merely eccentric, since it focused on aspects of England that have become so marginal that they look Irish rather than English. Instead, he argued that modern democratic arrangements and a thoroughly hmanized landscape were the real challenge for English poets:

> It was English poetry (with Wordsworth) that in modern times first expressed ideas of elemental sanctity and natural piety; and it seems it must be English poetry which asks what to do with those ideas in a landscape where virtually all the sanctuaries have been violated, all the pieties blasphemed.[32]

This, Davie suggests, is the challenge that Larkin takes up and Hughes evades. But it is unfair to dismiss Hughes as a writer who desperately attempts to continue a dead tradition against the odds of modernity. For one thing, not all his nature poems take English scenes as their subject. Like D.H. Lawrence, Hughes has not infrequently taken his nature-worship outside England – parts of *River* are even set in Alaska. This may be a way of recognizing, as Lawrence also did, that it has become increasingly difficult for England to coincide with nature. On the other hand, English landscapes and animals remain central to many of Hughes's poems, where they are sometimes made to assume the status of national totems – "Pike" is the most famous example. But Hughes's identification of England with nature represents a significant departure from the tradition which extolled the organic wholeness of natural life or the healing powers of the natural sublime. Only in his poetry for children can he be found continuing that tradition: in *Season Songs*, Hughes describes the wind as a "tenderness/Lifting through all the/Gently-breasted/Counties of England".[33] Such Georgian effusiveness is at best marginal in Hughes's other volumes. Instead, Hughes seems rather intent on disrupting the harmony that dominates mainstream representations of the English landscape. In the early "Wind", Hughes's imagination is drawn to the "woods crashing through darkness, the booming hills", "the fields quivering, the skyline a grimace". He thus finds aesthetic gratification in a landscape gone mad, where he can hear "the stones cry out under the horizon" (*The Hawk in the Rain*, 40).

"Horizon" is a favourite word of Hughes's, and its recurrence in the poems has prompted Tom Paulin to write that it gives his nature poems "a

---

[32] *Thomas Hardy and British Poetry*, 72.
[33] Ted Hughes, *Season Songs*, London, 1975, 20.

distinctively American turn".[34] However, Hughes himself has linked his use of the word with the landscape of his home town in Yorkshire, in a valley dominated by an oppressively tall, dark cliff:

> If any word could be found engraved around my skull, just above the ears and eyebrows, it would probably be the word "horizon". Every thought I tried to send beyond the confine of that valley had to step over that definite hurdle.[35]

Paulin can easily be excused: if Hughes's landscape belongs to English geography, it falls beyond the established boundaries of poetic England. Consequently, what looked Celtic to Davie looks American to Paulin. But Hughes's introduction of unfamiliar Northern landscapes in English poetry is more than a symptom of the growing importance of the North in English writing after the Second World War. Hughes is not simply claiming for his native geography the sort of central status which Southern landscapes had tended to occupy in English poetry (though the originating moment of that tradition was located in the Lake District). For although Northern landscapes may be more dramatic than Southern ones, they do not always meet the demands of Hughes's imagination. They may seem to do so in "Horses", whose ending relies wholly on the strengthening potential that Worsdworth attributed to memories of natural scenes:

> In din of crowded streets, going among the years, the faces,
> May I still meet my memory in so lonely a place
> Between the stream and the red clouds, hearing curlews,
> Hearing the horizons endure.
>
> (*The Hawk in the Rain*, 16)

But in "Pennines in April", the Hughesian impatience with static landscapes, expressed in "Wind" and underlined in "The Rock", surfaces again to destabilize Hughes's North: "If this country were a sea ... these hills heaving/Out of the east ... Must burst upwards and topple into Lancashire" (*Lupercal*, 28).

The Hughesian sublime is kinetic rather than static, it tends to generate fantasies of apocalyptic violence ("*If* this country") instead of offering regenerating visions which can persist in human memory.

---

[34] Paulin, *Minotaur*, 259.
[35] Ted Hughes, "The Rock", in *Writers on Themselves*, ed. Herbert Read, London, 1964, 90.

Hughes's imagination does not draw sustenance from its landscapes but rather imposes its violence on them. Similar nightmarish visions haunt the extravagant narrative of *Gaudete*: as flowers turn into "eruptions" in the distracted mind of one of the characters, "he imagines the still Sargasso of it, rising and falling, right across England" (71). The very ideal of an organic connection with the English soil almost becomes suspect: "the blueing bowl of landscape/Is a migraine of inescapable fixities" (157); "He sees the reeds sticking up out of the water/So conceitedly dull in their rootedness" (165).

Many of Hughes's landscape poems conspicuously lack the nostalgic plangency which had been distinctive of much English nature poetry. This could mean that nature can now become the subject of a poetry untainted by what Edward Thomas, in an ironic moment of self-analysis, called "the modern sad passion for Nature".[36] Its disappearance opens numerous possibilities for nature poetry, but Hughes often seems primarily concerned to shatter the clichés of the tradition he is subverting. Instead of presenting reassuringly organic images of natural settings, Hughes focuses on images of hyperbolic violence that distort or explode organicism. Farms now become "oozing craters in/Sheer sides under the sodden moors" (*Lupercal*, 14). Hughes's rural England is the scene where violence holds sway. The grim Northern landscape is aesthetically stimulating only in so far as it is the prey to destructive processes. "Heptonstall" illustrates this perfectly: the hill is a "collapsed skull", a landscape "Drained to sutures/Of cracked windowsills" (*Wodwo*, 165). This poem paves the way for *Remains of Elmet*, in which it was later included. There, farms become "stony masticators/Of generations that ate each other/To nothing inside them" (53). There is of course a certain melancholy about the descriptive poems of that collection. But the elegiac mood which runs through *Remains of Elmet* is not limited to the descriptions of rural scenes. It also embraces passages which are devoted to the vanished industrial glories of the Calder valley: "The sunk mill-towns were cemeteries/Digesting utterly/All with whom they swelled", they are reduced to "An absence, famished and staring,/To pick among crumbling, loose molars" (*Remains of Elmet*, 53). There is little sense here that the industrial revolution wrecked the harmony of the natural environment. Natural and industrial scenes are given the same treatment; Hughes's stark descriptions of decay make them almost interchangeable. The effect of his style is similar to that of the black and white photographs which accompany the poems, and where all distinctions

---

[36] Edward Thomas, *The Heart of England* (1906), Oxford, 1982, 66.

between nature and culture are abolished by their absorption in a single chromatic range.

Remains of Elmet makes it necessary to qualify Davie's contrast between Hughes's obsession with natural themes and the supposedly more authentic envisioning of England that Larkin developed in "The Whitsun Weddings".[37] The difference is not always one of focus, but one of attitude. Yet even here, matters are more complicated than Davie's account suggests. Larkin's tone in the second stanza of "The Whitsun Weddings", in which Davie recognizes "the congested England we have all inhabited", can indeed be described as "scrupulously neutral" – a neutrality which Davie finds refreshing after decades of sometimes cloying nostalgia.[38] But one may query whether Hughes's poetry is the best contemporary illustration of the perennial English tendency to mourn the disappearance of an idealized countryside. Indeed, Hughes was the leading English landscape poet of a time when the decline of the industrial spirit analysed by Wiener had been compounded by the conspicuous decline of the industries which that spirit had sustained.[39] This can explain why Hughes also strikes a melancholy tone when his gaze comes to rest on the vestiges of industrial activity.

Their elegiac mood of Hughes's landscape poems further coexists with a stylistic exultation in the possibilities offered by decay.[40] Its recurring images of broken spines, empty skulls, wasting mouths and distorted limbs exude an aesthetic fascination which Hughes acknowledged when he mentioned the "grim sort of beauty" and the "spectacular desolation" which followed the collapse of local industries (*Three Books*, 183). Hughes's poetry in fact colludes with the destruction which his own metaphors tend to magnify: the very rendering of the destruction of Elmet actually endows its scenery with an excess of presence. The effect is not dissimilar to that of Hill's description of England as "voiding substance like quicklime" (*Canaan*, 1), and in both cases the sheer vividness of the metaphors gives us a key to the real nature of the contrast between Hughes and Hill on the one hand, Larkin

---

[37] Davie, *Thomas Hardy and British Poetry*, 64-65, 73. One may add that Larkin had his ruralist moments too – "First Sight", for instance, is a touching poem about new-born lambs (*The Whitsun Weddings*, 36).

[38] *Thomas Hardy and British Poetry*, 64.

[39] In economic terms, the decline of British industry goes as far back as the beginning the century, but it was during Hughes's lifetime that closures and the decay of industrial sites really became a defining feature of British landscapes.

[40] David Gervais even writes that Hughes "greets rather than laments the decline he describes". See David Gervais, "Ted Hughes: An England Beneath England", *English*, XLII/172 (1993), 69.

on the other hand. The latter's scrupulously metonymic recordings of English scenes paradoxically led into visions of absence, whereas Hill and Hughes generate ontological value out of their metaphorical treatment of a vanishing England.

What is also striking about *Remains of Elmet* is that the images called up by rural decay and industrial decline are little different from those which are used in the description of a tree swaying in a storm in "Tree": "A priest from a different land" on the heath, the tree "Smote the horizons/With the jawbone of emptiness." "Tortured by huge scaldings of light", "Stripped to his root-letter, cruciform", the tree "tried to confess all" but eventually "Lets what happens to him simply happen" (*Three Books*, 50-51). The absence of any nostalgic dimension in this description casts further doubt on the nostalgia which may characterize other poems. In his metaphors, Hughes makes no distinctions between historical change, religious allegory and natural phenomena. Whether the violence perpetrated against the landscape is the result of specific historical processes or whether it originates in the environment itself ultimately seems to be of little relevance. Hughes's poetry depends on such violence for its effects and is ultimately less interested in its sources (indeed, it will create it if necessary) than in its intrinsic value. Hughes is not really mourning rural or industrial England; instead, he is investing in the aesthetic possibilities of its decay. Poetry becomes a last bid to endow England with an ontological intensity which exceeds nostalgia and its various ideological underpinnings. The substance of England is now to be found in the sheer pain and violence that its tormented landscapes radiate.

Hughes's sequence of poems about farming also illustrates his radical revision of English nature poetry. In the preface to the separate edition of *Moortown Diary*, he seems to prepare the reader for a poetic lament on the lost virtues of English rural life, with hints of reactionary xenophobia thrown in for good measure:

> The ancient farming community of North Devon was still pretty intact and undisturbed, more so than anywhere else in England. No industrial development or immigrant population had ever disrupted it (vii).

> How rapidly that changed within the next decade, how completely that ancient world and its spirit vanished (viii).

We were dragged ... into that seismic upheaval which has been,
probably, one of the biggest extinctions so far in the evolution of
English countryside and farming tradition (ix).

In these comments, Hughes's sympathy with the plight of the Devon
farmers coexists with a broader reactionary ruralism. The poems
themselves, however, provide little evidence of any nostalgia for the lost
organic wholeness of the farming community. The elegiac mode is
reserved for the poems dedicated to the memory of Hughes's father-in-
law Jack Orchard; it never spreads to his descriptions of farming life
proper. Instead, rural existence is powerfully evoked through a
deliberately blunt free verse that works against sentimentality. Hughes
seems committed to rendering his experiences as faithfully as possible.
This means that *Moortown Diary* has been hailed by some as an
unprecedented development in English nature poetry. David Gervais sees
it as an effort to do away with the pastoral mode in which a whole line of
English poets from Wordsworth to Thomas had approached a similar
subject matter:

> Pastoral poetry is notoriously artificial, and Hughes was seeking
> something even more artless than the down-to-earth kind of
> pastoral Wordsworth wrote in "Michael" .... Only through a non-
> literary language could rural life figure as a more basic kind of
> experience. This is what justifies his decision to write as a farmer
> himself and not, like Thomas, as a pastoral poet observing
> sympathetically from the outside. Only by eschewing the earlier
> poet's music was there any chance of recovering another England
> from beyond the great English landscape tradition .... The sense
> of his work as of something as immediate as the pulsing of blood
> is uncommon in poems about England.[41]

Gervais therefore concludes that those who regarded *Moortown Diary* as
a wistful celebration of a lost ideal are mistaken: Hughes's sharp accuracy
means that his sequence is thematically capacious enough to tackle
experiences which earlier poets had neglected. Quoting from Hughes's
description of the birth of a calf, Gervais observes that "one wouldn't
have guessed that this sort of thing also happened on Thomas's 'Manor
Farm'". Hughes's landscapes are indeed of a kind in which "no Georgian
poet would have lasted for more than five minutes".[42]

---

[41] Gervais, "Ted Hughes: An England Beneath England", 67, 49.
[42] *Ibid.*, 67, 52.

Yet, the originality of *Moortown Diary* may not quite lie in a supposed combination of stylistic bareness and thematic inclusiveness. Hughes seems to write "as a farmer", but he is still a poet turned farmer. Indeed, there is something ironic about his lamenting the effect of immigration in rural Devon when his very arrival constituted an invasion of some kind. Moreover, if Hughes rejects the music of pastoral writers, he doesn't quite write outside any tradition. Here are the first lines of the opening poem:

> Rain. Floods. Frost. And after frost, rain.
> Dull roof-drumming. Wraith-rain pulsing across purple-bare
>   woods
> Like light across heaved water. Sleet in it.
> And across the fields, miserable tents of their hedges.
> Mist-rain off-world. Hills wallowing
> In and out of a grey or silvery dissolution.
> ....
> Brown water backing and brimming in grass ...
>   (*Moortown Diary*, 1)

The alliterations and compounds show that Hughes has not forgotten the lessons of Hopkins. These reminiscences indicate that Hughes is substituting the robust sensualism of Hopkins for the sentimental pieties of mainstream nature poetry. But he is selective in his debt to Hopkins here. Indeed, he only adapts the techniques through which Hopkins worked to arrive at a renewed and more concrete rendering of natural scenes: alliteration and hyphenation twist language into a miming of the real. The musical drift of Hopkins's poems and the metaphysical unity with which the "instress" endows Hopkins's scenes,[43] on the other hand, are rejected together with the lyrical idealizations of other nature poets. Instead, Hughes's chopped-up, asymmetric free verse chastises their propensity towards abstraction by insisting on the fragmentariness and the separateness of what is described. The scene no longer dissolves into the unifying impulse of Hopkins's instress or in the emotional expansiveness of the traditional poet's subjectivity. It only dissolves in and out of itself in a movement that confirms its elusiveness and irreducibility.

If the rural reality of *Moortown Diary* resists traditional forms of poetic idealization, it does not quite resist poeticization altogether. Hughes claims to record his experiences like a faithful diarist, and yet he

---

[43] In Hopkins's poetry, the "instress" is the energy that holds a scene together and gives it its individual character and beauty.

still finds occasions to indulge in verbal and conceptual ingenuity. But his defamiliarizing metaphors challenge the very view of nature that had dominated pastoral poetry: his rural scenes no longer show a peacefully integrated mode of existence that persists against mechanization and artifice. Rather, the artifice itself is now subsumed into a continuum where the organic and the mechanical become interchangeable:

> Lifting of ice-heavy ewes, trampling anxieties
> As they follow their wide-legged tall lambs,
> Tripods craning to cry bewildered.
>
> (14)
>
> His machinery adjusted itself
> And his blood escaped, without loyalty.
>
> (37)
>
> But he got going finally, all his new
> Machinery learning suddenly ...
>
> (46)

As animals are described in mechanical terms, they stop providing alternatives to the alienation represented by mechanical culture. This is not to say that Hughes no longer contrasts the simplicity of natural life with the alienation of human existence, but the terms of the contrast have changed. This is best illustrated by the earlier poem "Thrushes": the birds are

> More coiled steel than living – a poised
> Dark deadly eye, those delicate legs
> Triggered to stirrings beyond sense ...

Humans are left to wonder what "Gives their day this bullet and automatic/Purpose?" (*Lupercal*, 52). The metaphors make clear that what separates animals from men is no longer their organic purity, but the almost mechanical power which allows them to "overtake the instant" (*Lupercal*, 52). What this nature poetry denounces is no longer the ignominies of a culture based on industrialism, but a human separation from the spontaneous violence through which the thrushes attain to a machine-like efficiency.

Hughes explained that the attacks launched by some critics on the violence of "Thrushes" partly stemmed from their indignation at seeing that violence "being committed by Browning's and Hardy's beautiful singer": "some blame, I suppose, is smudged on to the perpetrator of such a libel against one of the darlings of our pastoral idyll."[44] More than once, Hughes has expressed irritation at the charges levelled against him: "perhaps this whole debate is a fieldful of old-fashioned English windmills";[45]

> the role of this word 'violence' in modern criticism is very tricky and not always easy to follow. I wonder if it is used in other countries ... It's hard to imagine how the distinction can be made outside recent English poetry.

> I don't feel any bad conscience for what appears in what I write. It's more a case of being a witness. When the present quiet civil war in England has played itself out, I imagine my poems about Jaguars will look very tame.[46]

There is something slightly disingenuous about those remarks. Far from being indifferent to the "quiet civil war" that characterizes post-war England, Hughes often seems eager to join the fray. Although he affects a stance of objectivity, his recurrent references to English contexts suggest that his subversive appropriation of the symbols of English pastoral poetry is quite deliberate, and that it is inextricably bound up with his attempt to redefine English nationhood through a new relationship to nature. Thus, in *Moortown Diary*, Hughes insistently dwells on the less palatable, and sometimes frankly gruesome aspects of farming life. It is true that Hughes's language there is slightly less reliant on metaphor than in previous collections. But this only shows that Hughes had finally hit upon a reality that matched the requirements of an imagination which had hitherto slaked its thirst for violence in hyperbole. The very subject matter, this time, is hyperbolic.

After an immersion in the world of *Moortown Diary*, it almost becomes a shock to remember that rural England could ever have been the scene of poetic idylls. Its landscape is now a place where "fox corpses lie beaten to their bare bones/Skin beaten off, brains and bowels beaten out" (2). Many other poems lose themselves in the detailed descriptions of misshapen or still-born lambs and calves: "his eye just lay suffering the monstrous weight of his head/The impossible job of his marvellous huge

---

[44] *Winter Pollen*, 257.
[45] *Ibid.*, 263.
[46] "Ted Hughes and *Crow*", 197; Faas, *Ted Hughes: The Unaccommodated Universe*, 19.

limbs" (12-13);[47] "her lamb ... lay now/Without eyes, already entrails pulled out/Between his legs" (25); "the fine anatomy of silvery ribs on display and the cavity,/The head also emptied through the eye-sockets" (28). This culminates in "February 17th", where Hughes recounts how he had to extract the body of a still-born lamb from the ewe's womb by cutting off its strangled head, which hung blocked outside her rear-end, in order to pull out the rest of its body:

> ... it came.
> And after it the long, sudden, yolk-yellow
> Parcel of life
> In a smoking slither of oils and soups and syrups –
> And the body lay born, beside the hacked-off head.
>
> (31)

As Paulin suggests, the "oils" here are also a painter's.[48] This betrays the artistic nature of the gaze that registers the scene, and cautions us against a literal acceptance of Hughes's introductory remark about his method of composition:

> ... these improvised verses are nothing more than this: my own way of getting reasonably close to what is going on, and staying close, and of excluding everything else that might be pressing to interfere with the watching eye. In a sense, the method excludes the poetic process as well. This sort of thing had to be set down soon after the event ... by the next day, the processes of "memory", the poetic process, had already started (x).

On the basis of those remarks, one might consider that *Moortown Diary* exposes the tacit but indispensable link between the idealizing act of remembering natural scenes and the organicist assumptions that underpinned Wordsworthian representations of nature. But Hughes, by allegedly denying memory a role in his writing process, hasn't simply replaced the idealizing conventions of pastoral poetry by a more objective and immediate form of representation. In fact, the poems seem to correlate Hughes's rejection of the *re*membering process with the images

---

[47] One notes that, in this example, the sight of the dying calf is rendered with a stylistic ingenuity which breaks with the stylistic bareness that critics have celebrated.

[48] *Minotaur*, 273. Paulin's suggestion is borne out by Hughes's description of a setting sun as "glare light/mix[ing] its mad oils" in a later *Elmet* poem (*Three Books*, 6).

of *dis*memberment that pervade *Moortown Diary*. Hughes's thinking about nature is dominated by a radical opposition between the deceptive organicism of pastoral poetry and his own fascination with animal violence. What his poetry enacts is an inversion – and not a displacement – of that opposition: far from creating an entirely new kind of nature poetry that owes nothing to the pastoral mode, it is a violent reaction against that mode which remains negatively, but decisively indebted to it.

Through his attempt at closing the inevitable gap between perception and writing, Hughes claims for his poetry the perfection of the thrush's "ravening second". Hughes's style in *Moortown Diary*, like the bird whose violence he praised in *Lupercal*, "overtake[s] the instant": "No indolent procrastination" thwarts it (*Lupercal*, 52). But the thrush's immediacy was valued less for itself than for its admirable violence. That violence has remained central to *Moortown Diary* – in both style and content. Artistic creation has now been assimilated to the violence of nature, in a comparison that Hughes had already made in "Thrushes", where "Mozart's brain" shared the "bullet and automatic purpose" of the bird. Instead of "carving at a tiny ivory ornament for years" (*Lupercal*, 52), Hughes fashioned his poems with the blunt hammer of improvisation, but his hand remained guided by the same obsessions that dominated earlier volumes.

In *Moortown Diary*, Hughes was not simply recording a fragmentary reality by waiving the poetic privilege of a unifying memory. He was still, as elsewhere in his work, focusing on a fragmentation forcibly achieved by violent means. In the pastoral mode, memories of English natural scenes could bring relief in a reality degraded by the violence of industrialism. In Hughes's version, English nature has become the locus in which a violent imagination can rebel against the civilities of a society where conflict is being avoided. Even when it lays claim to the greatest objectivity, Hughes's poetry remains "a form of disguised social comment": a way of "expressing an impatience with the post-war consensus",[49] and more specifically with the decencies of the culture it produced.

Moortown Diary is set in North Devon. This shows yet again that, however close his connections with his native Yorkshire may be, Hughes's poetry is not the best example of a Northward displacement of the centre of gravity in English poetry. And yet, both Yorkshire and North Devon fulfil a similar role in that they fall outside the bounds of English pastoralism, whose Southern landscapes were often limited to the

---

[49] Tom Paulin, *Minotaur*, 252, 270.

Home Counties. In his preface to *Moortown Diary*, Hughes stresses the marginality of North Devon: "there was a palpable feeling here that England (along with South Devon and Cornwall) was another country and could be ignored in return" (vii-viii). This does not mean that Hughes does not think of North Devon as English, since he also contrasts it with "*the rest* of England" (viii, emphasis mine). On the contrary, it shows that Hughes is attempting to confer a central status on Englands that had remained marginal. Those Englands are plural; indeed Hughes is not, properly speaking, a regionalist. Marginality is not associated with any particular place; marginal locations are valued because they give access to a more primitive England which was obliterated in previous poetic versions of English nature.

North Devon also has a personal significance for Hughes, since he actually settled there; but biographical associations do not obscure literary ones. When Hughes moved to Devon, he actually entered the country of Henry Williamson, whose novel *Tarka the Otter* had played a key role in shaping his imagination: "Still spellbound by his magical book, albeit quite unconsciously, I had found myself where I still live, on Tarka's river, the Taw, in the middle of Devon." Hughes also says of Williamson that "it is not usual to consider him as a poet. But I believe he was one of the two or three truest poets of his generation".[50] Hughes's fascination with the feral and the primitive owes more to Williamson's vision than to any poetic model in the strict sense of the word. His nature poems admittedly invite comparison with Lawrence's and Clare's, who were already exploring and transgressing the limits of English nature poetry. Yet Hughes's primitivism is closer to Williamson's; not only because Williamson's vision of nature was more focused and more intense than Lawrence's or Clare's, but because its very intensity sometimes undermined the very definition of "nature". This is also true of Hughes, whose own paradoxes set him apart from Lawrence and Clare as well as from the pastoral mainstream.

Hughes's debt to Williamson is most evident in "An Otter" (*Lupercal*, 46-47). The poem reads like a summary of *Tarka*, although Hughes's description of the life and death of the otter de-individualizes it: Hughes's otter is first and foremost "the legend of himself" (46), rather than the animal protagonist of Williamson's tale. This allows Hughes to endow the otter with historical significance by comparing it to "a king in hiding" (46), which aligns the otter with the Royalist side in the English Civil

---

[50] Ted Hughes, "An Address Given at the Memorial Service at St. Martin-in-the-Fields", in *Henry Williamson: The Man, the Writings. A Symposium*, ed. B. Sewell, Padstow, 1980, 163, 161.

War, or at any rate with the underdogs of English history.[51] The metaphor surfaces in Hughes's discussion of the Civil War in *Shakespeare and the Goddess of Complete Being*, where Hughes talks of "the King ... hunted like an animal through the English landscape".[52] Williamson's novel itself occasionally harks back to an ancestral England, as in the passage where Tarka swims "under the Ancient Long Bridge, which the monks built across their ford two centuries before the galleons were laid down in the shipyards below to fight the Spanish Armada".[53] This can be compared with Hughes's description of the pond in "Pike", inhabited by creatures that have "outlasted every visible stone/Of the monastery that planted them" (*Lupercal*, 57).

"An Otter" is not only modelled on Williamson's novel, it also invites comparison with John Clare's poem "Badger", which Hughes discusses in *Poetry in the Making*. Clare's poem similarly describes the hounded animal's attempt to escape its pursuers, and its eventual failure: "kicked and torn and beaten out he lies/And leaves his hold, and cackles, and groans and dies."[54] Hughes's otter is also overtaken by pursuing hounds and "reverts to nothing at all,/To this long pelt over the back of a chair" (*Lupercal*, 47). Like Clare's, Hughes's nature poems are essentially poems of the wilderness. Both writers often render that wilderness with a concreteness and an attention to detail that are rare in other English animal poems, particularly those of the Romantics for whom larks or nightingales were essentially symbols. Still, if Clare's and Hughes's animals seem more real than symbolic, they certainly do not resist allegorical readings either. The connotations with which Clare and Hughes invest untamed nature, however, diverge significantly. Clare's poems about wandering animals were of a piece with his denunciation of the enclosures, which both ruined the sense of freedom which he associated with country life and consecrated the power of the landowning classes. The recent critical revaluation of Clare constantly stresses this radical aspect: thus, John Lucas writes that Clare's animal poems convey his own sense of being a "trespasser, fugitive [and] outlaw". Lucas

---

[51] Tom Paulin comments that this echo of the "broken king" of Eliot's "Little Gidding" manages to "combine the feral with Anglican royalism" (*Minotaur*, 264), The line may also recall Lawrence's "Snake": "for he seemed to me like a king,/Like a king in exile, uncrowned in the underworld". See D.H. Lawrence, *Complete Poems* (vol. 1), eds Vivian de Sola Pinto and Warren Roberts, London, 1967, 351.
[52] Ted Hughes, *Shakespeare and the Goddess of Complete Being*, London, 1992, 85.
[53] Henry Williamson, *Tarka the Otter*, Penguin, 1937, 63.
[54] Ted Hughes, *Poetry in the Making* (1967), London, 1969, 25.

consequently explains the relative neglect to which Clare's poetry was long confined as follows: "As an outlaw he cannot speak for England."[55]

It may then seem ironical that Ted Hughes, who in many ways has more in common with Clare than with other English nature poets, should have been Poet Laureate. But as we have seen, his otter is an aristocrat as well as an outlaw. Hughes's wanderers, like Clare's, are transgressors, but they are not marginal to the oppressive social order that disfigured Clare's English countryside in the first half of the nineteenth century. Instead, they embody a mode of existence that transgresses the democratic values of the Welfare State. In his defence of a poetics that could encompass Welfare State culture, Donald Davie famously had little time for Hughes's "tramps asleep in ditches", and not just because they are part of a natural scene which belongs to "a world well lost".[56] Davie's unease was probably compounded by the aristocratic nature of Hughes's tramps and animals. While the otter was a also a "king in hiding", the tramp of "Things Present" dreams that his "sires had towers and great names" (*Lupercal*, 9).

Hughes's fascination with marginal figures sometimes merges with actual social history. In "Billy Holt", social resistance becomes synonymous with the geographical marginality and the unconventional beauty of the Calder valley: "Badlands where outcast and outlaw/Fortified the hill-knowle's long outlook" (*Three Books*, 25). But what Hughes's focus on marginality really criticizes can be inferred from his 1963 review of Philip O'Connor's *Vagrancy*:

> the tramp is a free symbol, the shadow of the great prototype vagrants .... in what kind of society would there be no individuals misfitting to the point of vagrancy? .... Is our society as competitive, so exclusively a rat-race and dog-fight, as [the socialist Flannery] assumes? And is the spirit of competition picked up with such a difficulty, and so against nature? .... When non-competition is enforced, what sort of genetic torpor ensues, and worse?[57]

Retrospectively, Hughes's blend of proto-Thatcherism and eugenics makes for even more uncomfortable reading than it did in the 1960s, when an impatience with Welfare State values was not uncommon in the English cultural scene. But although Hughes's rhetoric seems to validate

---

[55] Lucas, *England and Englishness*, 151, 155.
[56] Davie, *Thomas Hardy and British Poetry*, 68.
[57] *Winter Pollen*, 36-37.

Tom Paulin's claim that his poetry "speaks for the freebooting private sector",[58] the fact remains that Hughes is more drawn to marginals than to entrepreneurs. Perhaps the two figures merge in Hughes's idealizing portrait of "Sketching A Thatcher" (no pun intended), but the poem ultimately praises the aesthetic intensity of the old man's labour rather than his efficiency (*New Selected Poems*, 182-83). He is primarily a figure of excess whose marginality is essential to Hughes's fascination. Like Dick Straightup in *Lupercal* and Hughes's other idealized country types, he is a descendant of the wanderer who regularly returned to haunt English nature poetry. However, the various incarnations of that figure have carried different associations.

In the case of Clare, wandering was a protest against a specific development in English rural life (namely the enclosures), and was largely a radical gesture. By the time the wanderer reappeared as the elusive Lob of Edward Thomas's eponymous poem, he had shed Clare's political urgency to blend in the quieter pastoral vision of Georgian poetry, in which Clare's struggles and protests had been forgotten:

> He is as English as this gate, this flower, this mire
> And when at eight years old Lob-lie-by-the-fire
> Came in my books, this was the man I saw.
> He has been in England as long as dove and daw ...[59]

Unlike Clare's wanderers, Thomas's Lob is explicitly a literary figure (he appeared in his "books"); the wanderer has now become a fantasy in the minds of alienated urban readers. Thomas's poem bears witness to the wanderer's popularity in the early twentieth century, a popularity that "relies upon the notional autonomy of the tramp and his or her supposed freedom from the confines of mass society".[60] Hughes's tramps and other rural types fulfil a similar function, but the "confines of mass society" are now identified with post-war social democracy rather than with urban life under early twentieth-century capitalism. This explains why Hughes's versions of the wanderer are often more marginal, primitive and violent than Thomas's: whereas Thomas's Lob is gently picturesque, Hughes's figures sometimes lapse into caricature: Dick Straightup, for instance, is a larger than life Falstaff who can down a "twelve-pint tankard at a tilt" or eat a "whole serving of thirty eggs", and who once spent a night buried in

---

[58] *Minotaur*, 270.
[59] Edward Thomas, *Collected Poems*, ed. R. George Thomas, Oxford, 1978, 161.
[60] See *Writing Englishness 1900-1950: An Introductory Sourcebook on National Identity*, eds Judy Giles and Tim Middleton, London, 1995, 74.

snow after keeling over in his drunkenness: "He was chipped out at dawn/Warm as a pie and snoring" (*Lupercal*, 17). The environment that Hughes's rural types inhabit is not the same world as Edward Thomas's either. Lob was still largely part of the rural peace that Thomas located at the "Heart of England". Dick Straightup, by contrast, spent "eighty winters on the windy *ridge*/Of England" (*Lupercal*, 17. Emphasis mine). His hyperbolic, animal vitality is of a piece with Hughes's primitive landscapes. The only moment when Thomas's and Hughes's natural worlds seem to meet is in Hughes's "Coming Down Through Somerset". In that poem, Hughes contemplates the body of a dead badger found on a road, during "the high moment/Of driving through England" (*Moortown Diary*, 40). Hughes lingers admiringly on the frozen perfection of the corpse, refusing to bury the animal, or even skin it or boil it "to liberate his masterpiece skull": "I want him/To stay as he is" (40). The badger's body is a glimpse of primitive nature caught in the English night; it recalls Thomas's rather atypical poem "The Combe", in which Thomas suddenly reached far beyond his pastoral "Heart of England", and thus prefigured Hughes:

> The Combe was ever dark, ancient and dark
> ... But far more ancient and dark
> The Combe looks since they killed the badger there,
> Dug him out and gave him to the hounds,
> That most ancient Briton of English Beasts.[61]

Beyond its gesture towards national allegory and the nostalgic sense of loss conveyed by its ending ("Something has to stay"), "Coming Down Through Somerset" is so engrossed in its vision of the badger's corpse that it becomes difficult to read it as ecological commentary. This is true of many other poems by Hughes, and sets him apart from another of his models, namely D.H. Lawrence. Hughes's poetry is characterized by an attention to detail and a scrupulousness of vision which, while not excluding metaphorical flights, nevertheless leave little room for the sentimentality and the speculations that one finds in Lawrence's animal poems.[62] Hughes is sometimes so focused on natural phenomena that he dispenses with the figure of an observer. When such a figure is present, he usually refrains from drawing philosophical, psychological or political

---

[61] Thomas, *Collected Poems*, 57.
[62] Keith Sagar makes much of the contrast between the "often sentimental" Lawrence and the supposedly more objective Hughes. See Keith Sagar, *The Art of Ted Hughes*, Cambridge, 1975, 45.

lessons from his observations. Lawrence's natural descriptions, however convincing in themselves, often end up looking like pretexts for such meditations. Hughes only gestures towards a myth of England through metaphors that are woven into the texture of the poems; rather than expounding his sense of nationhood, his nature poems are heuristic attempts at defining it.

Hughes's comparative lack of didacticism, however, raises further questions. While Lawrence's natural vision encompassed infinitely more than pastoral poetry did, it was still largely part of a general reaction against industrialism and the mechanical way of life it imposed. But as we have seen, Hughes is not loath to use mechanical metaphors in his nature poems. In this too, he reminds one of Williamson who, while railing against the desecration of the natural beauties of England, freely availed himself of the latest technical innovations. Thus, Williamson could "write, with an eloquent gesture, 'I had rejected civilization, just like Jefferies had, I was going to be a hermit', yet he made the journey from London to Devon on a motorcycle, intent upon setting a record time".[63] In Hughes as in Williamson, an ecological consciousness coexists with a Nietzschean exultation in excess that abolishes all distinctions between the natural and the mechanical. Lawrence's vitalism remained strongly organicist; the dichotomy between the natural and the mechanical is enforced with great regularity throughout his work. Lawrence can admittedly describe an animal through mechanical metaphors, as in this almost Hughesian passage about a bull:

> The great, roaring weight above
> Like a furnace dripping a molten drip
> The urge, the massive, burning ache
> Of the bull's breast.
> The open furnace-doors of his nostrils.

But Lawrence's last line justifies those industrial metaphors as it discloses the bull's allegorical nature: "The bull of the proletariat has got his head down."[64] It is only in rare poems like "Bare Almond-Trees" that Lawrence imaginatively mixes the natural and the mechanical in a way that points forward to Hughes: the trees are compared to "iron implements twisted, hideous, out of the earth": "Do you feel the air for

---

[63] William J. Keith, *The Rural Tradition*, Hassocks, 1975, 216.
[64] Lawrence, *Collected Poems*, 326-27.

electric influences/Like some strange magnetic apparatus?"; "Do you telephone the roar of waters over the earth?"[65]

By and large, however, Lawrence's nature poetry retains an explicitly allegorical dimension that Hughes hardly ever allows into his own work. But it is still possible to read Hughes's work as allegory, although of a more covert type: as has been pointed out, the visionary intensity that makes him collapse the natural with the mechanical is already a form of allegory in itself; it contrasts its own ontological excess with post-war blandness. Moreover, as we will now see, some of Hughes's mechanical metaphors reveal a historical subtext which remains at the heart of his imagination.

In Hughes's first collection, the hawk's sacrificial flight downwards in "The Hawk in the Rain" is paralleled by the fate of a pilot whose plane crashes in an English field in "The Casualty". The poems have a lot in common, from a contrast between the dullness of the surroundings and the thrilling violence of the event to the alliterative music borrowed from Hopkins:

> Farmers in the fields, housewives behind steamed windows,
> Watch the burning aircraft across the blue sky float
> As if a firefly and a spider fought

After the crash, the burned pilot among the wreckage still "Bulks closer greater flesh and blood than their own" (*The Hawk in the Rain*, 49). "The Casualty" not only refers back to "The Hawk in the Rain", it also adumbrates another poem which describes the accidental death of a motorcyclist. "A Motorbike" brings out more sharply the criticism of post-war English dullness that was half explicit in the hawk's collision with the "ponderous shires" (*The Hawk in the Rain*, 11). The motorbike of the title was confined to a shed during the Second World War: "thunder, flight, disruption/Cramped in rust." After the war, the demobilized soldiers "hung around limply,/Peace took them all prisoner": "The shrunk-back war ached in their testicles/And England dwindled to the size of a dog-track." It is against that background that a young man buys the motorbike: "He kicked it into life – it erupted/Out of the six year sleep." However, the young man finally "escaped/Into a telegraph pole" (*Moortown*, 104). His violent death both recalls the quasi-transcendence of the hawk's and the pilot's ends and confirms the inertia in which

---

[65] *Ibid.*, 300-1. It is not a coincidence that Hughes chose to discuss that poem in *Poetry in the Making*.

Hughes's post-war England is mired – an inertia compared with which violence and conflict appear more authentic.

The similarities between the motorbike's disruptive power and the violence of war also recall Williamson. Indeed, the First World War played an ambiguous role in Williamson's imagination. The author of *Tarka the Otter* also left powerful accounts denouncing the atrocity of trench warfare; but if he "settled in the Devonshire countryside 'in order to find peace and quiet'", he also rode "'at all hours of the day and night' on the motorbike which, he claim[ed] with obvious satisfaction, ma[de] 'a noise like a machine gun'".[66] Disturbingly enough, Williamson is not afraid to recreate warfare in the very countryside which he chose as a refuge. His undefiled England accommodates the very violence with which other war writers contrasted their visions of home. It is in those paradoxes and in the complex relation to England that they entail that Hughes is closest to Williamson, rather than in the authoritarian nationalism which some critics have read in Hughes's admiration for his model.[67]

Hughes's work is characterized by an ambiguity towards warfare similar to Williamson's. I have already discussed the role played by the Second World War in the development of his imagination. His many poems about his shell-shocked father, from the early "Out I" in *Wodwo* to "Dust As We Are" and "For the Duration" in *Wolfwatching*, show that the Great War was just as important to him. Those poems often express the horror of warfare as convincingly as any first-hand account, and show a degree of personal involvement that is only matched in *Birthday Letters*. Hughes also emphasized the prolonged impact of the Great War on English life when he described it as the "number one national ghost".[68] His poems reveal a strong impatience with the official attitude to the War, an impatience that he shares with Geoffrey Hill. In the first section of "Griefs for Dead Soldiers", Hughes untypically strings together resounding Latinisms to deride the spurious grandeur of official commemorations: ceremonies and cenotaphs only "Make these dead magnificent" and turn the "national sorrow" into "Permanent stupendous victory" (*The Hawk in the Rain*, 52). Hughes's irony is made clear by a deliberately inflated rhetoric of the kind found in Hill's poems on similar

---

[66] Keith, *The Rural Tradition*, 216.
[67] Tom Paulin accuses Hughes of complicitly evading the true nature of Williamson's pro-fascist politics in his memorial tribute to Williamson (*Minotaur*, 256), but he omits Hughes's open reference to his disagreement with Williamson: "we had terrible arguments about his politics" ("An Address Given at the Memorial Service at St. Martin-in-the-Fields", 164).
[68] *Winter Pollen*, 70.

subjects, not least in "A Pastoral". Like Hughes, Hill describes "Evidently-veiled griefs; impervious tombs". Those monuments are like the Pities of the poem which, "mobile, immaculate and austere", "Cleanse with a kind of artistry the ground/Shared by War", so that "the unedifying nude dead are soon covered" (*HCP*, 54). In the same way that Hill's poetry can break the surface of its parodic, Latinate decorum to restore war to its cruel intensity, the second section of Hughes's poem contrasts official commemorations with the private grief of War widows, while the third section imaginatively explores the realities of the battlefield. The following passage, with its mixture of grim irony, sharp realism, and plain language, points back to the War poets and prefigures Hill's *Funeral Music*:

> Among the flowers the dead wait like brides
> To surrender their limbs; thus of another body flung
> Down, the jolted shape of a face, earth into the mouth.
>
> (*The Hawk in the Rain*, 52)

Hughes stresses the centrality of the Great War in the national consciousness which he is trying to reshape, but his rejection of official mythography is so thorough that it occasionally leads to a wholesale rejection of England. "Out III" ends with precisely such a defiant, exasperated gesture:

> Goodbye to the cenotaphs on my mother's breasts.
> Goodbye to all the remaindered charms of my father's survival.
> Let England close. Let the green sea-anemone close.[69]
>
> (*Wodwo*, 157)

Hughes thus bids farewell to the poppy, that "bloody-minded flower" which is "whoring everywhere" on Remembrance Day. Earlier on, he had tried to align the poppy with his other symbols of natural violence: "The poppy is a wound, the poppy is the mouth of the grave, maybe of the womb searching" (*Wodwo*, 156-57). Those symbols do in fact regularly point back to war as well. War often remains the number one ghost in Hughes's imagination too, although it assumes the shape of a ghoulish spectre that will not be contained in cenotaphs.

---

[69] Hughes's valediction recalls Robert Graves' *Goodbye to All That* – both as a war writer and as the explorer of primitive myths in *The White Goddess*, Graves had an obvious appeal for Hughes.

Hughes's interest in violence inevitably raises questions as to the nature of his obsession with the war: Donald Davie, as we have seen, read his poetry as a form of morbid nostalgia for "the carnival of violence which World War legitimized".[70] In the programmatic "Tiger Psalm", Hughes seems to rebutt such charges by celebrating the violence of the natural world at the expense of modern human warfare. The poem consists of an extended, clear-cut comparison between a tiger and a machine-gun:

> The machine guns
> Permit themselves a snigger. They eliminate the error
> With a to-fro dialectic
> And the point proved stop speaking.
> The tiger
> Kills like the fall of a cliff, one-sinewed with the earth,
> ....
> Does not kill. The tiger blesses with a fang.
>
> (*Moortown*, 150-51)

This, however, is a distinction which many other poems seem strangely calculated to deconstruct. Hughes's metaphors often endow his natural scenes and animals with a violence that finds its roots in the cataclysm of the First World War. Thus, the mechanical metaphors of "Thrushes" include images that associate the instinctual efficiency of the bird with the perfection of modern weapons: their legs are "*triggered* to stirrings beyond sense", their days have a "*bullet* and automatic purpose" (*Lupercal*, 52. Emphases mine). "To Paint a Water Lily" describes how a dragonfly "bullets by/Or stands in space to take aim": "There are battle-shouts/And death-cries everywhere" (*Lupercal*, 29). Hughes's skylarks may have more substance than Shelley's, but if they are more resistant to symbolic interpretation, Hughes's metaphorical exuberance still hints at specific historical obsessions: his skylark is "barrel-chested for heights", "Leaden/Like a bullet", "shot through the crested head/With the command, Not die" (*Wodwo*, 168).

Hughes seems to insist that English landscapes should bear the marks of the battles that their inhabitants fought abroad: "The throb of the mills and the crying of lambs" in Elmet is "like shouting in Flanders" (*Three Books*, 31). However, it is not always clear whether the aim of that strategy is to inscribe the national consciousness with more urgent memories of war than cenotaphs, or whether Hughes is trying to bolster

---

[70] Davie, *Under Briggflats*, 220.

up the ontological intensity of his English landscapes by investing them with a violence in which they are found lacking. As was the case with Williamson, the moral and political dimension of Hughes's concern with war does not exclude a disturbing interest in the aesthetic possibilities that war affords.

War haunts the metaphorical networks of Hughes's poetry. Like an uncanny wraith, it paradoxically lends that poetry much of its stark, violent concreteness while opening it up to the more abstract interpretations it seems to resist. In this light, a late poem like "Dust As We Are" almost reads like an autobiographical account of Hughes's poetic development. Hughes describes his father's experience as his own "soul's food. A soap-smell spectre/Of the massacre of innocents". The end of the poem provides a link between Hughes's war-haunted imagination and his bestiaries: "So the soul grew. A strange thing, with rickets – a hyena./No singing – that kind of laughter" (*Wolfwatching*, 11). But for all its monstrosity, war is a spectre that fascinates. It is quite apposite that the war should emerge from the sea together with the "Ghost Crabs" that return each night to stalk the land in the eponymous poem: "Giant crabs, under flat skulls, staring inland/Like a packed trench of helmets." In Hughes's eyes, such ghosts are more real than our "nothingness", "to them, our cluttered countries are empty battleground". The last line of the poem asserts Hughes's belief in their greater authenticity, but simultaneously concedes that his protest at the degraded reality of modern life may be an expression of aesthetic playfulness rather than a form of political commentary: "They are God's only toys" (*Wodwo*, 21-22).

Although the countries of "Ghost Crabs" are plural, the similarities between that poem and "Mayday on Holderness" suggest that the spectres of past wars, whatever exotic shapes they may assume, are essentially part of Hughes's vision of England. Indeed, the latter poem both locates war in the sea that defines the East coast of England and identifies it with the feral members of Hughes's bestiary: Beneath the North Sea "Smoulder the wars: to heart-beats, bomb, bayonet". The "oozings of Gallipoli" are "curded to beastings":

> The expressionless gaze of the leopard,
> The coils of the anaconda,
> The nightlong frenzy of shrews.

> (*Lupercal*, 12)

Like the ghost crabs, the sea where Hughes's vision of war blends with his primitive world is presented as more authentic than his post-war

Northern England, which rivers evacuate into a superior reality: the sea "swallows it all", from "Sheffield's ores" to "dunghills, kitchens, hospitals" (*Lupercal*, 11). The very liminality of the North Sea, however, shows the ambiguity of Hughes's concern with the matter of England: like North Devon, it is both England and the limit at which England dissolves into its other; it thus stands for the necessary, but potentially extreme marginality of Hughes's authentic England. It encapsulates the contradictory impulses that cause Hughes either to reject England – as in "Out III" – or to pursue his quest for areas where a primitive England still persists.

Landscapes like Devon or the Calder valley are of course more than dramatic topographies which allow Hughes to deploy his poetics of violence. They are also the repositories of a primitive, remote English history that Hughes values as much as their rugged bareness and geographical marginality. It is now time to turn to a detailed examination of Hughes's poetic engagement with English history, which can be conducted in the light of the present conclusions. Indeed, the next chapter will analyse how Hughes's historical imagination largely remains an imagination of war, informed by the same obsession with violence and conflict that turned much of his nature poetry into a protest against post-war decency. It will also reveal how Hughes's vision of national history shares the paradox which is embodied in "Mayday on Holderness": Hughes's historical primitivism, like his natural primitivism, can lead either to a poetic transformation of England or to its rejection.

CHAPTER FOUR
TED HUGHES'S ENGLISH MYTHOLOGIES

When Ted Hughes became Poet Laureate in 1984, many sceptical eyebrows were raised. Hughes was described as "the most anti-establishment, black and acerbic poet to have become a court official".[1] However, he promptly dispelled doubts about the seriousness with which he would take his task. Less than eight years after his appointment, a volume collecting his Laureate poems (*Rain Charm for the Duchy*) appeared: few of his modern predecessors were as prolific. Hughes was not afraid to put his imagination in the service of an institution that has become increasingly controversial, and while his dedication put paid to the original reservations about his suitability for the post, his reputation also suffered in consequence. There is indeed something slightly grotesque about Hughes's recycling of his most powerful and disturbing images in poems written for royal occasions. The crow that drops the first two candles on Queen Elizabeth's birthday cake (*Rain Charm for the Duchy*, 18) may seem somewhat tame and ridiculous to readers of *Crow*.

Yet, it would be a mistake to think that Hughes's Laureate work was limited to the royal poems which earned him more scorn than praise. Since the office was created, the Laureateship has undergone a major transformation. The Laureate is now "less an articulator of royal praise than one who expresses national experience, a sense of nationhood and Englishness".[2] The blurb of *Rain Charm for the Duchy* informs us that the poems embody "a complete vision of royalty and nationhood". Hughes's controversial vision of royalty is indeed the gist of the collection, but he has developed his vision of nationhood in other works where he tried to fulfil the more informal, but perhaps more crucial task of the modern Laureate. Hughes's output of original poetic work had grown sparse before the publication of *Birthday Letters*, but the wealth of critical writings which he produced during his tenure include some of the most original attempts at reading the history of English poetry through the lens of nationhood. Taken together, the monumental *Shakespeare and the Goddess of Complete Being* and the essays on "Myths, Metres, Rhythms"[3] show Hughes trying to prove that E. M. Forster was wrong to ask "Why has not England a great mythology?".[4] In Hughes's hands,

---

[1] Michael Hulse, "The Laureate Business or the Laureateship of Englishness", *Quadrant*, XXIX (1985), 49.
[2] *Ibid.*, 47.
[3] "Myths, Metres, Rhythms" is included in *Winter Pollen*.
[4] E.M. Forster, *Howards End* (1910), Penguin, 2000, 262.

Shakespeare's *Complete Works* became "modern England's creation story, our sacred book, closer to us than the Bible".[5] Hughes also stressed the political, social and cultural dimensions of the competing poetic traditions which he brilliantly mythologized in his postscript to "Myths, Metres, Rhythms".

Although such writings are clearly the works of a self-conscious Laureate with a strong sense of his responsibilities, it would be wrong to suppose that Hughes was writing to order. The themes that those texts develop were already at the centre of Hughes's introduction to *A Choice of Shakespeare's Verse* (1971); more importantly, they also reflect the concerns that had always informed a great deal of his poetry. Hughes made no effort to conceal the link between his poetic imagination and his analyses of poetic and national history. He thus likened the interaction between poetic traditions in England to the couplings of male and female spiders[6] which he also described in his poem "Eclipse" (*Flowers and Insects*, 46-51), or to a tumultuous union between bride and bridegroom,[7] recalling poems like "Lovesong" (*Crow*, 88) or "Bride and Groom Lie Hidden for Three Days" (*Three Books*, 97). Those similarities invite us to read much of his work as, among other things, an extended meditation on English nationhood, a vast allegory where nature, history, sexuality and poetic form are all potential carriers of meaning in the signifying system of Hughesian Englishness.

It is not surprising that such a bold project as Hughes's should have met with scepticism or indifference. Apart from attracting charges of essentialism, attempts at theorizing or mythologizing Englishness also go against the empiricism and level-headedness that are felt to be key ingredients of the English character, although Hughes did much to question that stereotype by reverting to a Blakean, visionary Englishness. The prejudice accounts for the popularity of a Laureate like Betjeman, whose relaxed brand of anti-intellectualism Hughes could and would never make his.[8] But even if one agrees to read Hughes on his own terms, other problems arise. Indeed, if each individual expression of his vision of nationhood strives for internal consistency, I will show how they fail to cohere into a stable mythology. Far from providing a reliable hermeneutic key to his work, Hughes's formulations about nationhood are thrown into confusion by the echoes that they conjure up. The various texts which

---

[5] Hughes, *Shakespeare and the Goddess of Complete Being*, 85.
[6] *Winter Pollen*, 369.
[7] *Ibid.*, 369-72.
[8] A distinction must be made between the rationalism that Hughes has ceaselessly attacked and his profound intellectualism.

they seem to subsume constantly return to expose the contradictions within Hughes's project. Before those contradictions can be explored, Hughes's theoretical position must first be summarized.

At the heart of Hughes's poetico-national mythology lies his interpretation of Shakespeare's work as the expression of a key moment in the history of English identity: "the account of how, in the religious struggle that lasted from the middle of the sixteenth century to the middle of the seventeenth, England lost her soul."[9] The *Complete Works* become the allegory of a conflict in which each of the two contending persuasions is identified with attitudes to race, language and sexuality. Hughes can consequently defend his interpretation from charges of reductivism: if his "Shakespearean equation" brings everything down to a single theme, "singleness can be inclusive".[10] Thus, in the battle that Shakespeare dramatized, Catholicism stands for mediaeval English culture and, beyond it, the Celtic and pagan Britain which it had assimilated. It was also inherently feminine, the cult of the Virgin Mary having in some way perpetuated the pagan cult of the Celtic Goddess.[11] This in turn accounts for Hughes's conflation of Catholicism with a more instinctual way of life in which sensuality still had a place. Puritanism, by contrast, is rational, life-denying, obsessively masculine; it represents the development through which England severed its connections with the blend of older cultures which Catholicism had been able to absorb. Hughes writes that "to call that event a 'dissociation of sensibility' is an understatement. Our national poems are tragedies for a good reason".[12]

The Civil War was the moment when all the social, cultural and linguistic conflicts in the history of England came to a head in a cataclysmic confrontation that would reverberate in later crises, whether poetic or political. In Shakespeare's time, Hughes argues, the conflict was enacted within each Englishman, as the "front line [was] drawn across the solar plexus of each of Elizabeth's subjects".[13] It was also embodied and contained in the paradoxical figure of Elizabeth herself: as leader of the Reformed Church of England, she was a living symbol of England's rejection of Catholicism. Yet, she simultaneously appealed to the Catholic side of the English imagination, being by virtue of her sex a representative of the old Celtic Goddess. After her death, the balance was upset when James I "threw his weight against the old goddess and her

---

[9] *Winter Pollen*, 119.
[10] *Ibid.*, 106.
[11] *Ibid.*, 109.
[12] *Ibid.* 119.
[13] *Shakespeare and the Goddess of Complete Being*, 75.

idolatrous witcheries".[14] From then on, Catholicism and Puritanism radicalized, making the final explosion of the Civil War inevitable.

Hughes argues that the ambiguity of Elizabeth's reign was translated in the two poems which laid out the myth that governs Shakespeare's imagination: *The Rape of Lucrece* and *Venus and Adonis*. Those works are taken to dramatize the clashes between the Puritan and the Catholic/pagan minds that find expression in four "poles of energy": Lucrece, Tarquin, Venus and Adonis.[15] Adonis's rejection of Venus corresponds to the Puritan urge to escape from the grip of an older pagan culture. But the instincts that he represses grow more violent, until they rebel and overthrow the rational Puritanism that kept them at bay. In *Venus and Adonis*, this rebellion takes the form of Adonis's violent death. In *The Rape of Lucrece*, instinct, instead of destroying Puritanism, takes it over and perverts it into the murderous frenzy directed against both rational order and the forces of nature: Tarquin, the crazed Puritan, rapes Lucrece. Tarquin becomes the prototype for the heroes of the late tragedies, from Hamlet to Macbeth, the murderous regicide who uncannily prefigures Cromwell. Through these transformations, Shakespeare "conducted what is essentially an erotic poetry into an all-inclusive body of political action".[16] But Shakespeare himself tried to go beyond that conflict and looked for resolution in the romances, most notably in *The Tempest*. Prospero's banishment of the witch Sycorax, his treatment of the native Caliban, and the happy marriage between Miranda and Ferdinand represent the restoration of order after the final victory of Puritanism. By then, Shakespeare is then no longer the shamanic poet who wrote out the dreams of a nation in turmoil.[17] He becomes the cunning magician who casts his book in the sea and takes leave of the dream-world he had created. Prospero is the villain of Hughes's Shakespearean canon; he stands for England's final suppression of the older traditions that constituted its soul.

The make-up of that lost England was not only religious, political and sexual, but also linguistic. Shakespeare's poetics accordingly reflected the conflict between the native Anglo-Saxon stock and the incoming Latin and French vocabulary. Here too, an ancient form Englishness found its last expression in Shakespeare: his language was "somehow nearer to the vital life of English, still, than anything written down since". Shakespeare was still resorting to the "poetic instincts of English dialect", which

---

[14] *Winter Pollen*, 111.
[15] *Ibid.*, 116.
[16] *Ibid.*, 116-18.
[17] *Shakespeare and the Goddess of Complete Being*, 91.

brought out unsuspected dimensions in Latin words by exploiting their phonetic resemblance to Anglo-Saxon words.[18] Hughes's later translations of Ovid's *Metamorphoses* and of Racine's *Phaedra* show a similar desire to render Latin and French texts in a language free of all classical trappings and full of Anglo-Saxon vigour. Only Hughes could have made a line from Ovid sound like Old English verse: for instance, he describes how Pyramus "Brooded bewildered by the moods of manhood".[19] Hughes's model in those translations was partly the Shakespeare he described in his preface, whose language had "the air of being invented in a state of crisis"[20] and showed his awareness of the conflict that was played out on the physical surface of his words.

In this respect, however, Shakespeare's work is only one moment (albeit a crucial one) in a long series of poetic and political wars which Hughes has charted in his postscript to "Myths, Metres, Rhythms". The sensual, female principle which stood behind Catholicism is here associated with the native Anglo-Saxon poetic tradition, based on alliteration, sprung rhythm and dialect, whereas the rational, masculine pole is represented by the French and Italian modes that dominated courtly culture. Hughes describes the history of English poetry as the history of their marriage: "the old unorthodox tradition is the bride and the new, metrically strict orthodox tradition the groom." The marriage is actually a long series of quarrels that result in the growing alienation of the wild, sensuous bride. While in early and middle Shakespeare, she goes on the rampage, late Shakespeare corresponds to the stage where she "becomes a Sycorax, joins a coven, sleeps in her coffin to terrorize [her husband]". And just as Milton had thematically thrown "Delilah and Satan and the female spirit in general" "into the bottom of hell," so his work is the "lugubrious phase" where bride and groom live separated: "from his bedroom resounds the martial-domestic organ-toned doctrine and discipline of puritan wedlock, drowning out the last lamentings that emerge from hers."[21] The final suppression occurs when, with the Restoration, French style and rhythms more than ever became the norm for English literature. The marginalization of the native tradition was thus completed: only in brief moments, such as those which Hughes analyses in his study of Coleridge[22] or in the works of marginal figures (Clare, Hopkins), would it re-emerge – before, that is, Hughes's own attempt at

---

[18] *Winter Pollen*, 104.
[19] Ted Hughes, *Tales from Ovid*, London, 1997, 246.
[20] *Winter Pollen*, 215.
[21] *Ibid.*, 369-70.
[22] *Ibid.*, 390.

reviving it in his poetry. As he declared in an interview, "the difficult task of any poet in English has been to locate the force which Shakespeare called Venus in his first poem and Sycorax in his last".[23]

The metaphorical suggestiveness and consistency of Hughes's complementary accounts make them coalesce into a mythology where the transformations of the English nation are reflected in the history of its literature. The question that will concern me here is not whether Hughes's mythology makes historical sense: many a historian would no doubt scoff at his cavalier disregard of economic history and the blatant simplifications in which he has indulged. One sometimes senses an awareness of difficulties in Hughes's own prose. In the essays on Shakespeare and "Myths, Metres, Rhythms", the Restoration is described as a "historical accident", a "fluke".[24] The problem it poses for Hughes is all too obvious: the Restoration increased the French influence and further repressed the native sources of Anglo-Saxon poetry, but Hughes remains silent about the fact that it also brought England closer to Catholicism, which he identifies with mediaeval England. The beginning of a contradiction emerges when he speaks of the "Anglo-Saxon tradition, as idealized and politicized by Milton",[25] since the victory of Puritanism is supposed to correspond to the rejection of vital English sources.

The historical accuracy and coherence of Hughes's mythical account are inevitably debatable. As John Holloway had pointed out even before Hughes theorized his myth of English history, other Laureates like Austin and Tennyson had run up against similar problems when writing about the English past: "the trouble with English history was that there was too much of it. It was too long and varied to fit smoothly into a single myth."[26] Its explanatory power as Shakespeare criticism has been derided by many academic critics,[27] even though his readings can be intriguingly suggestive. Its greatest relevance, however, is of course to Hughes's own work. At first sight, it seems to possess a fair degree of internal consistency. Hughes records and bemoans the suppression of an older England which he associates with femininity, nature, the life of the

---

[23] "Ted Hughes and *Crow*", in Ekbert Faas's *Ted Hughes: The Unaccommodated Universe*, 197.

[24] *Winter Pollen*, 370, 119.

[25] *Ibid.*, 370.

[26] John Holloway, "The Myth of England", *The Listener*, 15 May 1969, 670.

[27] For a summary of the reception of *Shakespeare and the Goddess of Complete Being*, see Anthony Paul, "The Poet Laureate's National Poet", in *Reclamations of Shakespeare*, ed. A. J. Hoenselaars, Amsterdam, 1994, 159-72, and Neil Rhodes, "Bridegrooms to the Goddess: Hughes, Heaney and the Elizabethans", in *Shakespeare and Ireland*, eds Mark Thornton Burnett and Ramona Wray, London, 1997, 152.

senses, native poetic traditions, a blend of Anglo-Saxon, Norse and Celtic cultures, of Catholic and pagan religions. His condemnation of the opposite poles (male, rational, abstract, Frenchified or Latinate, Puritan) is just as constant, and it is not difficult to link his attacks on the debased version of Englishness that sprang from the Civil War with his denunciation of the condition of post-war England. When Hughes writes that "Puritanism, together with its accompanying materialist and democratizing outlook and rational philosophy, had very specific consequences",[28] he may be thinking of what he has termed "our psychotic democracy ... our materialist, non-organic democracy which is trying to stand up with a bookish theory instead of a skeleton".[29] Contemporary England, then, is yet another version (or perhaps the origin) of Hughes's Puritan villain, whose life-denying violence originates in the rejection of a more primitive, sensuous form of violence. This act of repression may be what Hughes meant by the "quiet civil war in England" which he held responsible for the hostility to his poems about violent animals.[30]

Hughes's historical thinking largely relies on the distinction between those two kinds of violence, which parallels the distinction between natural and mechanical violence in "Tiger-Psalm" (*Moortown*, 150-51). But as many other animal poems demonstrated, Hughes was unable to live up to that dichotomy (see chapter 3). The following analyses will show that what is true of his nature poems is also true of his historical vision. One of the questions that will have to be answered is why the distinction becomes blurred: does Hughes's search for maximal poetic effect in violence sometimes confuse his readers, or does that violence ultimately exceed a theoretical framework whose binary oppositions are deconstructed by the very workings of Hughes's imagination?

Among Hughes's early poems, "Witches" (*Lupercal*, 48) is ostensibly a fantasy about the female unconscious. It also condenses Hughes's national mythology in five quatrains. The poem runs the gamut of the contrasts between the authentic older England and its debased successor. The title makes it possible to identify the witches with the old goddess in her "Satanic" guise and with her "witcheries".[31] The opening line locates the equation in a distant past – "Once was every woman the witch/To ride a weed the ragwort road" – and the invocation of an ancestral feminine

---

[28] *Winter Pollen*, 110.
[29] "Ted Hughes and *Crow*", 198.
[30] Quoted in Faas's *The Unaccommodated Universe*, 19.
[31] *Winter Pollen*, 109, 111.

principle in the first stanza is significantly couched in strongly alliterative lines. Anglo-Saxon vocabulary and techniques are thus aligned with a feminine principle that is also connected with the Norse and Celtic elements in the national psyche: the witches are "Dancing in Ireland nightly, gone/To Norway". The witches thus come to stand for the cultural continuum that defined the largely pagan world of pre-Reformation England. The rational dismissal of witchcraft in the fourth stanza coincides with a return to present circumstances and modern colloquial English: "Did they dream it?/Oh, our science says they did." "Our science" is the legacy of Puritan rationalism and materialism to modern Britain, and the possessive adjective must also be interpreted as referring to a male collective subject. Indeed, the personal pronouns of the last stanza confirm Hughes's male/female dualism: although women may "weep/over our harms, who's to know/Where their feet dance while their heads sleep?". The last line also leaves open the possibility that the older England may still be reached through psychological exploration.

The poem is a fairly coherent expression of the conflict that Hughes locates at the heart of English nationhood. Had his writings on Shakespeare and on poetic traditions been available when *Lupercal* was published, the poem could have been interpreted as versified myth. As things stand, its reliance on sexual stereotypes goes some way toward showing how much Hughes's later elaborations, however complex, remained caught up in fairly rigid perceptions of gender. In this light, Plath's poem "The Shrike" makes for particularly disturbing reading, all the more because it may predate "Witches" ("The Shrike" was written in 1956, Hughes's poem was first published in *Sewanee Review* in 1958). Plath disturbingly reverses the oppositions that are central to Hughes's poem. "The Shrike" can indeed be read as a commentary on Hughes's mythologizing tendencies, although Plath herself comes close to accepting his terms:

> Such royal dreams beckon this man
> . . .
> To wing, sleep-feathered,
> The singular air,
> While she, envious bride,
> Cannot follow after ...[32]

Many other poems in Hughes's first two collections are constructed round some of the oppositions that dominate his thinking on England, but

---

[32] Sylvia Plath, *Collected Poems*, ed. Ted Hughes, London, 1981, 42.

they rarely coalesce into such compact clusters as "Witches". In retrospect, one can see that Hughes was already working out his mythology in *The Hawk in the Rain* and *Lupercal*. But although Englishness is one of the concerns of those early collections, it does not often emerge as a central theme: Hughes, like the angler of "Pike", was still casting his line in rather opaque waters that did not yield their secrets. In more senses than one, his England remained a mysterious depth (*Lupercal*, 57).

Hughes originally intended *Lupercal* to include a whole sequence about England: as Keith Sagar explains, "the controlling image was to have been a river, which metamorphoses freely with a snake, an adder standing for the rejected energies, the buried life of England, almost extinguished".[33] Eventually, this project was abandoned. *Wodwo* is also too varied to be described as an exploration of Englishness. Nevertheless, Hughes placed it under the aegis of his interest in the oldest sources of English poetry: the collection opens with an epigraph from *Sir Gawain and the Green Knight* where the word "wodwo" appears. The creature in the poem "Wodwo" is an existential quester wondering at his identity, and his search for self-knowledge can stand for Hughes's version of the modern English predicament:

> ... I suppose I am the exact centre
> but there's all this what is it roots
> roots roots roots and here's the water
> again very queer but I'll go on looking
>
> (*Wodwo*, 183)

The English are now experiencing their natural environment as a reality from which they have been alienated. The creature embarks on a quest for an identity to which mediaeval poetry still had access: that of the "wodwo".

The opening poem of *Wodwo*, "Thistles" (17), uses the alliterative devices of Anglo-Saxon poetry to suggest that natural cycles still embody a form of continuity with a submerged Englishness. Every thistle is "a revengeful burst/Of resurrection, a grasped fistful/Of splintered weapons and Icelandic frost...". "Burst of resurrection" achieves the same kind of effect as Shakespeare's use of the word "aggravate", which produced "a short-circuit to the concrete Anglo-Saxon 'gr' core of growl, grind, eager,

---

[33] Keith Sagar, "Fourfold Vision in Hughes", in *The Achievement of Ted Hughes*, ed. Keith Sagar, Manchester, 1983, 303.

grief, grate etc.".[34] In Hughes's poem, "resurrection" is caught up in the aggressively alliterative music of the lines, with their violent r's and consonant clusters.[35] The Latinate, Christian concept of resurrection is thus forcibly endowed with pagan and Germanic overtones. The word then paradoxically becomes an instrument through which a remnant of ancestral Englishness can be brought back to life. The thistles carry the Nordic heritage of Britain, the "gutturals of dialect", and they are also indestructible in their violence: they always reappear "Stiff with weapons, fighting back over the same ground".

"Thistles" has an obvious companion-piece in *Wodwo*, namely "The Warriors of the North" (159). The poem dispenses with natural allegory and deals directly with the place of the Nordic element in the multi-layered matter of England. Phonetically, its strong stresses, plosives, sibilants and consonant clusters work to create the same Germanic roughness that characterized "Thistles": the Vikings are "Bringing their frozen swords, their salt-bleached eyes, their salt-bleached hair". The poem, however, ends on a more pessimistic note than "Thistles". Cyclical rebirth has been replaced by degeneration: the Vikings' original violence eventually dissolved into the "relapse and prolongueur of their blood/Into the iron arteries of Calvin". Whereas "revengeful and "resurrection" had been absorbed into the Anglo-Saxon alliterative texture of "Thistles", the Latinisms of these lines take over from the Germanic quality of the poem's beginning; they linguistically re-enact the process through which the primitive violence of the Vikings was translated into the abstract, debased materialism of the Reformation. So far, the poem seems to conform to the pattern that Hughes would set down in his critical writings. Nevertheless, it is also the place where some complications begin to emerge.

Commenting on Hughes's predilection for alliterations, Seamus Heaney has written that "his consonants are the Norsemen, the Normans, the Roundheads in the world of his vocables, hacking and hedging and hammering down the abundance and luxury and possible lasciviousness of the vowels".[36] This is a view that Hughes must have found rather surprising; indeed, it goes against the grain of his own account of the struggle that poetic and cultural traditions have waged over the soul of England. Heaney's description of Hughes's consonants as "Normans"

---

[34] Hughes, *Winter Pollen*, 105.
[35] As discussed in chapter 2, Geoffrey Hill uses similar transitions from Latinate to Anglo-Saxon lexis in Hymn XXIII: "masterworks of treacherous thread. They trudged out of the dark ..." (*HCP*, 217).
[36] Seamus Heaney, *Preoccupations*, 154.

flies in the face of history: Hughes himself made much of the fact that the linguistic consequence of the Norman conquest was a marginalization of the alliterative tradition. Heaney's comparison is based on a purely political interpretation of Hughes's poetics: it is the roughness of his consonants, rather than their philological significance, that establishes the link with the violence of the Norman invaders in Heaney's imagination. The "Roundhead" element could seem rather out of place too: as Heaney himself points out, Hughes's alliterative music is indebted to Hopkins, and it would not seem fair to describe the latter – a convert to Catholicism – as a Roundhead.

Heaney's view of the consonants as "Norsemen", on the other hand, makes perfect philological sense, but it raises an interesting problem as well. Hughes himself conflated alliterative poetry with a cultural stratum where Celtic, Nordic and Anglo-Saxon influences merged into a sensuous, feminine, pagan-Catholic continuum. Heaney, on the other hand, upsets that balance of forces by wrenching both the Scandinavian input and alliterative poetics from Hughes's primitive England, and by aligning them with the Normans and Roundheads whom Hughes held responsible for loss of England's soul.

Heaney's account looks questionable, but he may well have hit upon a contradiction which Hughes himself acknowledged. One can see how, in the following passage from "Myths, Metres, Rhythms", Hughes was trying to do justice to Heaney's argument:

> to see the full irony of this Battle of Metrical Forms and that intertangled Battle of the Modes of Speech, in Britain, you have to be Welsh, Scots or Irish. You have to be one of those, that is, who failed, in successive defeats, to stop the Anglo-Saxon, the Scandinavian and finally the Norman invaders stealing the country from beneath them.[37]

Although he admits that Anglo-Saxon poetics dislodged Celtic forms in much the same way that it would later be displaced by continental conventions, Hughes tries to cling to the symbiosis on which his vision of a suppressed England is based: "for various reasons, the Celtic presence is usually found to be supporting the old English, and as time passes becomes less and less separable from it".[38] This has a glibness that is calculated to evade the implications of Heaney's reading, which reminds

---

[37] *Winter Pollen*, 368.
[38] *Ibid.*, 369.

us that in some parts of the United Kingdom time hasn't passed quite as fast as Hughes suggests.[39]

"Thistles" tries to merge its alliterative music with its thematic allusion to the "gutturals of dialect", but in Heaney's view Hughes can only imagine (and not revive) "the fundamental speech, uttering itself in gutturals from behind the sloped arms of consonants". Although he identifies Hughes's gutturals as Nordic,[40] Heaney's metaphors indicate that for him, gutturals belong to a Gaelic form of speech that was suppressed by Germanic consonants. He uses military images to describe the very Anglo-Saxon language which Hughes argued went underground when the "military garrison of the Empire" imposed its own idiom.[41] Heaney's own poem "Traditions" can then be read as a direct response to "Thistles":

> Our guttural muse
> was bulled long ago
> by the alliterative tradition
>
> (*Wintering Out*, 21)

The rare gutturals in Hughes's work are actually of Celtic origin, which may yet again point to Hughes's urge to blend the Celtic and the Germanic.[42] But, as the next chapter will discuss at length, the linguistic mythology that Heaney developed in his own work is based on a strategic misreading of Hughes's.

For Hughes, the conflict which Heaney makes central to his own politico-linguistic meditation must be attenuated; its protagonists must be united in the strife that opposed them both to those who really threatened the older England. This applies to mythology as well as poetics; indeed, in a review of Turville-Petre's *Myth and Religion of the North*, Hughes also argued that Nordic myths are

---

[39] In yet another text, Hughes took an opposite view and stressed the antagonism between Celt and Anglo-Saxon: the "Britishification" of the Normans "intensified in a real way the old polarization between Celt and Anglo-Saxon by clarifying the affinity and common interest of Anglo-Saxon and Norman". Hughes even speaks of a "Norman-Anglo-Saxon axis" (*Rain-Charm for the Duchy*, 62).

[40] Heaney, *Preoccupations*, 155.

[41] Hughes, *Winter Pollen*, 119.

[42] The "gutturals" of "Thistles" seem to emerge from the tomb of a "decayed Viking" (*Wodwo*, 17). But "Pibroch" (*Wodwo*, 177) is Gaelic (< Celtic "piobaireachd"), as is the verb "gralloch" (< Celtic "grealach") in "Esther's Tomcat", where an ageless cat "still grallochs/old dogs on the quiet" (*Lupercal*, 23).

much deeper in us, and truer to us, than the Greek-Roman
pantheons that came in with Christianity, and again with the
Renaissance .... It is as if we were to lose *Macbeth* and *King
Lear*, and have to live on *Timon* and *Coriolanus*; or as if a
vocabulary drawn wholly from the Greek-Roman brand were to
take over absolutely from our Anglo-Saxon-Norse-Celtic.[43]

Hughes also sees a manifestation of the old English poetic tradition in
Coleridge's interest in Norse and Celtic myths: Coleridge's work can thus
"be read as a large-scale, brilliantly concise, diagnostic, luminous vision
of England's spiritual/intellectual predicament".[44] In the landscape poetry
of *Remains of Elmet*, the erasure of more recent cultural accretions
uncovers older traces that are both Celtic (cf. "The Ancient Briton Lay
Under his Rock", 84) and Nordic:

> ... the children
> Of rock and water and a draughty absence
> ....
> Smashed all that would smash
> What would not smash they burned
> ....
> Then trailed away homeward aimlessly
> Like the earliest
> Homeless Norsemen
>
> (38)

The valley of Elmet itself, Hughes tells us in his note to the collection, is
a pass "between the Scandinavian pressures of the North Sea and the
Celtic pressures of the Irish Sea" (*Three Books*, 181). Hughes must keep
this Celtic-Germanic-Nordic continuum unified at all costs, despite the
violence that went into its making. His critical writings often show a
profound grasp of mythology and philology, but the demands of his
imagination almost made him repeat the historical blunders of the early
Romantics, who sometimes mixed up Gothic, Scandinavian and Celtic
elements in their mythological and bardic poems.[45] Hughes's own brand

---

[43] *Winter Pollen*, 41.
[44] *Winter Pollen*, 439. For discussions of Coleridge's use of Celtic and Nordic myths,
see 397-99, 429, 453.
[45] "The scholarship of the day was not always accurate in discriminating between
ancient systems of religion, and Gray, in his letters to Mason ... takes him to task for
mixing the Gothic and Celtic mythologies". Gray himself, however, "had not scrupled
to mix mythologies in 'The Bard' .... Mallet himself had a very confused notion of

of Romanticism forced him to smooth over contradictions of which he remained uneasily aware. But if his quest for an ancestral England seems to override historical considerations, it also relies on a wayward poetic logic which produces its own short-circuits. Indeed, Hughes's poetry itself was responsive to the arguments of those who, like Heaney, unwittingly exposed the fissures in his mythology of English nationhood.

Hughes repeatedly associated his sense of an authentic, primitive Englishness with femininity, through the figures of the bride and of the mediaeval Goddess. But in "Thistles", the task of perpetuating its spiritual legacy is clearly entrusted to male figures: when thistles turn grey, "like men", they are followed by "their sons" (*Wodwo*, 17). "The Warriors of the North" are also assertively male. Hughes suggests that their aggressive virility nevertheless merged with the feminine character of the land they invaded: their frozen armoury "thawed" when it cam into contact with the "fluttered bowels of the women" and the "gold of the Gaels" (*Wodwo*, 159). The alliteration in "gold of the Gaels" also attempts to merge a Celtic substratum with Germanic poetics. How persuasive Hughes's account of the fusion between feminine/Gaelic and masculine/Nordic elements actually is can be gauged by Heaney's effortless counter-interpretation, which radically separates them.

Heaney's analysis of Hughes can in fact be confirmed by other poems in *Wodwo*. In the third part of "Gog", the "hooded horseman of iron" is a "Holy Warrior" whose appearance is quite similar to that of the Viking warriors, or of the thistles that were "stiff with weapons". Hughes's knight, however, is battling against the feminine "wound-gash in the earth" from which he has emerged (*Wodwo*, 151). His "enemy" is the "womb-wall of the dream" "Suckling at the root-blood of the origins, the salt-milk drug of the mothers". He seems to enact the process by which the Vikings' energies were diverted into the Puritan ethics of Calvinism: "Bring him to the ruled slab, the octaves of order/The law and mercy of number" (152). Tom Paulin points out that, owing to the absence of mythological elaboration on Hughes's part,[46] the poem "stays obscure, indeed it collides with its own obscurity". Nevertheless, the critic has no difficulty in identifying the knight as a "Cromwellian figure", and only hesitates between different expressions of Puritan English materialism: "St. George? industrialist? colonist?".[47] Paulin's reading is part of a

---

the relation of the Celtic to the Teutonic race. He speaks constantly of the old Scandinavians as Celts". See Henry Beers, *A History of English Romanticism in the Eighteenth Century* (1899), New York, 1968, 195-96.

[46] Paulin is writing before the publication of *Shakespeare and the Goddess of Complete Being* and the new essays collected in *Winter Pollen*.

[47] Tom Paulin, *Minotaur*, 267.

broader analysis of *Wodwo* as a symptom of "the cult of the Nordic which is so central to the imagination of British Protestantism".[48] Once again, a Northern Irish critic has rushed into the cracks that open in Hughes's mythology.

Paulin is aware that Hughes is trying to contrast the authentic violence of the Vikings with the debased violence of the Puritans, but he refuses to make allowances for his attempt at blending the Celtic and the Nordic. Paulin rightly comments that Hughes often thinks "in terms of splits and polarities"; but like Heaney, he analyses Hughes's work in terms of dichotomies that do not always reflect Hughes's own. Paulin's reading thus pits the "salt-bleached warriors against the elaborate, patient gold of the Gaels" and "the Germanic/puritan/masculine" against the "Celtic-/Catholic/feminine". Consequently, Paulin gives short shrift to Hughes's two-tiered conception of violence: "The Warriors of the North" may "set one form of violence against the other, but it ratifies both".[49]

Wodwo is not only characterized by the historical contradictions that Irish misreadings reveal. It also shows the instability of the gender element in Hughes's mythology. In the light of Hughes's pronouncements on Shakespeare, the knight's hostility towards the feminine in "Gog" should obviously be condemned. But his struggle to escape from an "octopus maw" (*Wodwo*, 152) invites comparison with Hughes's praise of Keith Douglas as a poet who "seems to have no difficulties with the terrible, suffocating, maternal octopus of English poetic tradition".[50] Hughes is bold enough in his praise of Douglas to draw a daring comparison with Shakespeare.[51] And yet, Hughes would interpret Shakespeare's work as a constant engagement with the presiding female deity of pre-Reformation England. The resulting ambiguity makes it possible to account for readings of "Gog" as a celebration of masculinist heroism, rather than as an indictment of the Puritan rejection of pagan earth-cults.

Although several poems in *Wodwo* are clearly part of Hughes's development of a complete myth of nationhood, they already show that this project was doomed by the complexities and the excessive nature of his imagination of violence. They are admittedly not part of a collection that is articulated round the theme of Englishness – this can perhaps only be said of a sustained mythological narrative like *Gaudete*, which records the turmoil into which an unorthodox vicar plunges a small English

---

[48] *Ibid.*, 265.
[49] *Ibid.*, 266.
[50] Hughes, *Winter Pollen*, 213.
[51] *Ibid.*, 215.

village. But *Gaudete* does not subsume all the elements of Hughes's mythology in a framework that would prefigure the uneasy syntheses of *Shakespeare and the Goddess of Complete Being* and "Myths, Metres, Rhythms". Hughes's dilemma in that collection is not only that contemporary England simply isn't "a sufficiently plausible setting in which to enact his mythological drama".[52] Another problem of *Gaudete* is that it damages the very consistency of Hughes's mythology. When compared with *Wodwo*, *Gaudete* actually brings once more into focus the shifting place of the Nordic element in Hughes's thinking on England. Indeed, it recycles some of the images of "The Warriors of the North", but it also suggests that Hughes capitulated to Heaney's reading of that earlier poem.

Gaudete contrasts the sterile, Puritan rationality of the village's men with the sensuality of the reverend Lumb, who wants to restore Christianity to its former, more pagan aspects. In this, it is quite consistent with Hughes's account of religious changes in England. The hitch comes when religious oppositions are made to coincide with ethnic and sexual ones. One of the female characters seduced by the protagonist Lumb, Pauline Hagen, is meeting her lover: "her body's thirty-five year old womb-fluttered abandon/Warms his calming hands" (25). This recalls the way in which the invading Vikings had warmed at the "fluttered bowels of the women" in "The Warriors of the North" (*Wodwo*, 159). But Lumb is never associated with Nordic elements; instead, these attributes are now conferred on Major Hagen, who is observing the whole scene:

> Paradeground gravel in the folded gnarl of his jowls.
> A perfunctory campaign leatheriness.
> A frontal *Viking* weatherproof
> Drained of the vanities, pickled in mess-alcohol and smoked
> 　　dark.
> Anaesthetised
> For ultimate cancellations
> By the scathing alums of King's regulations,
> The petrifying nitrates of garrison caste
> 　　　　　　　　　　　　　　　(*Gaudete*, 24. Emphasis mine)

Here, Major Hagen's Viking quality is part of a cluster of associations which typify him as a sterile Puritan. The military rhetoric through which Hughes creates the stereotype ("parade-ground", "King's regulations",

---

[52] Robert Stuart, "Ted Hughes", in *British Poetry since 1970: A Critical Survey*, eds Peter Jones and Michael Schmidt, Manchester, 1980, 84.

"garrison caste") is exactly the one that he used in his dismissal of standard Victorian English.[53] Hughes himself commented in an interview that, when writing *Gaudete*, he tried to "maintain a balance between German/Scandinavian, and Ancient Britain/Celtic, between Puritanical suppressive and Catholic woman worshipping".[54] And indeed, it is only when he reappears in Ireland in the last section that Lumb starts singing hymns to a female deity. In *Gaudete*, Hughes himself jeopardized the unity of the historical continuum that constitutes his ideal England.

This shows how porous and shifty Hughes's dichotomies can be. Some of his most central symbols are liable to be contaminated by their very opposites, thus emphasizing the instability of Hughes's fables of nationhood.[55] Even Hughes's pike, perhaps his most potent totem of ancestral Englishness, turns out to be more ambiguous than it may seem. For although the pond it swims is apparently a sanctuary of the old pagan/Catholic England (it was originally part of a "monastery" – *Lupercal*, 57), the pike's "aged grin" also corresponds to its "jaws' hooked clamp and fangs/Not to be changed at this date/A life subdued to its instrument" (*Lupercal*, 56). Pike thus share the machine-like perfection of Hughes's thrushes (*Lupercal*, 52). But in the same way that his celebration of natural spontaneity in "Thrushes" paradoxically drew on mechanical metaphors, the connotations of the word "instrument" here turn the pike into an ambiguous symbol that undoes the opposition between pagan nature-worship and Puritan ethics. On the one hand, the mysterious, ancestral pike can be seen as an incarnation of the Goddess. But one of Hughes's most sympathetic critics, Leonard Scigaj, has read the phrase "subdued to its instrument" as an example of the "utilitarian blight that produced ecological and cultural devastation in favour of the Protestant ethic's 'Far, veiled gaze of quietly/Homicidal appraisal'".[56] This proves yet again that the propensity towards hyperbole in Hughes's treatment of violence ultimately defies the various cultural and historical frameworks that would give stable meanings to that violence.

---

[53] See *Winter Pollen*, 119.

[54] "Ted Hughes and *Gaudete*", Interview with Ekbert Faas, in Ekbert Faas's *Ted Hughes: The Unaccommodated Universe*, 215. This may be the comment which Paulin had in mind when he contrasted "the Germanic/puritan/masculine" with the "Celtic/Catholic/feminine" in Hughes (*Minotaur*, 266).

[55] *Gaudete* suggests that Hughes incorporated Heaney's negative interpretation of the Nordic element, but subsequent writings (*Remains of Elmet*, the essay on Coleridge in *Winter Pollen*) show a lingering fascination with the positive potential of Nordic themes.

[56] Leonard Scigaj, *Ted Hughes*, Boston, 1991, 48. The lines quoted by Scigaj are from the poem "For Billy Holt" (*Three Books*, 25).

Another problem which seems to have dogged Hughes is the constantly thwarted ambition to write a collection that would embody his vision of England. *Gaudete* comes closest to that ideal, but it fails to heal the rifts that open in Hughes's thinking. More surprisingly, perhaps, *Crow* was another mythological narrative which at some stage was intended to fulfil the role of national poem. But here too, the failure to carry out that plan is instructive. Some critics have seen Hughes's crow as a "totem of England".[57] Hughes's original plan shows that *Crow* was closely related to the national myth that found expression in his works on Shakespeare and poetic traditions: "Hughes originally conceived *Crow* to have a medieval epic plot where the protagonist, after many trials and ordeals, learns how to end his alienation from Nature and win Nature as his bride."[58] The optimism of that script was shattered by the deaths of Hughes's companion Assia Gutman and their daughter, and *Crow* has come to stand as Hughes's darkest collection. Nevertheless, it is possible to find traces of Hughes's national myth-making in the *Crow* poems, although the two clearest examples of national allegory were not included in the collection proper. These are "Crow's Song about Prospero and Sycorax" and "Crow's Song about England".[59] The first poem identifies Sycorax with Ophelia and Cordelia, and ends on a pessimistic note as the male figure repudiates his female counterpart:

> He has found
> Something
> Easier to live with ...
> His death and her death.

This double murder corresponds both to the denial of the female, life-giving principle that Hughes sees in *King Lear* and *Hamlet*, and to its suppression in the triumph of Reformation ethics in *The Tempest*.

"Crow's Song about England" likewise focuses on the desecration of England's feminine principle by Puritanism. In the poem, England is a girl who first tries to give her body ("mouth", "eyes", "breasts" and "cunt") and gets punished for it: "She was mad with pain she humped into a beast/She changed her sex he came back." This transformation into

---

[57] Keith Sagar, *The Art of Ted Hughes*, 106; Paulin, *Minotaur*, 264.
[58] Scigaj, *Ted Hughes*, 13. Graham Bradshaw considers "Crow and the Shakespeare essay" as "complementary investigations of Englishness". See his essay "Hughes and Shakespeare", in *The Achievement of Ted Hughes*, ed. Keith Sagar, 67.
[59] The poems are reprinted in Keith Sagar's *The Art of Ted Hughes*, 142, 144-45.

a male animal invites parallels with the emergence of the boar that kills the Puritan Adonis and with the frenzy that seizes the Puritan mind and makes it explode into the violence of Tarquin:[60] "When he saw her mouth he stabbed with a knife/Where he saw her eyes he stabbed likewise." Finally, England reverts to her female incarnation, and unsuccessfully tries to keep her body whole. Eventually, "she was sentenced/She did life" (145), like the incarcerated bride of native English poetry, "walled up" in her room by the "doctrine and discipline of puritan wedlock".[61]

Deprived of their mythological underpinnings, those pieces do not make for very impressive reading, as is confirmed by Hughes's decision not to include them in *Crow* itself. Only a handful of the poems that appeared in the collection deal more or less openly with the themes developed in Hughes's writings on England. One such poem is "Crow's Account of St George" (*Crow*, 31-32), which casts England's patron saint as a Puritan rationalist for whom "everything in the Universe/Is a track of numbers racing toward an answer". St George confronts a female monster which is even more hyperbolically threatening than the one fought by the knight in "Gog": "a belly-ball of hair, with crab-legs, eyeless .... a horrible oven of fangs." Filled with horror at the female principle, St George promptly hacks it up with a sword, only to realize his life-denying mistake: "his wife and children lie in their blood" (32). The value-system of the poem is less ambiguous than that of "Gog". Nevertheless, one wonders whether the sheer exaggeration of the style – from the all too obvious *vagina dentata* image to the description of St George's sword as a "ceremonial Japanese decapitator" – does not generate an irony that calls the seriousness of Hughes's myth-making into question.

"Criminal Ballad" (*Crow*, 38-39) similarly relates an anonymous man's tortured relation to the female principle. A Macbeth-like figure, he eventually "ran from the children and ran through the house/Holding his bloody hands clear of everything" (39). The following lines interestingly bring together various images that have proved central to Hughes's thinking on England:

> … the woman of complete pain rolling in flame
> Was calling to him all the time
> From the empty goldfish pond.

> (38)

---

[60] Hughes, *Shakespeare and the Goddess of Complete Being*, 8.
[61] Hughes, *Winter Pollen*, 370.

The "woman of complete pain" points forward to the elusive Goddess of complete being of Hughes's Shakespeare, the one who calls out from her depths to later English poets.[62] The pond refers back to the pond of "Pike", which was "as deep as England" and seemed to contain its buried energies (*Lupercal*, 57); the pond's emptiness may here convey a sense of environmental threat. However, Hughes's majestic pike has bathetically made way for goldfish. The pond's national meaning is also clear in "Crowego" (61) where, "Drinking Beowulf's blood", "Crow communes with poltergeists out of old ponds".[63] But Hughes's English myths here merge with others in a general parody of mythologies, which reduces Ulysses to a "worm, which Crow ate", and Hercules's remains to an "electrode in Crow's brain". As Paul Bentley writes, "echoes of the Anglo-Saxon alliterative tradition ... the poet's interest in shamanism, the poetry as fishing metaphor in the early poem 'Pike' – all here seem absurd".[64] Crow is feeding destructively on all human history, peering into it "Like a leopard into a fat land".

It is somehow surprising that *Crow* came out barely one year before Hughes first set out his ideas on English nationhood in his introduction to *A Choice of Shakespeare's Verse* (1971). Both works clearly echo each other. But, far from exemplifying Hughes's national mythology, *Crow* actually subjects it to the destructive gaze of sarcasm and despair. The vision of *Crow* is so hyperbolically dark that it also relativizes Hughes's concern with England by painting a picture of universal disintegration. The process through which England "lost her soul" almost becomes a comic episode in Hughes's cataclysmic account of human history since Creation. This is also reflected in the language of the collection. In *Crow*, the alliterative music of Hughes's earlier poems was subsumed into the "super-simple and super-ugly language" which he was now striving after.[65] Not only are most poems stylistically too bare to recall Hopkins or Anglo-Saxon models, but even Hughes's most successful alliterations are here divested of their historical significance. They become a mere stammer, the onomatopoeic equivalent of the universal chaos and violence that Hughes is describing:

> Black the blood in its loud tunnel
> Black the bowels packed in furnace

---

[62] *Ibid.*, 370-71.

[63] Tom Paulin regards those lines as an expression of the "occult nationalism" of *Crow* (*Minotaur*, 264), but he misses their parodic quality.

[64] Paul Bentley, *The Poetry of Ted Hughes: Language, Illusion and Beyond*, London, 1998, 49.

[65] Hughes, "Ted Hughes and *Crow*", 208.

...
Black also the soul, the huge stammer
Of the cry that, swelling, could not
Pronounce its sun.

(13)

God tried to teach Crow how to talk.
'Love,' said God. 'Say, Love.'
Crow gaped, and the white shark crashed into the sea
And went rolling downwards, discovering its own depth.

(20)

Crow may well drink of Beowulf's blood, but instead of reverting to the alliterative purity of Anglo-Saxon verse, it only regurgitates a meaningless, horrible laughter.

Hughes's thinking on language also has its paradoxes. Indeed, in the years that led up to *Crow*, he was not only emphasizing the importance of Anglo-Saxon dialect in Shakespeare, he was also involved in a project that would lead to the creation of *Orghast*, a play in an invented language. For Hughes, this did not imply any contradiction. For one thing, many of his remarks on *Orghast* refer to Shakespeare. Thus, the play was helped by director Peter Brook's "instinct for the all-inclusive, Shakespearean style of dramatic world, a giant rag-bag of everything possible, a colliding place of all human energies and polarities".[66] Nevertheless, a tension arises between Hughes's claim concerning Shakespeare's universality and his insistence on the fact that "Shakespeare's language is somehow nearer the vital life of English, still, than anything written down since". For Hughes also declared that "however rootedly national it may be, poetry is less and less a prisoner of its own language".[67]

This raises questions about the role of Anglo-Saxon and English dialect in Hughes's poetry. Hughes praised the "dialect instinct" in Shakespeare's language. Anglo-Saxon alliterative verse also appealed to the populist imagination he shared with Hopkins, since that tradition became "the poetry of the people – variously imprinted by the dialects of the provinces".[68] Hughes also commented on the importance of his West Yorkshire origins:

---

[66] *Winter Pollen*, 126.

[67] *Ibid.*, 104. The second remark is quoted by Michael Parker in "Ted Hughes and the Poets of Eastern Europe", in Sagar's *The Achievement of Ted Hughes*, 37.

[68] *Winter Pollen*, 104, 366.

They have a very distinctive dialect there .... Without it I doubt whether I would ever have written verse. And in the case of West Yorkshire dialect, of course, it connects you directly and in your most intimate self to middle English poetry.[69]

But if Hughes reached back to Anglo-Saxon verse via alliteration and sprung rhythm, dialect itself is largely absent from his poetry. Compared with the work of regionalist poets, or even with that of a more aestheticizing philologist like his model Hopkins, Hughes's poetry remains an attempt at subverting the Queen's English by internal means, that is by a strategic use of standard Anglo-Saxon lexis. It is of course significant that his alliterative thistles are only *"like* ... the gutturals of dialects" (*Wodwo*, 17. Emphasis mine).

Dialect in Hughes comes to resemble his ancestral pike: its presence may be acutely felt, but it never quite emerges from the waters which the poet is staring at. Hughes's interest in demotic English is largely divested of the social dimension it had for another of his models, John Clare. Tom Paulin's view of Clare strikingly recalls Hughes's own comments on standard English: "John Clare wrote before the long ice age of standard British English clamped down on the living language and began to break its local and vernacular energies."[70] But in the same way that Hughes turned Clare's wandering animals from symbols of social resistance into objects of aesthetic contemplation (see chapter 3), so does he rid Clare's idiom of the subversive dimension which radical critics are keen to stress. Hughes's subversion of standard English is a much more indirect and problematic affair; it does not rely on any specific regional or social energies, but on a historico-linguistic mythology that lacks consistency. Moreover, as I will now analyse, Hughes's interest in alliteration may ultimately spring from the same fascination with violence that underlies his animal poems.

Alliteration in *Crow* came to exceed the English framework in which Hughes had developed alliterative techniques in his first three volumes. But while some shift of priorities undeniably occurred between the Anglo-Saxon echoes of *Wodwo* and the "super-ugly language" of *Crow*, the uses of alliteration in the latter volume can also shed light on Hughes's earlier work. Hughes's cultivation of Anglo-Saxon poetics clearly points to a debt to Hopkins, but alliteration in Hughes often achieves effects that differ from Hopkins's in some key respects. Hughes's preference largely goes to consonant clusters that strain the

---

[69] "Ted Hughes and *Crow*", 202.
[70] Paulin, *Minotaur*, 47.

rhythm of his lines; for Hopkins, on the other hand, the repetition of consonants had an essentially musical function. Not many of Hughes's poems flow as musically as "The Windhover", with its interplay of sibilants, nasals, liquids and semi-vowels:

> I caught this morning morning's minion, king-
> > dom of daylight's dauphin, dappled-dawn-drawn falcon,
> > > in his riding
> > Of the rolling level underneath him steady air, and
> > > striding
> > High there, how he rung upon the rein of a wimpling wing
> > In his ecstasy!
>
> > > > > > > *(Poems, 69)*

Hughes's alliterations occasionally achieve a comparable musical felicity, as in the first line of "The Thought-Fox": "I imagine this midnight moment's forest" (*The Hawk in the Rain*, 14). However, Hughes's own version of "The Windhover", "The Hawk in the Rain", alternates between the harsher and more discordant consonantal rhythm of its first stanza:

> I drown in the drumming ploughland, I drag up
> Heel after heel from the swallowing of the earth's mouth,
> From clay that clutches my each step to the ankle

and the smoother alliterations of lines like

> His wings hold all creation in a weightless quiet
> Steady as a hallucination in the streaming air.
>
> > > > > *(The Hawk in the Rain*, 11)

When Hughes fuses Anglo-Saxon poetics with his interest in English history, his alliterations become even more distinctly aggressive, based as they are on blunt plosives, gnashing clusters and other awkward transitions between consonants. This is quite evident in "Thistles" and "The Warriors of the North":

> Every one a reve*nge*ful *burst*
> Of resurre*ct*ion, a *grasped* fis*tf*ul
> Of *spl*int*e*red wea*pons* and I*c*eland*ic fr*ost *thr*ust up ...
>
> > > > > *(Wodwo*, 17. Emphases mine)

*Bringing their *frozen* swords, their salt-*bleached* eyes,*
*their salt-*bleached* hair,*
*The *snow*'s *st*upefied a*nv*ils in rows,*
(*Wodwo*, 159. Emphases mine)[71]

This idiosyncrasy of Hughes's is perhaps best exemplified in the early poem "The Martyrdom of Bishop Farrar" (*The Hawk in the Rain*, 58-59), where it produces such lines as "... they see what/Black oozing twist of stuff bubbles the smell/That tars and retches their lungs ..." (58). The poem includes an impressive list of words beginning with "b" ("burn(ed)", "bone", "body", "bowels", "boil", "bare", "bargain" ...), as well as clusters containing that plosive: "blood" (twice), "bloody", "black" (twice), "bubble", "establish", "blazing", "blasphemous", "branded", "broke". Clusters beginning with "s" or "sh" are just as frequent: "smoke", "smell", "spared", "stamp", "struck" (three times), "stuff", "stump", "shrivel", "shrewd", "shrieks". The poem brings out the centrality of gruff, harsh, discordant sounds in Hughes's Anglo-Saxon poetics. It is not a coincidence that, in his discussion of the "dialect instinct" of Shakespeare's language, Hughes should have focused on Shakespeare's use of the word "aggravate": in Shakespeare's hands, the verb is "not merely a Joycean fusion of irritate, anger, exaggerate, but a much deeper short circuit to the concrete Anglo-Saxon 'gr' core of growl, grind, eager, grief, grate etc".[72] Hughes's philological reflections also bear the mark of a thematic obsession with violence.

In poems like "The Martyrdom of Bishop Farrar", Hughes recalls the Hopkins of the dark vision and the broken, discordant rhythms of the "terrible sonnets": "God's most deep decree/Bitter would have me taste: my taste was me/Bones built in me, flesh filled, blood brimmed the curse."[73] Musically as well as thematically, what Hughes found most useful in Hopkins was an expression of conflict and violent excess which he radicalized in his own poetry. If Hughes's prose presents Anglo-Saxon poetics as part of a historical locus of organic wholeness, the uses to which he put them in his poems are often radically anti-organic. His blunt, harsh consonants jostle with each other to create a phonetic equivalent of the violent conflicts that are at the heart of his poetry.

---

[71] The alliterative quality of the poem is underscored by the visual presence of the consonants that have disappeared from the pronunciation of words like "sword".

[72] *Winter Pollen*, 105. This supposedly Anglo-Saxon core nevertheless includes Latinate elements: "grief" (<OF *grief*) and "grate" (<OF *grate-r*) come from Old French.

[73] *The Poems of Gerard Manley Hopkins*, 101.

"The Martyrdom of Bishop Farrar" describes one of the key moments in the process through which England would "lose her soul", that is the Reformation. It is worth noting that the poem is actually sympathetic towards the Protestant bishop who was martyred on Mary Tudor's order. Years later, Hughes would speak of Mary Tudor's "bad luck": "she came at a moment when the opposition of the Nonconformists, pushing to complete the Reformation, drove her to react from the Satanic side of the old goddess, earning the name of Bloody Mary."[74] In this early poem, she is largely presented as the tyrant whose repression of Protestantism is defeated by Farrar's heroic attitude on the stake. Religious conflict transforms his Puritan "body's cold-kept miserdom of shrieks" into a violent spectacle that captivates both his flock and Hughes's imagination (*The Hawk in the Rain*, 59). This proves yet again that Hughes's mythology of English nationhood is not separable from an obsession with conflict and violence. It contradicts his urge to locate an authentic, organic England that disappeared at the end of a huge confrontation. In his poetry, conflict itself often seems to take over as a locus of authenticity, whether it informs his descriptions of nature or his treatment of English historical themes. Hence the paradox of denouncing "our psychotic ... non-organic democracy"[75] through a poetry that thrives on madness and anti-organic images. Hughes himself comes close to admitting as much when he writes of Shakespeare's crazed Puritans ("Richard III, Tarquin, Hamlet, Angelo, Othello, Macbeth"): "the peculiar fact is that it is just this man of chaos ... who is the mouthpiece of the poetry. Looking through the great passages, one sees that the mass of them belong to this possessed homicide ...".[76] Indeed, what is most distinctive about much of Hughes's poetry is its fascination with and exultation in chaotic violence.

Crow was the place where Hughes acknowledged that his thematic and formal concerns exceeded the myth of England that he never quite ceased to develop. The violent disintegration that had earlier served as a commentary on modern England became so hyperbolic that it strove for universal relevance. The Anglo-Saxon purity of alliterative poetry was dissolved in the stammer and laughter of Crow; after that collection, Hughes never quite returned to the full-blown Anglo-Saxon echoes of

[74] *Winter Pollen*, 109.
[75] "Ted Hughes and *Crow*", 198.
[76] *Winter Pollen*, 115. This Shakespearean antecedent bears out Neil Rhodes's comment that "Hughes's mission to rescue the Goddess ... is compromised by his need to give lavish accounts of the [male Puritan] figure". See Rhodes, "Bridegrooms to the Goddess", 155.

Wodwo. In *Crow*, Hughes's poetry also reached a paroxysm of destruction from which he could only retreat in subsequent collections. In some of these, Hughes actually tried to convey a sense of the organic wholeness which underlies his mythology. In *Gaudete*, he attempted to do so within an English context, but he could only succeed by locating the end of his quest in Ireland. Hints of reconciliation pervade the more cryptic and culturally indeterminate *Cave Birds*, particularly in "Bride and Groom Lie Hidden for Three Days": "Like two gods of mud/Sprawling in the dirt, but with infinite care//They bring each other to perfection" (*Three Books*, 98). Hughes's mysterious finale, however, undermines the optimistic thrust of the collection: "At the end of the ritual/up comes a goblin" (*Three Books*, 101). In *Shakespeare and the Goddess of Complete Being*, Hughes also uses that sentence to stress the artificiality of Shakespeare's vision of reconciliation in *The Tempest*: the betrothal of Ferdinand and Miranda is "as de-eroticized as heavenly help can make it," Hughes writes, but "according to the Ainu proverb, 'At the end of the ritual, up comes a goblin', the Masque itself produces its own destruction".[77] The implication of this for *Cave Birds* seems to be that, even if Hughes's betrothal is certainly not de-eroticized, his own poetic fable also destroys itself. Elsewhere, Hughes offered a traditional, organicist definition of what a poem should be: "an assembly of living parts moved by a single spirit." However, he also showed a quasi deconstructionist awareness of the elusive nature of words:

> It is this little goblin in a word which is its life and its poetry, and it is this little goblin which the poet has to have under control.
>   Well, you will say, this is hopeless. How do you control all that. When the words come pouring out how can you be sure that you do not have one of these side meanings of the word "feathers" getting all stuck up with one of the side meanings of the word "treacle", a few words later.[78]

The "goblin" of words, which is surprisingly close to the deconstructive instrument of *différance*, is what Hughes failed to keep under control in his own mythology of English nationhood. The dichotomies on which its various expressions rely deconstruct themselves, turning into their contraries or producing an excess of meaning that relativizes their national significance. As the goblin of *différance* ran riot in his writings,

---

[77] Hughes, *Shakespeare and the Goddess of Complete Being*, 446.
[78] Ted Hughes, *Poetry in the Making*, London, 1969, 17-18.

Hughes's hope of arriving at a stable mythology of Englishness receded further and further.

Unsurprisingly, the collection where Hughes overcame those tensions to suggest real images of integration and reconciliation is also the one where he rid himself explicitly of his obsession with a lost England. *River* may well succeed where *Lupercal* had failed in that it fulfils Hughes's ambition to write a whole sequence about rivers, but its central image does not quite stand for "the buried life of England, almost extinguished" which was to have been at the heart of *Lupercal*.[79] Admittedly, some of the poems in *River* recall Hughes's Shakespearean speculations about the struggle for England's soul. "Fairy Flood" reads like *King Lear* transformed into an ecological allegory where Lear's daughters are cast as an escaping river:

> The fatherly landscape upbraids and harangues,
> Claws weakly at her swollen decision and disarrayed
> With gaping beard and disarrayed robe
>
> (*Three Books*, 116)

But if the English landscape is shown disintegrating here, there are also moments when Hughes succeeds in capturing ecstatic visions that have been divested of his ambiguous cultivation of violent effects. What is most remarkable is that such visions sometimes arise from an explicit rejection of his mythical England. Whereas "Pike" had identified England with the depth of a pike-haunted pond, "That Morning" (strategically placed at the end of *River* in *Three Books*) shows that Hughes had deliberately stopped trying to equate nature with a sense of nationhood:

> We came where the salmon were so many
> So steady, so spaced, so far-aimed
> On their inner map, England could add
>
> Only the sooty twilight of South Yorkshire
> Hung with the drumming drift of Lancasters ...
>
> (*Three Books*, 178)

Hughes came full circle in that poem. In the same way that, as a child starting to write in wartime England, he "set [his] tales" in "places as far away as possible from the sooty town [he] lived in and the gloom of the

---

[79] See Keith Sagar, "Fourfold Vision in Hughes", 303.

war",[80] he has now given up trying to reconcile England with the primitivism that shaped his imagination. Instead, he now accepts and dramatizes the gap which his earlier poetry had often tried to bridge: that between England and primeval nature.

Another consequence of Hughes's liberation from his own English myths is that the very language of *River* achieves a quiet clarity that remains unmatched in other collections. The fish of "September Salmon" "ignores the weir's wrangle. Ignores/The parochial down-drag/Of the pool's long diphthong" (*Three Books*, 148). The collection is indeed largely free from the dour Anglo-Saxon music of Hughes's early poetry. What replaces his aggressive alliterations and drawn out, lugubrious vowels is the flowing, almost pristine language in which Hughes overcomes disintegration and celebrates his communion with nature in "Go Fishing":

> Join water, wade in underbeing
> Let brain mist into moist earth
> …
> Be assumed into glistenings of lymph
> …
> Crawl out over roots, new and nameless
> Search for face, harden into limbs
> …
> Heal into time and other people
>
> (*Three Books*, 136)

What alliterations there are in this poem are no longer dominated by plosives and harsh consonant clusters, but by the liquids, nasals, sibilants and fricatives that both recall Hopkins's most felicitous moments and suggest the murmuring flow of the river. Whereas "Pike" was characterized by the tension between the mutually spying gazes of the pike and the angler, "Go Fishing" merges the human and the natural, and dispenses with national myth-making altogether. Hughes is as it were crawling out over the same "roots" as the existential quester of "Wodwo" (*Wodwo*, 183), but he is also embarking on a "new and nameless/Search" which proves more successful. The last line, "Heal into time and other people", is an demand for final integration; it reaches out towards human community in a gesture that would have been unthinkable in the early stages of Hughes's career.

---

[80] Hughes, *Winter Pollen*, 4.

In *River*, Hughes relinquished both his ambition to define a mythical England and the cult of violence through which he had provided an indirect commentary on post-war England. This accounts for the sheer delight in nature that the collection expresses, as in the last poem where Hughes finds himself "alive in the river of light" (*Three Books*, 179). The fact that this river is an Alaskan one (*Three Books*, 186) shows that Hughes may have found it necessary to escape from England altogether in order to write a nature poetry genuinely based on ecological concerns. The primitivism that underlies *River* still contains a few echoes of his national mythologies, but these tend to merge into a much broader historical perspective. In "Milesian encounter on the Sligachan", the Celtic character of the locations Hughes is exploring opens out onto prehistory. The gaze that Hughes perceives is no longer that of a pike standing for a buried, Celtic or Germanic England, but simply that of primeval nature, as he now realizes with hints of self-irony:

> The loveliest, left-behind, most-longed-for ogress
> Of the Palaeolithic
> Watched me through her time-warped judas-hole
> In the ruinous castle of Skye
> As I faded from reality.
>
> (*Three Books*, 158)

The hyperbolic violence of *Crow* had laid everything waste from Creation onwards, and had engulfed Hughes's English myths in universal destruction. Likewise, the regeneration that takes place in *River* explicitly transcends any national framework.

As the national and historical categories of Hughes's thinking slide off into a broader primitivism, the organicist assumptions that underlie his myth of England are radically revised. The myth of an organic culture and the accounts of the "dissociation of sensibility" which wrecked that prelapsarian wholeness have had a long life in English culture. More particularly, they have assumed many guises in the history of English poetry. One of their leading exponents was T. S. Eliot, who eventually acknowledged that the causes of that dissociation remained elusive

> All we can say is, that something like this did happen; that it had something to do with the Civil War; that it would be unwise to say that it was caused by the Civil War, but that it is a consequence of the same causes which brought about the Civil War; that we must seek the causes in Europe, not in England

alone; and for what these causes were, we may dig and dig until we get to a depth at which words and concepts fail us.[81]

Hughes, undeterred, took up Eliot's challenge, and explicitly used his predecessor's vocabulary in his own analysis of the process through which England "lost her soul" through a "dissociation of sensibility".[82] However, the tensions that arise within his work show that he dug so far that he reached depths at which the very concepts of organicism and dissociation lose their validity. The complexity of English history and his own fascination with violence constantly destabilize Hughes's myth-making, as is best shown by the shifting place of the Nordic element in his work. Each invasion or upheaval potentially adds to a dissociation which is repeated so often that it becomes meaningless. Hughes' work is the place where, against Hughes's intention perhaps, the tradition of organicist thinking in English poetry finally fell apart, as organicism found itself shattered through the infinite regress of the dissociations that it posits. The endless dissociations that Hughes's work dramatizes suggest that organicism and dissociation are best explained in terms of human psychology rather than national history. Hughes himself repeatedly endeavoured to conflate these terms, but the opposed examples of *Crow* and *River* show that his most powerful expressions of dissociation and organic wholeness required him to abandon his attempt to fuse human predicament and national myth.

The celebratory mode of *River* was a new departure in Hughes's work, and it sometimes puzzled those who had admired his ability to write a nature poetry that escaped the pastoral mode. For some critics, the volume is tempted by "sentimentality and abstraction"; *River* is the collection where Hughes "lapse[d] into pastoral".[83] Whether or not this weakens the collection, what remains striking is that Hughes only turned to pastoralism when he gave up England, whereas for most previous English nature poets the pastoral mode was the proper way of writing about the national landscape. This new pastoralism was carried on in *Flowers and Insects*, which conveys a sense of sheer delight in the natural world and thus recalls the brighter side of Hopkins or even, as has been suggested, the occasional sentimentality of Lawrence's poetry (the very title of the collection echoes Lawrence's *Birds, Beasts and Flowers*).[84]

---

[81] *Selected Prose of T.S. Eliot*, 266.

[82] *Winter Pollen*, 119.

[83] Terry Gifford, "Gods of Mud: Hughes and the Post-Pastoral", in *The Challenge of Ted Hughes*, ed. Keith Sagar, New York, 1994, 138-39.

[84] Whereas Keith Sagar had insisted that Hughes lacked Lawrence's sentimental attitude to animals (*The Art of Ted Hughes*, 45), another critic writes that "with the

The extent to which Hughes had to rid himself of his obsession with England in order to achieve this is also evident in the poem "Big Poppy". Whereas in "Out III – Remembrance Day" Hughes had agonized over the status of the poppy as a national symbol (*Wodwo*, 156-57), "Big Poppy" does not even hint at Remembrance celebrations. Instead, the poem playfully strings together ingenious metaphors which retain Hughes's penchant for violent intensity, but divest it of historical connotations: "Her crucible/Is falling apart with its own fierceness", "Bleeding inwardly/Her maternal nectars into her own/Coffin" (*Flowers and Insects*, 53). "Saint's Island" also follows *River* (and *Gaudete*) in celebrating natural phenomena that are Celtic – in this case, "Irish" (*Flowers and Insects*, 30) – thus confirming that Hughes can only reach pure exultation when England is explicitly absent.

Flowers and Insects closes with a poem written for the Queen, where the figures that haunted Hughes's historical poems are caught up in a whirl of unrelated images. The poem is closer to the sheer ingenuity of Martian poetics rather than to the work of a tormented mythographer:

> A congregation of bells,
> Tiny domes
> Of serious worship –
>   all Cordelias.
> Or else all green-veined Gonerils
> under the empty frenzy of hoar-frost.
>
>   (60-61)

Hughes's Laureate poems often share this sense of playful improvisation. Many of them point back to Hughes's various English myths, but there is something casual about the way in which these are now rehearsed. This is not just because Hughes was celebrating a royal institution which is increasingly unable to sustain its own myth, let alone Hughes's. Salmon, Cordelia, wolf-heads, the "broad-vowelled women/Of the Dales ... Nursing the North/Sea's hard hacked edges", "Cromwell-/Macbeth reborn" (*Rain-Charm for the Duchy*, 14-15) do not gain much from being turned into puppets in a "Birthday Masque" for the Queen. But the very repetition and somewhat mechanical juxtaposition of earlier motifs and phrases also generates an impression of tiredness, as if none of those

publication of *Flowers and Insects* ... Hughes may have outsentimentalized Lawrence". See Rand Brandes, "Behind the Bestiaries: The Poetry of Lawrence and Hughes", in *D. H. Lawrence's Literary Inheritors*, eds Keith Cushman and Dennis Jackson, London, 199, 254.

images now had the power to absorb Hughes's imagination. *Rain-Charm for the Duchy* remains informative in that it confirms or completes Hughes's mythologies, and also because its longest and most personal piece, the "Masque for Three Voices" written for the Queen Mother, once again emphasizes the importance of the two World Wars in Hughes's vision of England: "The shiver of their battles my Shibboleth" (33). Hughes's syncretism, which draws on Asian, North American and Islamic sources (10-11, 55), and his awareness that the British are a "mixed-up gallimaufry of mongrels" (63) have made it possible for some to regard his Laureate work with something else than embarrassment by emphasizing its multicultural message.[85] Poetically speaking, however, its flaws remain obvious, and become even more so when one considers the disturbing effect with which Hughes recycled his myths and images in the very different context of *Birthday Letters*.

Hughes's last collection both confirmed and increased the complex symbiosis that existed between his and Plath's imaginations. The "gutturals of Thor" (*Birthday Letters*, 169), the "guttural" moon "mourning and remaking herself" (174), Hughes's reading of *The Tempest* ("Setebos", 132) became part of a private and painful myth against which Hughes's dreams of England were sometimes implicitly judged – altogether not to their advantage. Devon was "my dreamland./I sleepwalked you/Into my land of totems" (122). This was the alternative to the dinginess of post-war England: "an altogether other England – /An Avalon for which I had the wavelength,/Deep inside my head a little crystal" (155). However, what emerged from the landscapes of that alternative England was no longer the gaze of an ancestral pike, but other uncanny presences – those of Plath's own ghosts: "And here, at my feet, in the suds,/The other face, the real, staring upwards" (156). In *Wodwo*, Hughes's ghost crabs "recuperate[d] under the sea" (*Wodwo*, 22), but in *Birthday Letters* they too have assumed another identity: "Your Ogre lover/Who recuperated all day/Inside death, waited in the chasm/Under the tingling stars" (*Birthday Letters*, 159). In those poems, Plath's own myth takes over the images that Hughes had developed to sketch a myth of England; it gives them a new life in the very act of supplanting the myth in which they had first been used.

It might be tempting (but also spurious) to compare the authenticity of those two myths. The huge impact of *Birthday Letters*, to which Hughes's death has granted the status of last poetic will and testament, means that much of his work will inevitably be read through the lens of its interconnections with Plath's. But Hughes's place in the history of

---

[85] See Paul Bentley, *The Poetry of Ted Hughes*, 119.

English poetry is also, to paraphrase Geoffrey Hill, a case of dividing legacies. Indeed, his poetry was also crucial to another writer, who developed it in a very different direction from that in which Plath (and Hughes himself, in his last volume) decided to take it. It was Hughes's national (rather than psychological) myths that fed directly into the work of Seamus Heaney.

CHAPTER FIVE
SEAMUS HEANEY AND ENGLAND: A MAP OF MISREADINGS

If Hughes failed to forge a coherent myth of nationhood, his explorations nevertheless constituted the basis on which another, more confident and consistent myth was built. In a series of poetic and political transformations fraught with ironies, the problems that beset Hughes's national myth-making were solved in a work that completed Hughes's project through a powerful misreading – the poetry of Irish nationhood that Seamus Heaney developed in the 1970s. This chapter will analyse how Heaney's misreading of Hughes and other English poets simultaneously helped shape his own vision of Ireland and turned him into the main exponent of a new interpretation of English poetry and of its relation to nationhood.

The fact that Heaney's mythology of Irishness is inextricably bound up with Hughes's redefinition of Englishness has generally been either overlooked or played down in readings of his work. Hughes's influence on Heaney's nature poetry has been widely acknowledged (not least by Heaney himself), but the convergence of Heaney's and Hughes's historical imaginations has attracted much less attention.[1] One reason may be that, for several years, few readers discerned the importance of England in Hughes's poetry, or bothered to take it seriously. It seems that the first reader who gave it sufficient attention was none other than Heaney himself. However, the critical reluctance to explore Heaney's reading of Hughes may have other causes.

Poems that present a vision of nationhood invite readings that seek to place them within a national tradition. In that respect, the focus on Heaney's relation to Irish predecessors and contemporaries in criticism of his work is only understandable. But the complexity of Irish cultural politics means that any poetics of Irishness is bound to be controversial, perhaps more so than any other poetics of nationhood. Not only are there many definitions of Irishness, but some of the most vibrant poetic expressions of Irish nationhood can turn out to be radically at odds with the politics of Irish nationalism. This discrepancy between nationhood and nationalism is illustrated by recent changes in the reputation of W.B. Yeats, who was long regarded as Ireland's foremost national poet.

---

[1] One notable exception is Neil Rhodes's "Bridegrooms to the Goddess: Hughes, Heaney and the Elizabethans". Rhodes compares Hughes's and Heaney's adaptations of Elizabethan mythologies. My analysis complements some of his findings, but it will cast them in a new light by analysing Heaney's texts as strategic misreadings of Hughes. It will also correlate both poets' use of historical myths with their philological methods, which Rhodes does not consider.

Although he was explicitly concerned with the creation of an Irish national culture, Yeats also remained a poet writing in the English Romantic tradition, and his definitions of Irishness inevitably drew on nineteenth-century English discourses on the nature of the Celtic character. The debt that Yeats and other writers of the Celtic Revival owed to Matthew Arnold's celebration of the qualities of the Celtic race has been subjected to much scrutiny,[2] and the political implications of that influence have caused a radical reassessment of Yeats's contribution to Irish nationalism. Yeats's recycling of Arnold's essentialist ideas about Celtic races has raised the suspicion that he was advocating a peculiar brand of cultural nationalism that gestured towards, but eventually fell short of a full-blown Irish nationalism. This view of Yeats was largely developed by Seamus Deane and other Northern Irish critics affiliated to the Field Day project, in which Heaney is closely involved. Those critics admit that Yeats ostensibly supported Irish independence, which Arnold wanted to keep at bay by urging the British to integrate the Celtic dimension in their composite identity. But, in their view, the origins of Yeats's ideas in Arnold's Celticism betray his alienation from the realities of Ireland. His literary connections expose him as a member of the Protestant Ascendancy who was steeped in English Romanticism; they cast doubt on "how far [he] was a real nationalist and how far he truly escaped his Protestant, unionist background". After having been hailed for a long time as Ireland's national poet, the Yeats described by Field Day is thus "reborn as gentleman, unionist, Protestant, enemy of Catholic Ireland and, even if nationalist in some peculiar way, nevertheless at heart West Briton".[3]

Heaney, by contrast, is a Catholic nationalist poet for whom the Republic is an established reality, a reality which he hopes will eventually include his native North as well. These credentials appear to have largely protected him from the charges that Field Day critics have levelled at Yeats, despite the fact that his poetry "set[s] in verse notions of Ireland – female, mythic, undefeatable, boggy, resurgent – that the Republic of Ireland had all but abandoned and that ... resemble those of early Yeats".[4]

---

[2] See for instance John V. Kelleher, "Matthew Arnold and the Celtic Revival", in *Perspectives of Criticism*, ed. Harry Levin, New York, 1970, 197-221; Marjorie Howes, *Yeats's Nations: Gender, Class and Irishness*, Cambridge, 1996; Chris Corr, "Matthew Arnold and the Younger Yeats: The Manoeuverings of Cultural Aesthetics", *Irish University Review*, XXVIII/1 (1998), 11-27.

[3] John Wilson Foster, "Getting the North: Yeats and Northern Nationalism", in *Yeats Annual* 12, eds Warwick Gould and Edna Longley, London, 1996, 186, 190.

[4] *Ibid.*, 190. Heaney is more lenient towards the Celtic Revival than his Field Day colleagues; indeed, he writes that "although it has long been fashionable to smile

One important exception here is David Lloyd, who argues that Heaney's poetry and its popularity in the Anglo-Saxon world testify to "the continuing meshing of Irish cultural nationalism with the Imperial ideology that frames it", namely the British discourse on Irishness that originated with Arnold.[5]

This apparent contradiction in Heaney can be resolved by bringing his debt to Hughes into the equation. One could easily argue that Heaney is playing a modern Yeats to Hughes's Arnold. Indeed, for all their aesthetic and philosophical differences, both Arnold and Hughes both regarded Celticism as an antidote to the Protestant rationalism that dominates English culture, and Yeats and Heaney both proceeded to adapt this argument in order to develop their visions of Ireland. Arnold's influence has cast a shadow on the nationalist credentials of Yeats's poetry of nationhood. But the fact that Heaney mostly takes his cue from Hughes rather than from Arnold and the Celtic Revival makes it necessary to qualify Lloyd's assertion that Heaney's poetics too remain caught up in an "Imperial ideology". Indeed, Heaney's adaptation of Hughes's English mythologies took place in an ideological situation that was very different from the one in which Yeats set about using and transforming Arnold's Celticism. One could of course try to determine how much Heaney actually borrowed from Yeats and the Celtic Revival. However, my main purpose here will be quite different. My focus on Heaney's debt to Hughes will not lead to a radically different list of similarities, since the "Celtic" notes in both early Yeats and Hughes issue from the common matrix of English Romantic thinking.[6] But such an emphasis will bring out more specific and far-reaching intertextual connections in Heaney's work. It will also make it possible to take into account some key changes that have occurred in Britain and Ireland, in the literary history of both countries, and in the perception of nationhood in literary culture.

---

indulgently at the Celtic Twilight, it has to be remembered that the movement was the beginning of a discovery of confidence in our own ground, in our place, in our speech". See Seamus Heaney, *Preoccupations*, 135.

[5] David Lloyd, "'Pap for the Dispossessed': Seamus Heaney and the Poetics of Identity", in *Seamus Heaney: A Collection of Critical Essays*, ed. Michael Allen, London, 1997, 180.

[6] Tom Paulin rightly describes Hughes as "a type of Yeatsian changeling who has taken up residence as an English poet". See *Minotaur*, 252. The early Hughes owed much to Yeats, but it is conversely true that Yeats himself remained something of an English Romantic. English and Irish varieties of Romanticism are in fact almost impossible to dissociate, as the relationships between Hughes and Heaney only confirm.

Another similarity between Yeats's Celticism and Heaney's Irishness deserves more attention than it has hitherto received: what Seamus Deane has termed, with respect to Yeats, the Romantic "call to Englishness". Deane argues that

> for Yeats and Synge in particular, the Irish maintained their especial quality precisely to the degree that they remained loyal to those old beliefs and that old eloquence which had formerly characterized the seventeenth century English. This is the Coleridgean notion of the English community rephrased in an Hibernian idiom. The colony, Ireland, has now become the motherland of historical memory. The actual motherland, England, has become degraded past recognition.

Deane also writes that the call to Englishness

> has been a persistent one for almost two centuries. We find its contemporary forms in Donald Davie's espousal of Thomas Hardy, in Geoffrey Hill's *Mercian Hymns*, in the poetry of Ted Hughes. When transferred to Ireland, such a search for a national signature becomes colonial, on account of the different histories of the two islands.[7]

Deane's description of Yeats's and Synge's quest for nationhood as "colonial" may sound ambiguous, since the adjective has different meanings. In the context of Deane's discussion, it appears to be synonymous with "colonialist": the critic stresses the Ascendancy's separation from the Irish peasantry that they idealized; Yeats and Synge's descriptions of the Irish people betray their "colonialist mentality".[8] However, when Seamus Heaney calls Yeats a "colonial" writer, he seems to think of another meaning – one that is closer to "colonized". In Heaney's essay "Englands of the Mind", the adjective is tentatively applied not only to Yeats, but also to Ted Hughes and two of his English contemporaries, Geoffrey Hill and Philip Larkin:

> I believe they are afflicted with a sense of history that was once the peculiar affliction of poets of other nations who were not themselves natives of England but who spoke the English language. The poets of the mother culture, I feel, are now

---

[7] Seamus Deane, *Celtic Revivals*, London, 1985, 48-49.
[8] *Ibid.*, 49.

possessed of that defensive love of their territory which was once shared by those writers whom we might call colonial.[9]

The first example of those older writers is none other than Yeats. But the parallel is not just between Yeats and the three English poets whom Heaney discusses. Indeed, Heaney reads into his English contemporaries a sense of nationhood which informs his own experience of Irishness. In a paradox that is only apparent, Heaney too issues his own "call to Englishness". He tries to define a sense of nationhood that could redeem England from the oppressive role that Britain has played in Ireland – in other words, an English equivalent of his own Ireland of the mind. Heaney's aim is to inscribe both Ireland and England in a neo-nationalist project whose Irish version has gained an increasing popularity in contemporary criticism. Ideological factors may then explain why that criticism is not always prepared to consider the roots of Heaney's neo-nationalism in what remains at heart an English Romantic discourse.

When Heaney denounces British Imperialism, he is of course joining forces with a tendency at work within England, and which the previous chapters have analysed at length. Unlike Yeats and other Celtic Revivalists, Heaney writes in a historical situation which has been marked by Irish independence and the decline of Empire, although the Imperial legacy lives on politically in his native Ulster, and psychologically in the British neuroses that Hughes and Hill dissect in their works. That historical situation seems to foster the emergence of another England: a nation coterminous with the England on which generations of English and Irish Romantics had staked their hopes. Such an England has its place in the Romantic postcolonialism and neo-nationalism for which Heaney has become an influential spokesman. But if Heaney manages to develop a postcolonial vision of Ireland from his confrontation with Britain, his neo-nationalist interpretations of English poetry are much more problematic.

Crucially, the misreadings that Heaney performs in his poetry and in his criticism must always suppress the tensions that destabilize the poetry of English nationhood developed by his contemporaries Ted Hughes and (to a lesser extent) Geoffrey Hill. Heaney cannot contemplate the fact that their quests for an older, more authentic England ironically end up acknowledging their own defeats. While the similarities between their works and Heaney's point to remarkable degrees of influence and convergence, Heaney's blindness to the more ironic and unstable aspects of Hughes and Hill remains essential to his own project. His blindness, in

---

[9] Heaney, *Preoccupations*, 150-51.

other words, is the poetically and ideologically enabling condition of the version of nationhood that many of his writings promote. On the other hand, the fact that Heaney's poetry of nationhood is partly a successful version of Hughes's and Hill's projects forces us to reassess the terms in which Heaney's work has been hailed by various critics. Indeed, such critics' response to his English models would normally range from embarrassed indifference to downright hostility. Hughes's and Hill's Englishness may no longer be "Imperial" or "British" in the sense that Arnold's discourse was. But the irrational, conservative organicism to which both are drawn (and which they ironically fail to express coherently) remains stubbornly unpopular when it appears in an English guise. Heaney's organicism stems from a similar ideology, which his poetry articulates even more consistently. But unlike its English models, it has benefited from the positive status which a literary criticism based on the politics of identity often bestows on Irish nationalism. By stressing the extent to which Heaney engaged with English organicism, my analysis also purports to question the ideological assumptions of a critical discourse that presents neo-nationalism as a radical project.

That Heaney's early poems owe a debt to Hughes is widely recognized. Hughes's rough-hewn brand of nature poetry is rightly considered as a major influence on Heaney's first two collections. Heaney himself said that Hughes's nature poems showed him the way: "I am a different kind of animal from Ted, but I will always be grateful for the release that reading his work gave me."[10] The alliterative quality of Heaney's first collections also recalls Hughes, although it more probably points to a shared infatuation with Hopkins, whom Heaney discovered before he read Hughes.[11] Heaney's use of weapons as metaphors in some of his early nature poems has less to do with an uncanny prescience of the conflict that was about to break out in Northern Ireland than with Hughes's own penchant for such imagery.[12] It is also part of a wider Hughesian tendency to collapse the natural and the mechanical. The images that proliferate in Heaney's "Trout" ("a fat gun-barrel", "moths/that vanish, torpedoed" – *Death of a Naturalist*, 26) can all too easily be traced back to the metaphorical battlefields of Hughes's "To Paint a Water Lily" (*Lupercal*, 29). Heaney's "Storm on the Island", where the speaker is "bombarded by the empty air" inside his house (*Death of a Naturalist*, 38), reads like an Irish version of Hughes's

---

[10] John Haffenden, *Viewpoints*, 74.
[11] Neil Corcoran, *Seamus Heaney*, London, 1986, 18-19.
[12] *Ibid.*, 45.

"Wind" (*The Hawk in the Rain*, 40). Such examples could be multiplied, although at times Heaney seems to predict rather than imitate Hughes. Thus, "The Salmon Fisher to the Salmon" in *Door into the Dark* (6) actually points forward to Hughes's "Earth Numb" (*Moortown*, 95-96) and to *River*.

Heaney's first two collections offer many variations (some felicitous, some too clearly derivative) on Hughes's nature poetry. But while he retained the intensity of his Hughesian vision of nature in his next two collections *Wintering Out* and *North*, he also turned to myth, archaeology and philology in his quest for "images and symbols adequate to [the] predicament" of the Catholic community in Northern Ireland.[13] This shift, which followed the beginning of the Troubles, seemed to indicate that Heaney's Hughesian interest in nature became less important than a new and urgent need to explore the roots of the conflict in the historical unconscious of Ireland. Heaney suggested as much when he declared:

> my first attempts to speak, to make verse, faced the Northern sectarian problem. Then this went underground and I became very influenced by Hughes and one part of my temperament took over: the private county Derry childhood part of myself rather than the slightly aggravated young Catholic male part.[14]

One could infer from this account that Hughes's influence declined when Heaney turned once again to the cultural and political realities of Northern Ireland. Heaney's ambition was then to work out a more complex poetics that could explore those public themes in their historical, linguistic and mythical ramifications. However, I will argue that this was precisely the moment when Heaney's reading of Hughes was most intense and decisive. It was indeed the moment when Hughes's influence stopped spawning imitations and became an influence in a more Bloomian sense: Heaney identified a key problem in Hughes's poetics and solved it through a creative misreading of his English mentor.

The traumas of Irish history had never really been absent from Heaney's work. *Death of a Naturalist* and *Door into the Dark* include poems that are haunted by the famine ("At a Potato Digging", "For the Commander of the Eliza") and the defeats suffered during Irish rebellions ("Requiem for the Croppies"). Present-day sectarian tensions are reflected

---

[13] Heaney, *Preoccupations*, 56.

[14] Seamus Heaney, "Unhappy and at Home", Interview with Seamus Deane, in *The Crane Bag Book of Irish Studies 1977-1981*, eds Mark Patrick Hederman and Richard Kearney, Dublin, 1992, 66.

in the unsympathetic portrayal of a brutish Protestant worker in "Docker" – a figure that Michael Parker suggestively called "a Unionist cousin of the miner in Ted Hughes's 'Her Husband'".[15] Both poems contain suggestions of domestic violence, and the similarities reveal a shared dislike of Puritan masculinity on the part of both authors. Heaney's poem clearly derives from his own anxieties as an "aggravated Catholic" rather than from his reading of Hughes ("Docker" predates "Her Husband"); and yet his description of the docker also recalls the imagery of Hughes's "Pike". The docker is "staring at his drink ... Speech is clamped in the lips' vice" (*Death of a Naturalist*, 28). Heaney's lines curiously echo the words of Hughes's poem: "The jaws' hooked *clamp* and fangs"; "The outside eye *stared*: as a *vice* locks" (*Lupercal*, 56-57. Emphases mine). Like some analyses of "Pike",[16] Heaney's poem would seem to identify Hughes's elemental creature with the oppressive Puritanism that Hughes's work attacked.

   Door into the Dark is also the collection that shows the first signs of what would become Heaney's archaeological and mythological methods. The collection ends with "Bogland", a landscape poem which prefigures the poetic excavations that Heaney would perform in the bog poems of *Wintering Out* and *North*. Hughesian influences are perceptible in hyperboles – the ground of the bog is "Missing its last definition/By millions of years" (40). Another poem, "Whinlands" (35) has been fruitfully compared with Hughes's "Thistles" as a poem in which nature is both vividly realized and "ablaze with identity": the gorse that "Persists on hills, near stone ditches,/Over flintbed and battlefield" represents an endurance that survives the various defeats of the older Irish culture.[17] The interaction between natural landscapes and national history that is central to some of Hughes's *Wodwo* poems is a more direct source for the irruption of ghostly presences in Heaney's "Shoreline":

> Listen. Is it the Danes,
> A black hawk bent on the sail?
> Or the chinking Normans?
>
> (*Door into the Dark*, 38)

Neil Corcoran writes of Heaney's Danes that "Heaney's ear has perhaps been schooled to hear them ... by Hughes's 'Thistles', and by ... 'The Warriors of the North'" – a poem that deals specifically with the Vikings'

---

[15] Michael Parker, *Seamus Heaney: The Making of the Poet*, London, 1993, 72.
[16] See Leonard Scigaj, *Ted Hughes*, 48.
[17] Michael Parker, *Seamus Heaney: The Making of the Poet*, 85.

invasions of Gaelic areas.[18] The Normans did not figure explicitly in Hughes's mythologies at this stage. The most likely source for their appearance in this poem is Austin Clarke's poetry, which criticized the Norman influence on the Celtic Catholicism of mediaeval Ireland.[19] The hesitation that the poem describes ("Is it ... or ...") may well express a more basic indecision: the ancestral Ireland that Heaney is about to explore has its sources in both English and Irish mythologies; it is defined in opposition to both Hughes's Vikings and Clarke's Normans. Although they remain elusive at this stage, these figures laden with historical significance will come to play a crucial role in Heaney's searches for symbols adequate to Northern Ireland's predicament in *North*. Meanwhile, *Wintering Out* would also develop a philological reading of the historical poems in Hughes's *Wodwo*,[20] through which Heaney would invest the very surfaces of his own verse with political meanings.

One of the poems that are central to Heaney's new linguistic myth is of course "Traditions", which the previous chapter showed to be a strategic misreading of Hughes's "Thistles". Both poems refer to gutturals. The gutturals of Hughes's dialects were, as Heaney himself recognized in "Englands of the Mind", connected with the "Nordic [that is consonantal] stratum of English speech", and yet Heaney's account also suggested that they represented a "fundamental speech" that was distinct from Hughes's consonants.[21] The reason behind this apparent contradiction in Heaney's account is the use to which he had put Hughes's poem a few years earlier in *Wintering Out*. In "Traditions", Heaney had already identified his own "guttural muse" as the tradition of Gaelic poetry that was "bulled long ago/by the alliterative tradition" (21) – hence his later clumsy insistence on keeping Hughes's gutturals somehow separate from his consonants. Heaney discerned that Hughes's music was part of a reversion to a fundamental speech, but his own fundamental speech had to be different. Thus, in *Wintering Out*, Heaney came to regard alliteration as a cultural manifestation of Ireland's oppression at the hands of its invaders.

---

[18] Corcoran, *Seamus Heaney*, 61.

[19] See for instance Clarke's poem "The Loss of Strength" in *Collected Poems*, Dublin, 1974. Clarke bemoans "the Norman invasion which submerged the national uniqueness of the Celtic-Romanesque". See Susan Halpern, *Austin Clarke: His Life and Works*, Dublin, 1974, 86.

[20] Edna Longley's percipient suggestion that *Wintering Out* "owes a debt to the Ted Hughes of *Wodwo*" is a point that needs much developing. See Edna Longley, "'Inner Emigré' or 'Artful Voyeur'? Seamus Heaney's *North*", in *Seamus Heaney: A Collection of Critical Essays*, ed. Michael Allen, 53.

[21] Heaney, *Preoccupations*, 155.

Alliteration had been one of the most notable and successful features of *Death of a Naturalist* and *Door into the Dark*. In those two volumes, Heaney had displayed a virtuoso's ability to use alliteration for quasi-mimetic effects:

> Right down the dam, gross-bellied frogs were cocked
> On sods; their loose necks pulsed like sails. Some hopped:
> The slap and plop were obscene threats.
>
> (*Death of a Naturalist*, 3-4)

> The plash and gurgle of the sour-breathed milk,
> The pat and slap of small spades on wet lumps.
>
> (*Death of a Naturalist*, 10)

But in *Wintering Out*, this very music becomes the symbol of an alien presence in Heaney's cultural make-up. Heaney will not quite discard alliteration, but he will strive to transform it so as to reconcile it with the original speech which his linguistic excavations have unearthed. This fusion is what the other philological poems of *Wintering Out* are designed to achieve.

The speech to which Heaney has shifted allegiance is that to which the poem "Broagh" (*Wintering Out*, 17) gives both formal and thematic expression. It is a speech dominated by the "abundance and luxury and possible lasciviousness of the vowels" that Hughes's consonants allegedly repress.[22] Heaney thus deliberately fills his lines with the drawn-out diphthongs and long vowels that the poem explicitly celebrates:

> ... the black *O*
>
> in *Broagh*,
> its low tattoo
> among the windy boortrees
> and rhubarb-blades.

The "last/*gh* the strangers found difficult to manage" is then typographically fused with the "*O*" of "*Broagh*". Their merging symbolizes the alliance between a Gaelic guttural and the vowels whose dark, feminine sensuousness Heaney will henceforth contrast with the

---

[22] *Ibid.*, 154.

British and masculine qualities of alliteration.[23] Heaney thus strategically appropriates the linguistic, sexual and natural symbolism that underlies Hughes's English mythologies; he then proceeds to develop a language that will prove easier to reconcile with the feminine/natural pole of Hughes's dichotomies than the harsh consonants which dominate Hughes's poems.[24] This operation will also enable Heaney to define the very origin which Hughes's self-deconstructing quests kept gesturing towards in vain. Heaney's vision of Ireland will consequently possess the organic coherence which Hughes's contradictions denied to his own vision of England.

The "guttural muse" of "Traditions" is of course feminine: "her uvula grows//vestigial" (*Wintering Out*, 21). In "A New Song", the "vanished music" that re-emerges when Heaney meets a "girl from Derrygarve" is "Poured by this chance vestal daughter" (23). This original speech is also a "dialect" which, like Hughes's dialects in "Thistles", is a part of a natural landscape: "a snipe's bleat is fleeing/its nesting ground/into dialect" (19).[25] In "Gifts of Rain", the "tawny guttural water" is "breathing its mists/through vowels and history"; it is also "a swollen river,/a mating call of sound" (15). Like "Broagh", the poem thus unites gutturals and vowels. By stressing their erotic potential even more, it also gives rise to what Harold Bloom described as Heaney's "central trope"[26]: what Heaney would call the "vowel of earth" in his next collection (*North*, 36).

This vowel, springing from the boggy earth of Heaney's native landscape, is crucial to his vision of Ireland. A sister to the guttural muse,

---

[23] This change is also perceptible in Heaney's 1974 essay on Hopkins, "The Fire I' the Flint". By contrasting Hopkins with the "feminine" Keats, Heaney characterizes Hopkins's creative processes as masculine: "There is a conscious push of the deliberating intelligence, a siring strain rather than a birth-push in his poetic act" (*Preoccupations*, 85). R.J.C. Watt observes that "in all these ways, [Hopkins] is 'English' not 'Irish'. To that extent, Heaney's early affinity with him was an affinity with the other, the alien". See R.J.C. Watt, "Seamus Heaney: Voices on Helicon", *Essays in Criticism*, XLIV/3 (1994), 219. However, Heaney's revision of Hopkins does violence to the reality of his native speech: as he pointed out elsewhere, "the Ulster accent is generally a staccato consonantal one" (*Preoccupations*, 45).

[24] Of course, Heaney is not the first Irish poet to identify Ireland as feminine – the trope has been a familiar one since the Celtic Revival. What is new here and clearly points back to Hughes is the insistently primitive nature of Ireland's femininity, its openly sexual character and its systematic association with social, historical and philological tropes.

[25] Whereas the dialects of "Thistles" remained imagined, Irish dialect is actually part of the poetics of Heaney's collection.

[26] Harold Bloom, "The Voice of Kinship", Review of *Field Work*, *Times Literary Supplement*, 8 February 1980, 137.

it was bulled by alliteration, "hack[ed] and hedg[ed] and hammer[ed] down"[27] by the very consonants that Hughes tried to identify with his female natural principle. "Traditions" contrasts the guttural speech of origins with the "furled/consonants of [Protestant] lowlanders" (*Wintering Out*, 21), which are lumped together with the "Elizabethan English" and the "Shakespearean" language (20) in which Hughes still read traces of his mediaeval, pagan-Catholic England. "The Wool Trade" (*Wintering Out*, 27) records how the Irish wool industry was wrecked by Imperial economic demands. In that poem, "spools" and "vowels" are intimately associated, they evoke a "lost syntax of looms and spindles". But Heaney's indulgence in the long, sprawling vowels of the poem is finally cut short by a reminder of the economic, political and linguistic changes that British rule brought about in Ireland: "And I must talk of tweed,/A stiff cloth with flecks like blood." The curt alliterations of the last two lines mingle with a suggestion of enforced economic change (the British tweed has replaced the native wool) and of political violence ("flecks like blood").[28]

Wintering Out inaugurated a new phase in Heaney's poetic career since, as Henry Hart put it, "even the vowels and consonants [now] conveyed mythic significance". However, most critics analyse that new departure in an exclusively Irish context. Hart argues that Heaney's "poetymologies" owe much to the example of illustrious Irish predecessors:

> with Joyce in his wake, Heaney's allegories of vowels and consonants seem traditionally Irish rather than eccentrically English …. Heaney knows, if for no other reason than because he has read Joyce, that philology and myth have walked in tandem throughout Western tradition.[29]

Neil Corcoran also believes that Heaney's method is typically Irish when he points out that his etymological poems

> may have been sanctioned by the Gaelic tradition of *dinnseanchas* which Heaney defines in "The Sense of Place" as

---

[27] Heaney, *Preoccupations*, 154.

[28] The etymologies of that poem are thoroughly analysed by Michael R. Molino in "Flying by the Nets of Language: Seamus Heaney, the 'English Language' and Ulster's Troubles", *Modern Philology*, XCI (1993), 180-201.

[29] Henry Hart, *Seamus Heaney: Poet of Contrary Progressions*, Syracuse, 1992, 49, 55.

"poems and tales which relate the original meanings of place-names and constitute a form of mythological etymology".[30]

Blake Morrison refers to the same essay in order to suggest that Heaney's "is a more political etymology" than that of the *dinnseanchas*, since "its accents are those of sectarianism .... it uncovers a history of linguistic and territorial dispossession".[31]

Such analogies are indeed suggestive, and partly justified by Heaney's own pronouncements and allusions in his essays and poems. Another Irish source would be Austin Clarke, to whom Heaney refers in "The Sense of Place". Heaney discusses Clarke's poetics, and more particularly the view that "the note of Irish poetry is struck when the rhythms and assonances of Gaelic poetry insinuate themselves into the texture of the English verse". He comments: "I am sympathetic to the effects gained but I find the whole enterprise a bit programmatic."[32] Written in the very year when the philological exercises of *Wintering Out* appeared, that last note of criticism sounds rather paradoxical: some of Heaney's poems are every bit as programmatic as anything that Clarke ever wrote. Perhaps Heaney's criticism reflects his sense of a greater complexity in his own enterprise; what makes it more complex may be the fact that the method of *Wintering Out* derives from Hughes as well as from Irish traditions. Indeed, if Heaney is reverting to a "vowel-music" similar to that which Clarke was reviving in his own poetry, he does not use a form of internal assonance that follows regular patterns, as it does in Clarke's poems.[33] In *Wintering Out*, assonance is more irregular, it infiltrates the whole texture of the poem much as Hughes's alliteration does – without creating patterns of its own. Instead, it is thematized through the foregrounding of the "black *O*" of "Broagh" (17); it becomes the very substance of the poem, like the suppressed gutturals of "Traditions" (Clarke, by contrast, is largely silent about gutturals). In this respect, Heaney's linguistic allegories also echo the self-reflexivity of Hughes's "Thistles", the poem whose gutturals Heaney appropriates.

If Heaney returns to a Celtic vowel music, it is largely in response to Hughes. Not only are the etymological meditations of *Wintering Out* based on a misreading of the historical poems of *Wodwo*, but the various

---

[30] Corcoran, *Seamus Heaney*, 87.

[31] Blake Morrison, *Seamus Heaney*, London, 1982, 41.

[32] Heaney, *Preoccupations*, 36.

[33] Assonance in Clarke's poems "occurs when the tonic syllable at the end of the line is supported by an assonance in the middle of the next line", or when rhyme relies primarily on the vowels of the last syllable rather than on its consonants. See Susan Halpern, *Austin Clarke*, 51, 71.

archetypal connotations with which Heaney invests his linguistic allegories are borrowed from Hughes as well. Contrary to critical opinion which sees Heaney's allegories as "Irish rather than eccentrically English",[34] the method of *Wintering Out* actually originates in Heaney's response to one of the most eccentric of his English contemporaries. Heaney's aim in fathoming the linguistic and historical strata of Irish history may well be "a restoration of the culture to itself".[35] But if he reaches back beyond the legacy of the British occupation to uncover an original Irishness, his debt to Hughes reveals that this primeval, feminine Ireland of sensuous vowels and gutturals has largely been wrested from the mythological fumblings of England's last Romantic. The English presence in *Wintering Out* is not limited to the layers that were superimposed during centuries of British domination; indeed, the very framework within which Heaney worked out his contrasting myths of Irishness and Englishness can be identified as the by-product of an English imagination.

This fact has all too understandably escaped the notice of critics who want to confer a sense of local authenticity on Heaney's poetic response to the Troubles. Heaney has never quite advertised the extent of that debt to Hughes, and yet his work contains enough clues to encourage such a reading. This is not only due to the closeness with which Heaney's poetic misreadings followed the appearance of the relevant poems by Hughes.[36] Heaney's remarks on Hughes in "Englands of the Mind" reveal how sensitive he has been to the importance of England in Hughes's poetry. Hughes's own critical writings on the subject were still rather scant in the early 1970s, but the seminal remarks he made in his edition of *A Choice of Shakespeare's Verse* had become available by 1971. Heaney explicitly refers to Hughes's afterword in an essay written in 1974;[37] and other pronouncements show that he had also digested the preface.

---

[34] Henry Hart, *Seamus Heaney: Poet of Contrary Progressions*, 55.

[35] Heaney, *Preoccupations*, 60.

[36] *Wintering Out* (1972) appeared five years after *Wodwo* (1967), but Heaney's response to that collection was already prefigured in the two poems from *Door into the Dark* (1968) discussed above. One should note that Hughes's "Thistles" and "The Warriors of the North" had appeared several years before they were included in *Wodwo*: "Thistles" appeared in *TLS* in 1960, "The Warriors of the North" appeared in *The Observer* in 1962.

[37] Hughes's afterword is mentioned in "The Fire in the Flint" (*Preoccupations*, 91). The words Heaney quotes do not have a bearing on myths of nationhood. Personal exchanges of views on such questions remain a matter of conjecture; the friendship between the two poets encourages one to think that some must have taken place.

It is not difficult to see what elements of Hughes's preface Heaney responded to most. Hughes's denunciation of the catastrophic legacy of Puritanism obviously struck a chord; it actually found an echo in Heaney's prose. In a 1974 review of David Jones's *The Sleeping Lord*, Heaney wrote of the Catholic Anglo-Welsh poet that "his effort has been to graft a healing tissue over that wound in English consciousness inflicted by the Reformation and the Industrial revolution".[38] Although Jones himself found a confirmation of his views in Eliot's anti-Puritan organicism, Heaney's rhetoric more probably derives from Hughes. Hughes himself was adapting Eliot's theory about the "dissociation of sensibility"; but unlike the pre-dissociation England of Eliot's writings, Hughes's original England is based on the cult of the "old goddess – the real deity of Medieval England", whom he identifies with "the Celtic pre-Christian goddess, with her tail wound round those still very much alive pre-Christian and non-Christian worlds", "the goddess of all sensation and organic life": "she is Nature."[39] In his review, Heaney similarly observes that Jones's work feeds on "the insular Celtic and British traditions".[40] In Heaney's analysis of the section entitled "The Tutelar of Place", "the nurturing centre of the whole book" is the point "where the tutelar is both madonna and earth-mother": although this comment can be borne out by a reading of Jones's text,[41] it also closely follows Hughes's assertion that "the Isis behind the Virgin Mary and the Celtic goddess behind Medieval England had originally been one".[42]

Such pronouncements were received with great interest by Heaney, who has often stressed the importance of Marian devotion in his own Irish Catholic background. Hughes's equation of mediaeval Catholicism with a female-oriented Celtic religion also shows that Heaney's interest in Hughesian energies was quite compatible with Irish Catholic pieties – a point overlooked by critics who argue that "after twenty years of intense exposure to Catholicism, the 'primeval' feel of Hughes's world appealed to the Oisin in [Heaney]".[43] Catholicism is after all present in Hughes's early poems, albeit as a vague reality that mingles with Anglicanism as well as Celtic paganism – it is simply one part of Hughes's anti-Puritan

---

[38] Seamus Heaney, "Now and in England", Review of *The Sleeping Lord*, *The Spectator*, 4 May 1974, 547.

[39] Ted Hughes, *Winter Pollen*, 109, 110, 112.

[40] Heaney, "Now and in England", 547.

[41] "... she is but one mother of us all: one earth brings us all forth, one wombs receives us all, yet to each she is other, named of some name other ..." (*The Sleeping Lord*, 59).

[42] Hughes, *Winter Pollen*, 109.

[43] Michael Parker, *Seamus Heaney: The Making of the Poet*, 44.

equation. In "Nicholas Ferrer", Hughes's contrast between Puritanism and a nature-worshipping Catholicism is evident from the reference to "the tree that crabbed/In Cromwell's belly as it bloomed in Rome" (*Lupercal*, 27-28). Hughes's ancestral pike were also remnants of a suppressed Catholic culture; they had "outlasted every stone/Of the monastery that planted them" (*Lupercal*, 57).

Heaney's Catholicism undoubtedly has a cultural specificity which Hughes's rather vague sympathies may lack; nevertheless, the poetic uses to which Heaney put the faith he was born into show a remarkable convergence with Hughes's thoughts on Catholicism. Heaney's first bog poems were met with great enthusiasm by Hughes, who encouraged Heaney to write more of them.[44] This is no coincidence: "The Tollund Man" articulates the very conflation between Catholicism and a feminine, primitive religion that Hughes theorized. The victim of the fertility ritual described in the poem is a "bridegroom to the Goddess" of earth who "work[ed] him to a saint's kept body" (*Wintering Out*, 36): Heaney's metaphors thus provide smooth transitions from paganism to the Catholic cult of saints. The conflation of Catholicism with Celtic primitivism would also be a major structuring element in the mythology of *North*, to which we will return. Hughes's religious syncretism is also echoed in Heaney's comment that "Irish Catholicism is continuous with something older than Christianity".[45] However, Heaney's statement also deviates strategically from Hughes's theories. Indeed, in the same way that "Traditions" turned Hughes's Nordic gutturals into Gaelic ones, Heaney's reference to *Irish* Catholicism implies that the real repository of the primitive values described by Hughes is not a long-suppressed England, but Ireland. By making a primeval Ireland central to his own mythology, Heaney simultaneously made Hughes's meditations relevant to his own historical predicament and turned them into an more coherent project. Paradoxically, Heaney's project also blurred the traces of its derivative nature by encouraging readers to regard it as a nativist Irish strategy.

Heaney's misreading was of course facilitated by the fact that the female deity of Hughes's primitive world already had a Celtic dimension. This qualifies Michael Parker's assertion that the world of Hughes's

---

[44] *Ibid.*, 123.

[45] Heaney also makes clear his preference for "a religion that has a feminine component and a notion of the mother in the transcendental world". Although not a "pious Catholic", Heaney "never felt any need to rebel or to do a casting-off of God or anything like that, because I think in this day anthropologists and mythologists have taught us a lot, to live with our myths". See John Haffenden, *Viewpoints*, 60. My suggestion is that Hughes was one of the mythologists who helped Heaney to make poetic sense of his Catholicism.

Lupercal "may have actually become 'celticized' in Heaney's imagination".[46] Hughes's primeval world does not simply look Irish, as it did to Donald Davie; it sometimes *is* Irish. Parker underestimates this when he writes that although Heaney "learnt his craft from [Hughes and other English poets], his technique and full poetic voice were achieved ... as a result of his relationship with the 'feminine', Celtic influences".[47] Indeed, that relationship was mediated by none other than Hughes himself. As we have seen, Hughes's witches celebrated their pagan rituals in Ireland (*Lupercal*, 48). In "Wilfred Owen's Photographs", Hughes paid a quasi-Arnoldian tribute to the Irish influence on British culture. The poem describes how the flogging of sailors in the Royal Navy was abolished thanks to the intervention of "Parnell's Irish in the House" (*Lupercal*, 45). But the Arnoldian bent of that poem also points to Hughes's longing for a blend of Celtic and old English elements which is unblemished by the influence of British Puritanism. Hughes's Celticism remains part of a mythological continuum that must also include Nordic and Anglo-Saxon influences. In more recent writings, Hughes came close to acknowledging that the Celtic element should logically be at the centre of his primitive England, as when he spoke of the "enveloping, nurturing Celtic matrix" without which "English poetry would be unrecognizably different and vastly deprived". But his assertion that "the Celtic presence is usually found to be supporting the old English"[48] betrays his unwillingness to relegate the Anglo-Saxon and Nordic elements to a secondary status. Indeed, too much was at stake for Hughes's poetic imagination: his primeval England is associated with the excessive violence that held his post-war imagination in thrall and got translated in the rough Anglo-Saxon quality of his lines. Those very Anglo-Saxon and Nordic elements, however, displayed a shiftiness that threw Hughes's dichotomies into disarray. In the same way, some key aspects of Hughes's primitive violence were contaminated by the very connotations carried by the mechanical, Puritan culture that he denounced.

It was left to Seamus Heaney to provide the solution to Hughes's quandary. Whereas Hughes's dream of a primeval England inevitably deconstructed itself, Heaney's mythology of Irishness is firmly anchored by the emergence of a feminine, watery, naturalized and Gaelic "vowel of earth". Hughes's primitivism is here divested of its mechanical and hyperbolically violent undertones. Those destabilizing elements are exchanged for the coherence of a quieter and seemingly home-made Irish

---

[46] Parker, *Seamus Heaney: The Making of the Poet*, 45.
[47] *Ibid.*, 21.
[48] Hughes, *Winter Pollen*, 369.

organicism. Heaney's careful reading of Hughes had given him an insight shared by few others at the time, namely that Hughes's apparently very masculine imagination was imbued with a longing for an elusive feminine principle, and that this longing informed the meditations on England which Hughes's readers often neglected. Heaney's own poems gave full expression to the pagan/feminine principle and the primal speech that Hughes theorized, but only gestured towards in his poetry.

While Hughes's poetic voice essentially remained that of an anxious male quester, Heaney felt confident enough to write fantasies of erotic satisfaction spoken by a female voice. The early "Undine" is a perfect illustration: the poem is the song of water itself, a female presence that warms to the digging of a male worker (*Door into the Dark*, 14). What Heaney does is to stress the identification of that female sensuality with a primeval Irishness. Heaney's feminine symbolism is not different from that of Hughes's "Gog III", with its "root-blood of origins,/The salt-milk drug of the mothers" (*Wodwo*, 152). But Hughes's poem is a chaos of half-symbolic hints thriving on the violence which renders them obscure. Heaney's excavation work in "Bogland", by contrast, charts a progression towards its glimpse of origins, a quasi sexual "wet centre" which is "bottomless" (*Door into the Dark*, 41). Heaney also has little difficulty in identifying this sensuous Ireland as *"our* unfenced country" (41, emphasis mine). When Hughes's poems catch glimpses of his older England, the first person plural remains excluded from his vision. Hughes's primeval England thereby appears to be a deeply personal, possibly unreal vision; Heaney's Ireland, by contrast, is presented as a timeless organism. The "wet centre" of "Bogland" may still have lain so deep as to dizzy Heaney, but the archaeological poetics of *Wintering Out* and *North* showed a firmer grasp of Irish origins.

Ironically enough, the first fully-fledged articulation of Heaney's Irish organicism emerged shortly after Hughes's own attempt at integration with the feminine principle was wrecked by the cosmic disintegration of *Crow*. At the time when Hughes's violent machinery went into overdrive, Heaney was bringing Hughes's defeated organicism to fruition in his own work.[49] It is significant that *Wintering Out* is virtually free from the Hughesian mechanical metaphors that characterized some of Heaney's earlier nature poems.[50] Instead, Heaney now "pushes into a souterrain"

---

[49] Heaney barely discusses *Crow* in "Englands of the Mind", except to mention how it "verges on the grotesque" (*Preoccupations*, 157). The extreme violence of that collection and its occasional repudiation of Hughes's myths explain why it did not appeal to Heaney's imagination.

[50] Examples include "Trout" or "The Outlaw", in which a bull was compared to a "steam-engine shunting" (*Door into the Dark*, 4). Some metaphors in Heaney's "First

till he is "sleeved in/alluvial mud" (*Wintering Out*, 16). The only traces of industry that remain here are the tools of the local wool trade, which gets contrasted with the British industrial revolution that supplanted it, and can thus be safely naturalized into "spools/Of ... vowels" and a "lost syntax of looms and spindles" (27). *Wintering Out* is replete with suggestions of the watery softness of the Irish landscape; the word "soft" actually recurs throughout the volume (6, 15, 16, 27), culminating in the significant phrase "the soft fontanel/Of Ireland" (63). Ireland is already being thematized as the soft feminine body that would be raped by British invasions in the sexual allegories of *North*.

However, Ireland's feminine sensuousness is not only that of a rape victim. Its erotic potential underlies a trope that Heaney deploys insistently in his work: the trope of seduction. If the guttural muse was brutally bulled by consonants, the "tawny guttural water" of Moyola is also a turgid, "swollen river//a mating call of sound" (*Wintering Out*, 15), and "A New Song" shows that the objects of its seduction are the very consonants which used to oppress it. The "river tongues" must "flood, with vowelling embrace/Demesnes staked out in consonants" (23). Indeed, the philological contrasts that Heaney derived from his misreading of Hughes are not only part of an exploration of Irish history: they are also part of the way in which Heaney allegorizes the contemporary sectarian conflict in Ulster. Heaney, like his colleagues of Field Day, has been attempting to define a sense of Irish identity in which Northern Protestants might recognize themselves.[51] Field Day came into existence in 1980, but one can see how its project was already adumbrated in *Wintering Out*. "A New Song" derives its symbolism from Heaney's philological investigations, but its title indicates that the poem is also a utopian vision. It is the allegory of a culture in which the harsh, aggressive consonants of Protestant culture are integrated in the resurgence of a primeval Ireland, symbolized by the poem's "vowelling embrace".

Heaney explained that those linguistic dichotomies provided "a metaphor for the split culture of Ulster". He added: "I think of the

---

Calf' are still rather Hughesian, and seem to prefigure Hughes's *Moortown Diary*: a cow's snout is compared to a "warm plaque", while her afterbirth becomes "semaphores of hurt" that "swaddle and flap on a bush" (*Wintering Out*, 62). However, this poem belongs to the second part of *Wintering Out*, where Heaney's historical and philological method is much less prominent.

[51] His position has been more recently summarized in "The Frontiers of Writing", where he invites Protestants to "re-enter the whole country of Ireland imaginatively, if not constitutionally, through the northern point of the quincunx". See Seamus Heaney, *The Redress of Poetry*, London, 1995, 202.

personal and Irish pieties as vowels, and the literary awareness nourished on English as consonants. My hope is that the poems will be vocables adequate to my whole experience."[52] But the poems of *Wintering Out* do not reflect a split, they actually thematize a healing process in which the English part of Heaney's experience is folded back into his sense of Irishness. This is the theme of "Anahorish": the name of the poem is a "soft gradient/of consonant, vowel-meadow" (*Wintering Out*, 6); its etymology is Gaelic, but it is also a linguistic utopia in which the phonetic symbols of the British/Protestant presence have been inflected into soft sounds that harmonize with its native, grassy vowels. It would thus be wrong to suggest that Heaney turned his back on the alliterative technique that contributed to the success of his first two collections. A poem like "Servant boy" still draws heavily on Anglo-Saxon alliteration in lines like "the back-end of a bad year" or "a straggle of fodder/stiffened on snow" (*Wintering Out*, 7). But Heaney declared that "in some senses these poems are erotic mouth-music by and out of the anglo-saxon tongue".[53] That consonantal music is now turned into a "soft gradient", infiltrated as it is by the seeping vowels that are central to *Wintering Out*. The "black *O//in Broagh*" is literally central to the eponymous four-stanzas poem, since it straddles the enjambement between the second and third stanzas. It sends echoing ripples into the neighbouring alliterative lines that would stake it out: the long semi-open vowels and diphthongs in lines like "its l*ow* tatt*oo*/among the windy b*oo*rtrees/and rh*u*barb-blades" are its reverberations (*Wintering Out*, 17. Emphases mine).

By absorbing Hughes's consonants into a linguistic realm dominated by feminine vowels, Heaney rebuilt Hughes's fragile Celtic-Saxon alliance along firmer lines and turned it into a cultural allegory for Irish unification. In his preface to *A Choice of Shakespeare's Verse*, Hughes praised Shakespeare for turning an "erotic poetry into an all-inclusive body of political action",[54] but it was Heaney rather than Hughes who found the means of translating those Shakesperean myths into contemporary political terms.[55] In Heaney's hands, Hughes's confused

---

[52] Heaney, *Preoccupations*, 35, 37.

[53] Quoted by Neil Corcoran in his *Seamus Heaney*, 87.

[54] Hughes, *Winter Pollen*, 116.

[55] Terry Gifford and Neil Roberts miss Heaney's indebtedness to Hughes by relating both poets' mythologies to Graves, but this analysis confirms their suggestion that "whereas for Heaney, the relevant meanings of the Celtic mythology of *The White Goddess* are immanent in contemporary history, for Hughes they have to be encountered through a more radical imaginative journey". See Terry Gifford and Neil Roberts, "Hughes and Two Contemporaries: Peter Redgrove and Seamus Heaney", in *The Achievement of Ted Hughes*, ed. Keith Sagar, 96.

nostalgia for primeval nationhood became a coherent primitivist organicism; it was also made to look politically relevant by Heaney's Irish neo-nationalist rhetoric.

Heaney's neo-nationalism, like that of Field Day, purports to be inclusive. But if it proposes to integrate the English dimension of the Irish experience, the ways of achieving that integration are rather ambiguous. Indeed, if the trope of seduction dominates "Anahorish" or the lines from "A New Song" quoted above, the latter poem also suggests that erotic tactics may be complemented by a more muscular approach. The resurgent Irishness that the poem envisages can not only "embrace", but also "enlist" (*Wintering Out*, 23). As Blake Morrison comments, the verb "enlist" suggests "a more forceful and even violent kind of takeover".[56] Like Hughes's goddess, Heaney's primitive Ireland can either seduce or show her more violent side. But in Heaney's hands, her ambiguity no longer accounts for shifts in Shakespeare's "tragic equation": it underlies his own mythological account of the Northern Irish conflict. As Heaney explained in 1974, he was now looking for a poetics that would allow him to

> grant the religious intensity of the violence its deplorable authenticity and complexity. And when I say religious, I am not thinking simply of the sectarian division. To some extent the enmity can be viewed as a struggle between the cults and devotees of a god and a goddess. There is an indigenous territorial numen, a tutelar of the whole island, call her Mother Ireland, Kathleen Ni Houlihan, the poor old woman, the Shan Van Vocht, whatever; and her sovereignty has been temporarily usurped or infringed by a new male cult whose founding fathers were Cromwell, William of Orange and Edward Carson.[57]

These remarks paved the way for the publication of *North*, a volume which translated the Troubles into mythological terms by adding further twists to the misreading of Hughes that Heaney had developed in *Wintering Out*.

Hughes's enthusiasm for Heaney's first bog poems had made him encourage his Irish counterpart to write more of them. Some of the poems in *North* were published separately as *Bog Poems* by Hughes's sister

---

[56] Morrison, *Seamus Heaney*, 42.
[57] Heaney, *Preoccupations*, 57.

Olwyn,[58] but I would argue that *North* also bears Hughes's imprint in more significant ways. Hughes's blessing may have been prompted by the intuition that Heaney had solved the tensions which were perceptible in *Wodwo*. For if Hughes's myth was centred on the figure of a primitive goddess, it was Heaney who gave her successful expression. Only Heaney could have had the confidence to let the "bog queen" of the eponymous poem speak in the first person: "I lay waiting" (*North*, 25). In "Come to the Bower", the female presence that Heaney ventriloquizes in "Bog Queen" emerges "out of the black maw/Of the peat" (24). Hughes's "Gog" also features a similar "maw" (*Wodwo*, 152), but Hughes's Puritan knight hastens away from that place of origins, and often seems to drag the whole poem with him. Heaney's male persona, by contrast, is a seasoned Prince Charming who "unpin[s]" the "dark-bowered queen" and reaches "to the bullion/Of her Venus Bone" (*North*, 24).

Heaney's scenes of seduction in *North* can be read as a response to Hughes's "The Warriors of the North", in which the frosty Vikings first "thawed" at their contact with the Gaelic culture they invaded, only to "relapse" later into the "iron arteries" of Puritanism (*Wodwo*, 159). The Nordic theme is of course one of the keys to *North*; Heaney himself explained that the collection was inspired by his reading of P.V. Glob's *The Bog People* and by the Viking exhibitions held in Dublin in the late 1960s.[59] Glob's book about the Iron Age and its rituals contains photographs and descriptions of corpses preserved in peat that underlie much of Heaney's imagery. However, I suggest that Heaney was also drawn to *The Bog People* because it helped him adapt Hughes's myths for his own ends.[60] The Nordic element was one of the factors that destabilized Hughes's vision of a primeval England. Heaney himself indirectly exposed Hughes's problem by aligning the Vikings with Protestantism in "Englands of the Mind". His reading emphasized the pessimistic end of "The Warriors of the North", and overlooked Hughes's attempt at reconciling the Nordic and the Celtic. The reason behind this silence, I suggest, is that Heaney had actually chosen to express that reconciliation in his own poetry and to put it in the service of his Irish neo-nationalism.

---

[58] See Corcoran, *Seamus Heaney*, 33.

[59] *Ibid.*, 33.

[60] Although he does not analyse how Heaney's poetry deviates from its Hughesian model here, Neil Rhodes quite rightly points out that "the bog poems and other related poems on Elizabethan themes emerge as much from Hughes's ideas about Shakespeare, Elizabethan England and rescuing the goddess, as they do from P.V. Glob and his treasure trove". See Rhodes, "Bridegrooms to the Goddess: Hughes, Heaney and the Elizabethans", 160.

At first sight, Heaney's decision to give the Viking element such prominence in his archaeology of Ireland seems to complicate the opposition between Celtic and Anglo-Saxon that was central to *Wintering Out*. In "Belderg", the dualistic etymologies of Heaney's previous collection are called into question. The poem revolves round the discussion of the word "Mossbawn", for which Heaney proposes two etymologies – one English, the other Irish. His interlocutor, however, introduces another possibility: "'But moss?'/He crossed my old home's music/With older strains of Norse" (*North*, 5). The Nordic element reveals a further dimension to the history of conflict in Ireland, but the ambiguity it introduces is not of a nature to pose insuperable problems for Heaney's mythologizing impulse. In *Wintering Out*, Heaney's linguistic allegories had seduced and absorbed the English element into a whole dominated by a Celtic, feminine, guttural-vocalic presence. It is a similar strategy that informs Heaney's use of ancient Nordic religion in *North*.

According to Edward Larrissy, Heaney's "savage, feminine, northern religion dissolves the boundaries between the opposites it comprises: Celt and Teuton, Catholic and Protestant, male and female".[61] This would be a brilliant analysis if it were applied to Hughes. Larrissy's statement is actually prompted by Heaney's description of Hughes's masculine Norsemen in "Englands of the Mind", which he thinks makes the mythology of *North* ambiguous. But it is best seen as a trace of the misreading through which Heaney extracted his own coherent myth from Hughes's ambiguities. Heaney achieved this through the trope that Larrissy misses: the trope of seduction, which Heaney's *North* manages to express while Hughes's "The Warriors of the North" ultimately failed.

Heaney's readings in Nordic history confirm this. He once wrote of the Viking raids on Celtic Ireland and Orkney: "Both populations *sustained* and *seduced* their invaders: have lived mostly on the land, possess an old culture that is vital to their identity but difficult for outsiders fully to sympathize with."[62] Like the "*gh*" in "Broagh", that "the strangers found/difficult to manage" (*Wintering Out*, 17), the Celtic culture that absorbed its Nordic invaders remains resistant to the understanding of modern non-Irish observers. The phrasing also points forward to Hughes's later assertion that the Celtic presence usually supported the old English in its fight against later cultural invasions.[63] But

---

[61] Edward Larrissy, *Reading Twentieth Century Poetry: The Language of Gender and Objects*, Oxford, 1990, 155.
[62] Seamus Heaney, "Celtic Fringe, Nordic Fringe", *The Listener*, 21 August 1969, 254. Emphases mine.
[63] Hughes, *Winter Pollen*, 369.

Heaney once again insists on the centrality of the Celtic presence. He is comforted in this by Glob's discussion of Northern religion:

> The goddess is to be seen in all her majesty, splendidly fashioned, on Celtic bronze and silver vessels offered sacrificially in Danish bogs. Although these vessels were not manufactured in Denmark, and show us the Celtic peoples' concept of their gods and goddesses, the rich world of pictorial imagery represented by the cauldrons cannot have failed to impress the northern, Germanic people also.[64]

The gold and women of the Gaels also had their attractions for Hughes's Vikings. But whereas they eventually relapsed into a Puritan masculinity, Heaney's Norsemen ultimately remain faithful to the Goddess. They sometimes appear to be Hughesian caricatures of swashbuckling masculinity, driven by "Thor's hammer" to "thick-witted couplings and revenges" (*North*, 10-11). They are "killers, haggers/and hagglers, gombeen-men" (15). But as their longship "enters [Heaney's] longhand" (14), some transformations occur.

The "longship's swimming tongue" commands Heaney to "Lie down/in the word-hoard" (*North*, 11). The "word-hoard" is closely associated with the Anglo-Saxon of *Beowulf*, and yet, as Blake Morrison writes, Heaney's excavations "retrieve an extraordinary number of linguistic finds, many of Gaelic origins".[65] However, it should be pointed out that these linguistic finds are organized hierarchically, according to a progression charted in "Bone Dreams". Heaney, like Hughes, begins by dismissing Latinate forms such as "Norman devices" and "ivied latins". He reaches back "to the scop's/twang, the iron/flash of consonants" (*North*, 20). Anglo-Saxon and Nordic consonants are thus separated from "Norman devices", whereas Heaney would later conflate them in his discussion of Hughes in "Englands of the Mind".[66] The reason behind this contradiction is once again that Heaney's consonants, unlike Hughes's, are a station on the way to a yet more fundamental speech. This is the speech that Heaney uncovers "In the coffered/riches of grammar/and declensions":

> ... a cauldron

---

[64] P.V. Glob, *The Bog People*, London, 1969, 171.
[65] Morrison, *Seamus Heaney*, 60.
[66] "His consonants are the Norsemen, the Normans...". See Heaney, *Preoccupations*, 154.

of generation
swung at the centre:
love-den, blood-holt,
dream-bower.

(*North*, 20-21)

Philology here turns into mythology, as Heaney's etymological broodings blur into a contemplation of primitive origins. The "centre" of "Bone Dreams" prefigures the centre of "Kinship": finally "facing a goddess", Heaney acquires enough confidence to name the missing centre of Hughes's mythologies and to snatch the mantle of Irishness from the shoulders of a doubting Yeats: "This centre holds", "This is the vowel of earth/dreaming its root" (*North*, 36). Few contemporary poets have dared to contradict Yeats's "The Second Coming" ("the centre cannot hold") so boldly.[67] Heaney fuses a vision of origins with the vowel of primeval Irishness, and offers the rough beast of his Celtic primitivism as the centre that holds *North* together. Heaney's synthesis also consecrates the naturalization of language that is a hallmark of his early poetry.[68] The poet of *North* decodes the "porous/language of touch" (19), the "braille" of bog corpses (25), and the "hieroglyphic/peat" (33).

The source of this natural language is the Celtic vowel of earth, "dreaming its root" in a primeval soil (*North*, 36). The relation between ancestral nationhood and primitivism has long been problematic. Yeats already accused Matthew Arnold of mistaking the primitive religion of Europe for a Celtic idiosyncrasy.[69] Yeats himself, however, regarded Ireland as the repository of universal ancient wisdom, and could sometimes put his fascination with primitive mythologies in the service of his Romantic nationalism. Hughes, as we have seen, eventually abandoned his hope of reconciling his own sense of English nationhood with primeval energies, and explicitly discarded England in his celebration of primitive nature in *River*. The only national signature that his primitivism retained was indeed a Celtic one, similar to that which Heaney asserts through his misreading. Heaney's own Celtic primitivism moves smoothly between nature and culture, between prehistory, ancient history and Irish history. Both Arnold and the Celtic Revival identified

---

[67] W.B. Yeats, *The Poems*, ed. Daniel Albright, London, 1990, 235.

[68] For an adversarial reading of Heaney's linguistic realism that explores its broader theoretical implications, see Antony Easthope, "How Good is Seamus Heaney?", *English*, XLVI/184 (1997), 21-36.

[69] Yeats wrote of Arnold: "I do not think he understood that our 'natural magic' is but the ancient religion of the world." See W.B. Yeats, *Essays and Introductions*, London, 1961, 176.

Ireland with the lost culture of antiquity – a tendency that Joyce subjected to hilarious parody through the parallels between Ireland and ancient Greece in *Ulysses*. But in "The Toome Road", Heaney disregarded Joyce's ironies and reverted to those time-hallowed parallels. He thus challenged the trespassers on his native landscape with the words: "It stands here still, vibrant as you pass,/The invisible, untoppled omphalos" (*Field Work*, 15). For Heaney, "Omphalos" means "the navel, and hence the stone that marked the centre of the world".[70] This is the centre which Heaney identifies with his primeval Ireland, and in which the tensions of the present can be imaginatively absorbed. The Troubles are explained as the recurrence of an archetypal conflict whose religious intensity challenges the understanding of contemporary commentators, in the same way that it originally baffled Tacitus: "And you, Tacitus,/ observe..." (*North*, 38).[71]

That religious intensity, however, is the preserve of Heaney's Catholicism. Like Hughes, but with more poetic consistency, Heaney contrasts the primitive violence of a pagan/Catholic culture with the debased, rational violence of Puritanism. Heaney's approach to the history of conflict in Ireland not only draws on ancient myth, but also on tropes that clearly derive from Irish Catholicism. Tacitus and other observers are thus challenged to survey the "mother ground" on which blood is shed, and which is also a "sacred heart" (*North*, 38). This had drawn criticism form Northern Protestant critics like Edna Longley, who argues that Heaney "defines the battlefield in astonishingly introverted Catholic and Nationalist terms". Longley also discerns Catholic overtones in Heaney's use primitive rituals: according to her, the patient descriptions of bodies found in bogs "incline to rosary beads"[72] – a view borne out by Heaney's likening of the Tollund Man to "a saint's body" (*Wintering Out*, 37). Moreover, Heaney punningly underscores the Celtic origin of the rituals in which the bog victims were sacrificed by a Nordic

---

[70] Heaney, *Preoccupations*, 17. Joyce's use of the word "omphalos" is altogether different: in "Oxen of the Sun", Malachi Mulligan "proposed to set up ... a national fertilizing farm to be named *Omphalos* with an obelisk hewn and erected after the fashion of Egypt and to offer his dutiful yeoman services for the fecundation of any female of what grade of life soever who should there direct to him with the desire of fulfilling the function of her natural". See James Joyce, *Ulysses*, 526.

[71] Heaney wrote of the religion of the Iron Age: "there are satisfactory imaginative parallels between this religion and time and our own time. They are observed with amazement and a kind of civilized tut-tut by Tacitus in the first century and by leader-writers in the *Daily Telegraph* in the 20th century" (quoted in Morrison, *Seamus Heaney*, 63).

[72] Edna Longley, "'Inner Emigré' or 'Artful Voyeur'? Seamus Heaney's *North*", 46, 43.

tribe. The "bog queen" thus relates how her skull "*hibern*ated/in the wet nest of my hair" (*North*, 26. Emphasis mine). Heaney's explorations of Danish bogs do not contradict his native Hibernian concerns: as the conclusion of "The Tollund Man" announced, he always ends up feeling "at home" (*Wintering Out*, 37). "Kinship" further reminds us that "*bog*/mean[s] soft" (*North*, 34), and thus points back to the softness that *Wintering Out* had insistently associated with Ireland.

The boggy softness that lies at the centre of *North* belongs to a female deity who seduces the very language of violence into a soothing, erotic music:

> Earth-pantry, bone vault,
> sun-bank, embalmer
> of votive goods
> and sabred fugitives.
>
> Insatiable bride.
> Sword-swallower ...

(North, 34)

By eroticizing the violence of fertility rituals, Heaney's deployment of the trope of seduction also rids Nordic violence of the destabilizing ambiguity which it had in Hughes's work. If, in Heaney's view, Hughes's Norsemen were fighting the "lasciviousness" of vowels,[73] the violence of Heaney's own Goddess-worshipping Vikings has a sensuousness which makes it lasciviously pagan: "they spread out your lungs/and made you warm wings/for you shoulders" (*North*, 15). Heaney's Nordic invaders are folded back into the primitive, Celtic world they came to conquer, "like Gunnar/who lay beautiful/inside his burial mound/though dead by violence" (9).

The mythical structure of *North* is designed to articulate the paradox of a masculine violence that originates in a feminine religion. Hughes, despite his avowed interest in the Goddess, often gave the impression that his fascination with violence was a very masculine obsession. Heaney, on the other hand, does not find it incongruous to explain IRA violence as the resurgence of "feminine" cults – even when its victims are the real Catholic women of the controversial "Punishment", who end up shaved and tarred for their sexual betrayals. The end of the poem shows that the "tribal, intimate revenge" has claims on Heaney's imagination that can outweigh any "civilized outrage" at the violence it mythologizes (*North*,

---

[73] Heaney, *Preoccupations*, 154.

31). Heaney sometimes shows unease with his success at adapting Hughes's religious primitivism: he is aware of being an "artful voyeur" (31), and in other poems the victims of violence can also be found "outstaring/axe and beatification" (32). The mythical framework that gives meaning to Heaney's primitive violence is less ambiguous than its sources in Hughes's work; but its implacable coherence generates a moral hesitation. The end of "Kinship", however, suggests that the ambiguity of Heaney's response to past and present atrocities is resolved through an ultimate recourse to the female deity that presides over his mythology:[74] observers of the conflict are challenged to report how, in the midst of various atrocities, "the goddess/swallows our love and terror" (38-39).

In the second part of *North*, Heaney turns from the mythical method of the first part to a more straightforward treatment of the Troubles, but the rejection of the "'voice of sanity'" persists (52). The last poem proposes an "Exposure" of his ambiguous stance as a Northern Irish poet newly settled in the Republic. But while the lines "I am neither internee nor informer;/An inner émigré, grown long-haired" seem to combine a disenchanted suggestion of political impotence with a declaration of neutrality, Heaney's self-description as a "wood-kerne/Escaped from the massacre" (67) actually shows this to be a strategic retreat. As Morrison notes,

> "wood-kerne" has quite definite political overtones (wood-kernes were the shadowy Gaelic outlaws who put up resistance to the Protestant colonization of Ireland, and of whom later Republican gangs of "boys" are the natural successors).[75]

Moreover, as Heaney blends into his native landscape by "taking protective colouring/From bole and bark" (67), he reinforces the primitivism of *North* by identifying once more with his native natural environment.

North sparked off a heated critical debate that centred on its mythologizing approach to the Northern Irish problem. Seamus Deane,

---

[74] Heaney's adaptation of Hughes's primitivism thus allows him to breathe new poetic life into the familiar Irish nationalist trope of blood sacrifice, which culminated with Pearse's sacrifice during the Easter Rising. For an analysis of the history of that trope, see Richard Kearney's "Myth and Terror" in *The Crane Bag Book of Irish Studies 1977-1981*, eds Mark Patrick Hederman and Richard Kearney, 273-287.
[75] Morrison, *Seamus Heaney*, 57.

although critical of Yeats's myths of Ireland,[76] took a more lenient view of Heaney's: "although it is true that the Viking myths do not correspond to Irish experience without some forceful straining, the analogy between the two was at first thrilling." His response to *North* reproduces Heaney's own wavering between civilized outrage and tribal irrationalism in "Punishment"; unsurprisingly, his conclusion likewise surrenders to irrationalism as he speaks of "what writing, to remain authentic, must always face – the confrontation with the ineffable, the unspeakable thing for which 'violence' is our helplessly inadequate word".[77] In an interview with Heaney, Deane also suggested that "rational clarity" and "humanism" were "being used as an excuse to rid Ireland of the atavisms which gave it life even though the life itself may be in some ways brutal".[78] Asked whether the mythical poetics of *North* may not imply the "danger of sentimentalizing a world ... which in its own time may have been nasty, brutish ...", Heaney first recognized the risks, but went on to produce the familiar organicist argument: "I am not sure whether it was any nastier. I think it was hard, maybe, but there was a kind of rhythm to it and a completeness to it."[79]

On the other hand, Edna Longley's scepticism echoed Ciaran Carson's denunciation of Heaney's pose as a "mythmaker, an anthropologist of ritual killing, an apologist for 'the situation', in the last resort, a mystifier".[80] Such responses became paradigmatic of a diffidence towards Heaney's method. Other critics were not slow to take Heaney's sceptics to task. According to Eamonn Hughes, critical unease with Heaney's contrasting treatments of Protestant and Catholic violence suffers from ideological short-sightedness: in his view, a poem like "Punishment" is simply "an admission of the power of the communal over the individual for which [a] liberal conscience does not allow".[81] Henry Hart argued that Heaney was following the modernists in substituting a mythical method for an impossible objectivity. He also expressed disbelief at Longley's suspicion of "a profoundly Catholic slant

---

[76] See Deane's attack on Yeats's mythicizing tendencies in *Heroic Styles: The Tradition of an Idea*, Derry City, 1984.

[77] Seamus Deane, "Seamus Heaney, The Timorous and the Bold", in *Seamus Heaney: A Collection of Critical Essays*, ed. Michael Allen, 69, 76.

[78] Seamus Heaney, "Unhappy and at Home", Interview with Seamus Deane, 69.

[79] See Haffenden, *Viewpoints*, 66-67.

[80] Carson's words are quoted by Henry Hart in his *Seamus Heaney: Poet of Contrary Progressions*, 77.

[81] Eamonn Hughes, "Representations in Modern Irish Poetry", in *Seamus Heaney: A Collection of Critical Essays*, ed. Michael Allen, 85.

to *North*": according to Hart, the poems are confessions of "allegiances to
both tribes", since Heaney

> lovingly addresses the victims of prehistoric fertility cults,
> elegizes murdered Catholics, but also finds himself admiring the
> heroic traditions of the ... victors, even though they belong to the
> English colonizer, Viking conqueror, or Norse raider.[82]

But Hart overlooks Heaney's misreading of Hughes, which subsumes the
Norse element under the Celtic primitivism that sustains and comforts
Heaney's Catholic bias. As we will see in a moment, Heaney's treatment
of the "English colonizer" is quite different: the integration of the English
element is not a historical fact, but a utopian project that runs parallel to
the enlistment of Protestant vowels envisaged in "A New Song". Hart's
other claim that Heaney "embraces a complex dialectic" between tribal
allegiances and rational response is deconstructed by his own description
of Heaney's "*apocalyptic* desire for both rational and intuitive
judgements".[83] Hart, like Deane and Heaney, only envisages a synthesis
that effectively tips the balance in favour of irrationalism.

Critical neglect of the role played by Hughes in the making of *North*
has seriously distorted the perception of its politics. Michael Parker
regards Heaney's mythical method as a genuine attempt at transcending
sectarian differences. According to him, "Heaney's attitude towards his
Catholic inheritance is not by any means uncritical or unquestioning"; for
in *North* Heaney

> felt compelled to examine other modes of feeling and perception
> – *in addition to* Catholic and Christian ones – and to employ pre-
> Christian mythic material to enable him to confront and interpret
> the slaughter of innocence.[84]

My focus on Heaney's misreading of Hughes makes it possible to refute
such claims, since the mythical structure that Heaney borrows from
Hughes conflates Catholicism with pre-Christian religion and excludes
Protestantism.

As with *Wintering Out*, the major irony that has gone unnoticed in the
reception of *North* is that Heaney's myth of Ireland emerged from the
internal contradictions of the writer who would become England's

---

[82] Hart, *Seamus Heaney: Poet of Contrary Progressions*, 77-78.
[83] *Ibid.*, 82. Emphasis mine.
[84] Parker, *Seamus Heaney: The Making of the Poet*, 151, 116.

eccentric Poet Laureate. The debate that surrounds *North* has sometimes been presented as a conflict between Irish atavisms and English liberalism, but it must eventually centre on attitudes towards a Romantic neo-nationalism that is not specifically Irish. Heaney's neo-nationalism does not spring from any innate, mystically conceived Irishness. It is an ideological construct which he imported from England via his misreading of Hughes, and which he re-exported through his treatment of England in *North*, as we will now examine.

"Ocean's Love to Ireland" and "Act of Union" once again allegorize Ireland's history in sexual terms. But whereas the Norse poems and the bog poems were dominated by the trope of seduction, the dominant trope here is that of rape and insensitive male domination. Seduction in Heaney is often expressed through metaphors of rising rivers and a seeping boggy moistness that is associated with Ireland. In "Ocean's Love to Ireland", by contrast, it is the English presence that is translated into more violent and threatening waters[85]: "Ralegh has backed the maid to a tree/As Ireland is backed to England", "He is water, he is ocean." This invader, unlike the Vikings, resists the imaginative integration into the ancestral culture: "Iambic drums/Of English beat the woods where her poets/Sink like Onan" (*North*, 41). The rift in the English soul that Hughes had associated with the Reformation and would later associate with the iambic tradition[86] corresponds to the invasion that Ireland could not sustain. The poem itself fails to articulate the eroticized consonantal music which was wedded to the vowel of earth and the gutturals of *Wintering Out* and poems like "Kinship"; its very language reflects the loss of Celtic sensuality that it thematizes.

The same is true of "Act of Union", in which the "imperially/Male" persona has left his wife with "the pain,/The rending process in the colony". This turns out to be an allegory for the creation of Ulster, which now hosts "an obstinate fifth column/whose stance is growing unilateral". Britain is a "tall kingdom" over Ireland's feminine shoulder, and their encounter is characterized by a warped, incomplete eroticism: faced with England's ambiguous caresses, Ireland would "neither cajole nor ignore" (*North*, 43). The damage is apparently irreparable, since "no treaty" "will

---

[85] Although his reading does not focus on the political implications of that theme, R.J.C. Watt analyses Heaney's water imagery in similar terms: "despite his deep attachment to spring and well and stream, Seamus Heaney is afraid of water *en masse*". See Watt, "Seamus Heaney: Voices on Helicon", 225.

[86] Hughes described how Spenser "lines up his own syllables on the parade-ground and drills them to march in iambics" (*Winter Pollen*, 356). He also wrote that the Romantic attraction to Anglo-Saxon poetics ended when "iambics restored public calm" (*Winter Pollen*, 371).

salve completely [her] tracked/And stretchmarked body" (43-44). However, Heaney does propose a solution: namely, to rid England of its Puritanism and its modernity, and rediscover the mythical England that Hughes idealized. This is the neo-nationalist utopia that the extended metaphor of "Bone Dreams" expresses.

The poem opens on a hostile note. Heaney finds a bone lying on the ground and imaginatively throws it at England, following its "drop/to strange fields" (19). The first lines thus seem to voice resentment. In the sections that follow, however, Heaney casts himself as an imaginative explorer of England's riches and, most importantly, as a seducer who would re-awaken her buried sensuality. After hitting upon the "love-den, blood-holt/dream-bower" of primeval origins, Heaney orders himself to

> re-enter the memory
> where the bone's lair
> is a love-nest
>
> (*North*, 21)

This sets the scene for the poem's seduction of England: the poet "holds [his] lady's head" and turns himself into a primitive symbol of fertility: "a chalk giant/carved upon her downs". This enables him to engage an archaic England in an erotic game that seals the triumph of his Celtic seduction, as his hands "move towards the passes" and he ad England end up "cradling each other" (21).

Whereas the Britain that leans over Ireland's shoulder in "Act of Union" is an Imperial male imposing his violent sexuality and its unwelcome consequences, Heaney's Celtic male displays the more seductive approach of his Romantic neo-nationalism and reinvents the primitive England of Hughes's poetry. It can hardly be a coincidence that the geographical references in the last section of "Bone Dreams" lead back to Hughes's England. Heaney describes the dead body of a mole he found "One morning in Devon". Inspecting it, he likens its shoulders to "small distant Pennines" (*North*, 22-23). No one seems to have made much of the fact that Heaney is here alluding to places that have definite Hughesian associations.[87] Hughes's longing for a primitive, sensuous England has in fact come full circle – in Heaney's work. The misreading is completed, but its result has been to make the neo-nationalism that both

---

[87] Hughes comes from the Pennines, and had moved to Devon in the 1960s. He may well be the interlocutor who invites Heaney to touch the mole in this section of "Bone Dreams".

poets share look primarily Irish, and to give it the ideological respectability that is often granted to Irish nationalism.

Heaney's work has thus been welcomed as a postcolonial manifesto to which the English should turn for inspiration. In an article that praises the linguistic subversiveness of *Wintering Out*, Stan Smith concludes:

> The contestation of Irish dialect and "Standard English" says enough. If the English are truly the last people to be decolonized, then the politico-cultural *logomachia*, the darkened English, of such poets as Heaney ... will show us the way.[88]

This chapter has shown that there already was an English poet to whom England, like Heaney, could turn in its search for a post-Imperial sense of nationhood: its late Poet Laureate, Ted Hughes. One can only wonder what response Hughes's work would have got, had his own "politico-cultural *logomachia*" been sustained by a primitivist organicism as coherent as Heaney's. As things stand, Hughes remains mysteriously neglected by Heaney's English supporters.[89] Heaney himself, after all, had shown the way quite explicitly when he greeted Hughes's appointment as Poet Laureate:

> Britain today is a country apparently obsessed with its fatigued class war and its self-wounding industrial crises, a country whose destiny is debated in terms of economics; whose official church is almost embarrassed by the mention of God; whose universities falter in their trust in the traditional humanist disciplines. That such a country should turn to a poet with an essentially religious vision, without a word to say on contemporary politics but with a strong trust in the pre-industrial realities of the natural world, is remarkable. In fact, it is a vivid demonstration of the truth of the implied message of Hughes's poetry that the instinctual, intuitive side of man's, and in particular the Englishman's, nature has been starved and occluded and is in need of refreshment.[90]

---

[88] Stan Smith, "Darkening English: Post-Imperial Contestations in the Language of Seamus Heaney and Derek Walcott", *English*, XLIII/175 (1994), 55.

[89] Smith himself balks at the "feudal ethos of cruelty, superstition and half-barbarous grandeur" of Hughes's primitive England. See his "Wolf Masks: The Early Poetry of Ted Hughes", in *Critical Essays on Ted Hughes*, ed. Leonard Scigaj, New York, 1992, 78.

[90] Seamus Heaney, "The New Poet Laureate", in *Critical Essays on Ted Hughes*, ed. Leonard Scigaj, 46. One should note the transition from Heaney's diagnosis of a *British* disease to an invocation of the *Englishman*'s instinctual side.

For some reason, the critics who commend Heaney as a guide to the decolonization of the English mind have failed to take the hint and to celebrate Hughes's primitive England. But if they remain unwilling to refresh themselves in Hughes's energies, the time may have come for them to reassess the terms in which they praise Heaney.

Although his comment on Hughes's appointment shows that he is sympathetic to his colleague's efforts, Heaney himself, as we have seen, is partly responsible for stressing Hughes's difficulties in articulating a coherent vision of English nationhood. It sometimes looks as though Heaney recognizes the longing for an older England in some English poets, but finds their poetics somehow inadequate for its expression. Thus, his praise of Hughes's Anglo-Saxon primitivism is counterbalanced by a distrust of the masculine violence of Hughes's consonants, which do not submit to the influence of his own Celtic vowels. Only on rare occasions does Hughes reach what Heaney considers to be a true vision of primeval origins, as in the vocalic line from "The Thought Fox": "A widening, deepening greenness" (*The Hawk in the Rain*, 14). This, for Heaney, is the "epiphany" during which Hughes briefly becomes "the poet-warden, the vowel-keeper".[91] A similar ambiguity characterizes Heaney's relation to Hopkins. His view of Hopkins's poetics as "masculine" is tempered by approving comments on Hopkins's vision of a remote English past. Hopkins's experiments, Heaney writes, "were part of a patriotic urge to keep all of English at work". Although Hopkins's strategy is still too intellectual and masculine for Heaney, his motivation was ultimately feminine and sensuous. Indeed, "there may be more of the lexicographer in Hopkins but there is still earth under the nails of his hand turning the dictionary pages"; his poetry is "grounded in the insular landscape which, in the month of May, blooms and greens in a way that is still Marian, sacramental, mediaeval English Catholic".[92]

Heaney also dwells on the archaic, Celtic traces in the English landscapes of Thomas Hardy. His reading of "Channel-Firing" focuses on the last stanza of Hardy's poem:

> Again the guns disturbed the hour,
> Roaring their readiness to avenge
> As far inland as Stourton Tower,
> And Camelot, and starlit Stonehenge.

---

[91] Heaney, *Preoccupations*, 154.
[92] Seamus Heaney, "Place, Pastness, Poems: A Triptych", *Salmagundi*, LXVIII-LXIX (1985-1986), 45.

Heaney argues that, in those lines, "we are at the tribe's centre of feeling and belonging, where the spirits of the ancestors are pressing actively in upon the consciousness of the living". Hardy also describes how, at the sound of the guns, the worms "drew back into the mounds". According to Heaney, those "mounds" have associations that "reach back to the hill-forts and earth-works of Celtic Britain".[93] In Heaney's analysis, the threat posed to a modern England by the oncoming war makes it possible to reassert the nation's Celtic origins – no allowances are made for a reading in which the resounding guns would threaten those origins as well. The Hardy whom Heaney favours is not the sceptic or the pessimist whom Larkin presented as his model, nor is he the decent English liberal championed by Donald Davie in *Thomas Hardy and British Poetry*. Rather, he is a poet who asserted a sense of ancestral continuities at a time when modern Britain was in crisis, and Heaney implies that an ancient nationhood may emerge from the dislocation of the modern order that Hardy envisages.

Heaney's Hardy thus becomes comparable to David Jones, in whose work Heaney sees "a version of pastoral, based on a visionary nostalgia for an early British Golden Age".[94] Such concerns would mean that both Hardy and Jones somehow prefigured Hughes's own interest in things Celtic; yet Heaney's characterization of Jones's work as "pastoral" makes it necessary to qualify this apparently simple equation. Indeed, Hughes's work is noted for its rejection of the English pastoral idyll. Heaney's nature poetry, on the other hand, is marked from the outset by an oscillation between the opposite poles of traditional pastoralism and Hughesian anti-pastoralism.[95] This hesitation no doubt springs from an ambiguity in Heaney's personal response to the natural world; it was already perceptible in *Death of a Naturalist*, where he was both fascinated with and repelled by natural processes, sentimental and tough in turns – "Blackberry Picking" and "The Early Purges" stand at both extremes of that spectrum. But since Heaney invested natural processes with the political connotations developed in *Wintering Out* and *North*, the relations between pastoral and anti-pastoral modes in his work can also illuminate his relation to Hughes, and to the latter's own attempt at equating nature and nationhood.

---

[93] *Ibid.*, 42.

[94] Heaney, *Preoccupations*, 180.

[95] See Henry Hart's chapter "Pastoral and Anti-Pastoral Attitudes" in his *Seamus Heaney: Poet of Contrary Progressions*.

As we have seen, Hughes's anti-pastoralism and his interest in violence were both essential to his vision of a hidden England *and* damaging to its coherence. By contrast, Heaney's own mythologizing of historical violence succeeded in containing the more destabilizing aspects it had in Hughes's work. His ability to negotiate between pastoral and anti-pastoral modes achieves a similar effect. In the conclusion to his essay on pastoral, "In the Country of Convention", Heaney suggests that the term should be given a broad definition that could encompass David Jones's poetry as well as works by Irish writers like Synge, Kavanagh and Montague, to which Heaney considers applying the label "frontier pastoral". Heaney is interested in the limits of the genre and appears to favour a "tough" version of pastoralism. He nevertheless implicitly draws the line at Hughes himself, whose name is never mentioned in the essay.[96] The reason is that, while some of Heaney's early nature poems read like pastiches of Hughes, Heaney's relation to nature remains, in the last analysis, more conventionally Romantic.

Heaney's nature poetry indeed manages to blend Hughesian intensities with a Wordsworthian sense of dwelling. Hughes's "spirit of place", as Keith Sagar writes, "is emphatically not the loving mother of post-Wordsworthian nature poetry".[97] Heaney, on the other hand, has often defined poetry's relation to place in explicitly Wordsworthian terms. In "The Sense of Place", Heaney recognizes the Romantic poet's seminal influence: "Wordsworth was perhaps the first man to articulate the nurture that becomes available to the feelings through dwelling in one perpetual dear place."[98] English though he was, Wordsworth does not represent an alien mode of feeling for the insistently Irish Heaney. Heaney's essay "Place and Displacement", which examines some Northern Irish poets' treatments of place, begins with considerations on Wordsworth. The tension between the attachment to place and the necessity of displacement is first presented in terms of a Jungian dialectic which leads to the development of a "new level of consciousness". Heaney then adds that "Jung might have found in Wordsworth's *Prelude* a working model for that evolution of a higher consciousness in response to an apparently intolerable conflict".[99]

This synthesis of Jung and Wordsworth is quite remarkable, and reveals once again how Heaney deviates from Hughes. Indeed, when

---

[96] The essay is reprinted in *Preoccupations*.

[97] Sagar, *The Achievement of Ted Hughes*, 3.

[98] *Preoccupations*, 145.

[99] Seamus Heaney, "Place and Displacement: Reflections on Some Recent Poetry from Northern Ireland", in *Contemporary Irish Poetry*, ed. Elmer Andrews, London, 1992, 124, 125.

Heaney explained that he was "Jungian in religion", he came very close to Hughes's definition of poetry as a form of shamanism.[100] Heaney also approvingly quoted Anna Swir's characterization of the poet as "an antenna capturing the voices of the world, a medium expressing his own subconscious and the collective unconscious".[101] But if Hughes regularly made similar statements, his own brand of shamanism remained too saturated with violent energies to be accommodated by a Wordsworthian idiom. Heaney, by contrast, has sought to reconcile his Wordsworthian relation to place with his mythical sense of Irishness. In the second part of *North*, the poems that make up "Singing School" are placed under a Wordsworthian epigraph that sums up Heaney's feelings about his own move to the South of Ireland:

> *Fair seedtime had my soul, and I grew up*
> *Fostered alike by beauty and by fear;*
> *Much favoured in my birthplace, and no less*
> *In that beloved Vale to which, erelong,*
> *I was transplanted ...*

(North, 56)

The method of "Singing School" itself owes little to the Hughesian investigations of the first part of *North*. But the Wordsworthian note it introduces was later picked up in *Field Work*, where Heaney blended it with his Celtic primitivism.

In his *Glanmore Sonnets*, a sequence which is part of *Field Work*, Heaney celebrates his new Irish home in a poetic idiom which, unlike the Anglo-Saxon music of the first part of *North*, is indebted to more recent English traditions: the sonnet, the pentameter, the iamb (or, rather, variations on the last two forms). The poems, as Morrison observes, are "self-consciously pastoral".[102] Heaney even indulges in a rather artificial nod to Wordsworth in the third sonnet, where the pastoral scene strikes the poet as "all crepuscular and iambic". He turns to his wife and starts comparing their lonely situation to that of Wordsworth and his sister, "Dorothy and William" – at which his wife breaks in: "'You're not going to compare us two...?'" *(Field Work*, 35). The *Glanmore Sonnets* thus explicitly adapt an English Romantic sense of dwelling which Hughes resisted. Heaney is now settled in a pacified Irish landscape, in which his

---

[100] Seamus Heaney, Interview with Frank Kinahan, *Critical Inquiry*, VIII/3 (1982), 409.
[101] Seamus Heaney, *The Government of the Tongue*, London, 1988, 93.
[102] Morrison, *Seamus Heaney*, 85.

myth of Irishness takes on a new dimension. The fifth sonnet reminds us that Heaney is still an "etymologist of roots and graftings" and a poet of philological broodings, exploring the origins and connotations of words: "Elderberry? It is shires dreaming wine./Boortree is bower tree ..." (*Field Work*, 37). The underlying element is still recognizably Irish, as the major trope that controlled the violent myths of *North* now re-emerges in a much quieter guise: "Vowels ploughed into other: opened ground" (*Field Work*, 33). This "opened ground" is no longer that of Ireland's raped body in "Act of Union" (*North*, 44). The equation of a primitive Celtic idiom with nature takes place within the confines of an Irish "haven" (*Field Work*, 39), where "Words [are] entering almost the sense of touch". The "voice" that Heaney is trying to find here is one that "might continue, hold, dispel, appease" (34).

"The Guttural Muse" similarly resumes the reflection initiated by "Traditions" in *Wintering Out*, but it focuses on the healing potential of a recovered Irishness rather than on its historical humiliations. The voices that Heaney overhears in "The Guttural Muse" are "thick and comforting/As oily bubbles the feeding tench sent up" – the tench's slime is "said to heal the wounds of fish that touched it" (*Field Work*, 28). Heaney himself is such a wounded fish, an appropriately chosen pike escaped from the Hughesian myths of violence that the poet had explored in *North*: "I felt like some old pike all badged with sores" (28). The guttural muse is here offered as the local balm that heals all rifts: Heaney explained that the real voices that prompted the poem were "absolute dialect voices ... I felt the redemptive quality of the dialect, of the guttural, of the illiterate self".[103] Gutturals and dialects are now more firmly Irish than ever, as Heaney's misreading of Hughes is brought to completion in the harmonies of *Field Work*.

The pastoralism of *Field Work* does not exclude glimpses of a harsher reality. The idyllic mode of *Glanmore Sonnets* is occasionally disturbed by the rats which already haunted *Death of a Naturalist*:[104] they leave their "Blood on a pitch-fork, blood on the chaff and hay". Such visions raise questions that the poet cannot evade: "Did we come to the wilderness for this?"; "What is my apology for poetry?" (*Field Work*, 41). The sequence ends with Heaney turning for comfort to the soothing certainties of marital love that the last sonnet celebrates. For, as the

---

[103]   Haffenden, *Viewpoints*, 58.
[104]   See poems like "The Barn" (with its Gothic metaphor "the two-lugged sacks moved in like great blind rats"), "The Advancement of Learning" and "Personal Helicon", where a rat "slapped across [the poet's] reflection" in a well (*Death of a Naturalist*, 5, 6-7, 44).

Yeatsian allusion in "The Harvest Bow" proclaims, *"the end of art is peace"* (*Field Work*, 58).[105] Heaney's poetry strives for resolution on all levels – an idea that is also reflected in the very title of his third collection of critical essays, *The Redress of Poetry*. His misreading of Hughes, whose imagination thrived on conflict, has logically resulted in a resolution of the tensions that informed the work of his model.

Hughes was not the only English poet on whom Heaney drew in his poetic treatment of historical violence. Heaney also seems to have learnt something from Geoffrey Hill's descriptions of English battlefields in the sonnets of *Funeral Music*. Another of Heaney's darker intimations in his own *Glanmore Sonnets* is the vision of raindrops that come down "Spattering dark on the hatchet iron". The spectacle of a magpie inspecting the body of a sleeping horse conjures up sinister thoughts: "I thought of dew on armour and carrion" (*Field Work*, 40). These associations may have been prompted by the lines where Hill shows "carrion birds/Strutt[ing] upon the armour of the dead" (*HCP*, 76), whereas the line "Spattering dark on a hatchet iron" recalls the blow of the axe "spattering block-straw with mortal residue" (*HCP*, 70) in the opening sonnet of *Funeral Music*.

An earlier sonnet of Heaney's, "Requiem for the Croppies", already ended with a blend of formal Latinisms and Anglo-Saxon words that seem to point back to Hill's sonnets:

> ... the fatal conclave.
> Terraced thousands died, shaking scythes at cannon.
> The hillside blushed, soaked in our broken wave.
>
> (*Door into the Dark*, 12)

Heaney's metaphor of a blushing hillside, like Hill's line "Reddish ice tinged the reeds" (*HCP*, 76), paradoxically combines a displacement which avoids a direct treatment of death in battle with a hyperbole that magnifies the horror of the scene. But a key difference remains: in *Funeral Music*, the ghostly speech of an anonymous soldier only appears between quotation marks. Heaney's sonnet, by contrast, is entirely spoken by a collective "we" who clearly stands for the side with which Heaney identifies, namely the Irish rebels known as the Croppies. Like Hughes's ancestral England, Hill's visions of English battlefields, for all their sensuous detail, appear definitely remote. Heaney's use of similar poetics

---

[105]   The allusion is to Yeats's poem "To a Wealthy Man...", *The Poems*, 159.

in an Irish context gives them the greater sense of historical urgency with which he also endowed Hughes's mythologies.

Heaney's debt to Hill remains less extensive and less verifiable than his misreading of Hughes. As we saw, Hill's exploration of the matter of England, unlike Hughes's, explicitly excludes the Celtic dimension. It thus makes it difficult for Heaney to find a thematic point of purchase in Hill's work, although Hill's sympathy for the English recusants and his unease with the excesses of Puritanism may have been congenial to Heaney. On the whole, it remains hard to decide whether similarities between Hill and Heaney should be explained as cases of influence or of convergence. The resemblance that Heaney's *Stations* bear to *Mercian Hymns*, however, offers a clearer case. Heaney explained that the prose poems of *Stations*

> were begun in California in 1970/71 although the greater part of them came rapidly to a head in May and June last year [1974]. The delay was partly occasioned by the appearance of Geoffrey Hill's *Mercian Hymns*: what I regarded as stolen marches in a form new to me had been headed off by a work of complete authority (*Stations*, 3).

Eventually, Hill's example seems to have been more stimulating than inhibiting for Heaney. Both *Mercian Hymns* and *Stations* largely consist of childhood memories which connect the poets back to a vividly apprehended landscape infused with national history. Like Hill's language, Heaney's prose poetry is characterized by its sensuousness, a propensity towards apposition, and a relish in the precision of its alternately Latinate and Anglo-Saxon lexis: "primroses grew in a damp single bunch out of the bank, imploding pallors, star plasms, nebula of May ... He knelt and reached the stems. Pod ridges. Legs of nestlings" (*Stations*, 6). Heaney's self-conscious exploration of his "catechism with its woodcut mysteries and polysyllabic runs, its 'clandestine solemnizations', its morose delectation and concupiscence" (10), almost reads like a parodic description of the more sophisticated aspects of Hill's idiom. And indeed, the very words of *Stations* recur in "Englands of the Mind", where Heaney imagines "Hill as indulging in a morose linguistic delectation".[106]

---

[106] Heaney, *Preoccupations*, 160. Hill seems to have been wryly amused by the description: "*Morosa/delectatio* was his expression, that Irish/professor of rhetoric – forget his name" (*The Triumph of Love*, 39).

Heaney's descriptions of nature oscillate between a loving attention to detail and Gothic fantasizing: in "Sweet William", the blooms of "gooseberry bushes, strawberry plants and shot leeks" can "infuse themselves into the eye like blood in snow, as if the crumpled growth had been spattered with grapeshot and bled from underneath" (*Stations*, 11). The effect is comparable to what Hill achieves in his description of an English landscape after a storm in *Mercian Hymns*:

> Earth lay for a while, the ghost-bride of livid Thor, butcher of strawberries, and the shire-tree dripped red in the arena of its uprooting.
>
> (*HCP*, 131)

However, what largely remains an aestheticizing fantasy of violence in Hill's poem opens onto a more definite and pressing sense of history in *Stations*: "Sweet William" is not only a flower, but a name laden with ominous significance for Heaney, referring as it does to the Protestant king who subjugated Catholic Ireland: "the words had the silky lift of a banner on the wind, where that king with crinkling feminine black curls reached after the unsheathed flare of his sword" (11). Similarly, the end of Heaney's poem "July" recalls both *Mercian Hymns* and *Funeral Music*. But Heaney once again gives contemporary relevance to the ancient battlefield that, in Hill's idiom, remains implacably distant: "The air grew dark, cloud-barred, a butcher's apron. The night hushed like a white-mothed reach of water, miles downstream from the battle, skeins of blood still lazing the channel" (15). Unlike Hill's own morbid contemplation the blood that "flowed along the furrows and ditches" after the battle of Towton (*HCP*, 201), Heaney's vision is conjured up by the Orange Drummers' contemporary celebration of the battle of the Boyne (15).

Heaney's fusions of childhood memories and national history in *Stations* can also be read as a less ironical version of the way in which Hill introduced mediaeval references into contemporary scenes. In "Kernes", Heaney remembers how a Protestant boy

> balanced upright on the bicycle, a saddled declamatory king of the castle .... The bicycle, with its chrome insignia and rivetted breastplate of Sir Walter Raleigh in his inflated knickers, motioned (14).

The method here is similar to that which blurred the identities of child and mediaeval king in *Mercian Hymns*. Hill's method, however, remains tentative, and lacks the clear political motivation with which Heaney invests his own poems. Hill's childhood persona "was taken to be a king of some kind, a prodigy, a maimed one" (*HCP*, 109). But as I suggested in chapter 2, Hill's identification with Offa is ultimately an act of aesthetic recreation. Heaney's own early identifications, by contrast, have a more specific historical resonance. In *Stations*, Hill's example helped Heaney reconcile "the private county Derry childhood part of [him]self" with "the slightly aggravated young Catholic male part",[107] but the reconciliation between the private and historical dimensions of his experience goes beyond what Hill himself could achieve. *Stations* thus eschews the more blatant anachronisms and ironies of *Mercian Hymns*.

Heaney, however, would probably disagree with this view of Hill's work. He appears to discern no irony in Hill's description of Offa as "overlord of the M5" (*HCP*, 105). Instead, he argues that Hill

> follows the Joycean precedent set in *Ulysses* of confounding modern autobiographical material with literary and historic matter drawn from the past. Offa's story makes contemporary landscape and experience live in the rich shadows of a tradition.[108]

Heaney's likening of his native place to an "omphalos" in "The Toome Road" already showed his disregard for the parodic dimension of Joyce's parallels between Dublin and ancient Greece in *Ulysses* (see above, note 70). His comments on Hill point to a persistent blindness to the self-conscious arbitrariness of Joyce's and Hill's mythical methods. Heaney takes historical myths seriously – a fact that also explains his successful adaptation of Hughes's problematic mythologies. But it also causes him to simplify Hill's stance. Heaney's Hill is no ironist;[109] on the contrary, he is an English poet who is "celebrating his own indomitable Englishry, casting his mind on other days, singing a clan beaten into the clay and ashes, and linking their patience, their sustaining energy, with the glory of England".[110] This misreading also informs Heaney's treatment of Hill's

---

[107]   Heaney, "Unhappy and at Home", 66.

[108]   Heaney, *Preoccupations*, 160.

[109]   Comparing Heaney's use of myth with Hill's, David Annwn observes that "Heaney's intentions are simple in relation to Hill's goals". Heaney is not "as concerned with the stance of self doubt as Hill is". See *Inhabited Voices: Myth and History in the Poetry of Geoffrey Hill, Seamus Heaney and George Mackay Brown*, Frome, 1984, 7.

[110]   Heaney, *Preoccupations*, 163. This description of Hill draws heavily on one of Yeats's most imperious poems about Ireland, "Under Ben Bulben" (*The Poems*, 375).

language. Few critics have been as sensitive as Heaney to the etymological subtleties of *Mercian Hymns*. Heaney's method for fathoming the depths of Hill's words is that of the philologist, which uncovers ancestral roots. Heaney's philological analyses can be quite impressive, but he neglects the sheer linguistic playfulness of *Mercian Hymns* – the punning method of Hymn II, where the sounds of "Offa" give rise to a multiplicity of arbitrary variations: "a laugh; a cough ... Scoffed-at horned phonograph" (*HCP*, 106. See also chapter two). In Heaney's view, the links between Hill's contemporary and ancient Englands are always validated by the certainties of philology; the possibility that Hill simultaneously invites us to question the arbitrariness of his parallels has no place in such a reading.

Heaney's critical and creative misreadings of English poetry are guided by a neo-nationalist agenda that stresses the importance of the link with an ancestral England. That England is mostly defined along firmly organicist lines; it is a mirror image of the primitive, Gaelic and Catholic Ireland which lies at the centre of his own preoccupations. His misreading of Hughes, however, suggests that this Ireland of the mind owes not a little to its interaction with Hughes's mythical England. One might imagine Heaney and Hughes holding up mirrors at each other, although the surface of Heaney's looking-glass has a smoothness which cancels the distortions that appeared in Hughes's.

Heaney's response to Hughes and Hill interprets their re-creations of a primitive England in essentially postcolonial terms. He regards them as attempts to replace a discredited British identity with a more ancient and authentic sense of English nationhood. While this shows an undeniable sensitivity to important aspects of the English poets' works, it also tends to obscure their problematic relation to Welfare State culture. In Heaney's view, Hughes's and Hill's calls for the rebirth of a primitive Englishness are serious interventions in the identity politics of contemporary Britain, rather than aesthetic protests against the decencies of the post-war cultural consensus. Characteristically, his various misreadings also dispel the tensions and ironies that inform the works of his English counterparts; the threat that those deconstructive elements might pose to Heaney's poetics of identity must be banished or contained. However, the next chapter will show that Heaney's strategy ran into problems when applied to another and rather different English poet, who has nevertheless kept claiming his attention.

CHAPTER SIX
NEITHER HERE NOR THERE: LARKIN AND HIS MISREADERS

The third poet whom Heaney discusses in his essay "Englands of the Minds" makes a rather unlikely companion to Ted Hughes and Geoffrey Hill. Philip Larkin, as Heaney himself acknowledges, is in many ways the antithesis of his slightly younger contemporaries. Both Hughes and Hill partly defined their poetics in the 1950s in reaction against values that were defended by or associated with Larkin. As chapter two has shown, Hill's attitude to the English past set him consciously and radically at odds with Larkin. The discrepancy between Hughes and Larkin is no less considerable. One could hardly imagine a more clear-cut contrast than that between Hughes's absorption in myth and natural energies, and Larkin's dismissal of "Blinding theologies of flowers and fruits" in his poem "I Remember, I Remember" (*The Less Deceived*, 38). References to Hughes and Hill in Larkin's letters are often less than complimentary.

Larkin's work also confronts Heaney with a poetics that is less congenial than Hughes's or Hill's. It is therefore not surprising that Heaney's should mostly describe Larkin through a series of negatives.[1] Larkin is a poet who is "neither a race memory nor a myth-kitty nor a mason", whose language is "neither a dialect nor a pulpit language", who speaks in a "stripped standard English voice" that "leads back neither to the thumping beat of Anglo-Saxon nor to the Gregorian chant of the Middle Ages". Heaney's unease becomes perceptible in his remarks on what he calls the "seaside-postcard Larkin", namely the four-letter words of poems like "Sunny Prestatyn", "This Be the Verse" or "Sad Steps". His critical bafflement is also evident from his rather frantic and not always convincing attempts at linking Larkin with various traditions in English poetry. *Everyman*, Skelton, the Cavaliers, the late Augustans, Tennyson, Hardy, Imagism, Hopkins, Shakespeare and Sidney all follow in rapid succession. In "Englands of the Mind", Heaney's attempts at coming to terms with Larkin[2] thus never match the searching (if sometimes misleading) analyses that one finds in his paragraphs on Hughes and Hill.

Other references in Heaney's prose show that he places Larkin in a tradition of English poetry which is alien to the one that interests him most. Heaney's view of Hardy as the rediscoverer of a buried England

---

[1] Larkin himself was of course very fond of that mode, as is best shown by the title of the unfinished poem "Negative Indicative" (*LCP*, 79).
[2] Seamus Heaney, *Preoccupations*, 164-67.

results in a contrast that pits Larkin against one of his professed models: Heaney's Hardy, as we have seen in chapter five, is a poet of continuities, whereas "Auden and Larkin, two of his natural heirs, are much more at a remove from their emotions when they come to feel about a past which they know to be, among other things, a construction of the literary imagination".[3] Some of Heaney's interpretations of Hardy may be questionable,[4] but they nevertheless point to a real difference between Hardy's poetry of haunting memories and the work of Larkin who, while presenting himself as Hardy's successor, made his desire for oblivion or his inability to remember central to his own work.

Heaney's comparison of Larkin to Auden is also telling. Another poet who loomed large in Larkin's development, Auden is one of the whipping boys of Heaney's critical writings. Auden's definition of the poem as a "verbal contraption" clearly jars with Heaney's own idea of poetry, which leans towards Romantic organicism.[5] In *The Government of the Tongue*, Auden's "strategic intelligence" is once again found to be "too much in control of things". The Auden who appeals to Heaney is the young Auden of *The Orators*, whose Anglo-Saxon alliterations also influenced Hill's *Mercian Hymns*, and in whom some have seen an Englishness leading back to *Beowulf*. Heaney is left to regret that Auden's rationalism suppressed an early cultivation of vernacular energies: the price of Auden's "active intelligence", in Heaney's view, was "a certain diminution of language's autonomy, a not uncensorious training of its wilder shoots".[6] The rational mode in English poetry is also under attack in Heaney's essay on Stevie Smith (another poet whom Larkin admired): if her poems match Auden's definition of poetry as "memorable speech", they nevertheless are found to represent a "retreat from resonance": "you have been persuaded to keep your head at all costs".[7]

When Heaney discusses Dante's influence on modern poetry, he takes Eliot to task for his conversion to a similar poetic rationalism. The discursive mode of *Four Quartets* (for which Eliot had drawn on Auden's example) is unfavourably contrasted with the visionary mode and the demotic energies of *The Waste Land*. The older Eliot is berated for

---

[3] Seamus Heaney, "Place, Pastness, Poems: A Triptych", 44.

[4] See James Booth, "The Turf Cutter and the Nine-to-Five Man: Heaney, Larkin and 'the Spiritual Intellect's Great Work'", *Twentieth Century Literature*, XLIII/4 (1997), 392; Edna Longley, *The Living Stream: Literature and Revisionism in Ireland*, Newcastle, 1994, 150.

[5] Heaney has repeatedly contrasted Auden's definition of a poem with Wordsworth's poetic practice. See *Preoccupations*, 49, 63.

[6] Seamus Heaney, *The Government of the Tongue*, 114, 119, 126.

[7] *Preoccupations*, 201.

preferring a stately, Dantean classicism to a Shakespearean cultivation of the vernacular. Heaney's view of Shakespeare's language here betrays his Hughesian concern with the power of demotic speech: he refers to Shakespeare's "opportunistic dash through the high world of speculation and policy, still fresh from the folk-speech and hedge-school of the shires".[8] Eliot is further criticized for underestimating "the untamed and thoroughly parochial elements" of Dante's Italian vernacular, which according to Heaney can be "as barbarous as Hopkins". Heaney is disappointed by Eliot's substitution of a Latinate idiom for the demotic speech he had used in *The Waste Land;*[9] and while this complaint recalls Hughes's dramatization of the struggle between Anglo-Saxon and Latin modes, it also coincides with Geoffrey Hill's marked preference for early Eliot over *Four Quartets* and his comparison between later Eliot and Larkin. Heaney's remarks on Auden, Eliot and Larkin are both informed by Hughesian concerns and confirmed by Hill's analysis of transitions in mid-twentieth century English poetry. Through critical writings that display a remarkable similarity of purpose, Hughes, Hill and Heaney have been seeking to re-write modern English poetic history for a couple of decades.

The overlaps between their writings concur to propose an alternative to an English poetic line that includes Auden, the older Eliot and Larkin. If one considers that Larkin proposed his own history of modern English poetry through his *Oxford Book of Twentieth Century English Verse*, the contrast is confirmed by his grudging inclusion of some poems by Geoffrey Hill and his omission of David Jones – an exclusion that Heaney lamented.[10] The largely negative views of Hughes and Heaney expressed in Larkin's letters seem to complete the picture: Larkin should logically stand for a version of English poetry that is alien to the one which Heaney is trying to promote. Nevertheless, Heaney curiously insists that Larkin, like Hill and Hughes, is "one of the hoarders and shorers of what they take to be the real England". For all his insistence on Larkin's modernity, Heaney's rhetoric cannot help but discern in Larkin's work the quasi-tribal sense of nationhood which he ascribes to Hughes and Hill. Larkin is "the insular Englishman, responding to the tones of his own clan". Larkin must in fact be made to comply with Heaney's interpretation of contemporary English poetry as a moment akin to that

---

[8] Seamus Heaney, "Envies and Identifications: Dante and the Modern Poet", *Irish University Review*, XV/1 (1985), 11. Heaney's words strongly recall Hughes's comments on Shakespeare's language in his introduction to *A Choice of Shakespeare's Verse*. See *Winter Pollen*, 104-5.
[9] "Envies and Identifications", 12-13.
[10] Seamus Heaney, "Now and in England", 547

previously traversed by "those poets whom we might call colonial".[11] Heaney's Larkin is a "poet ... of composed and tempered English nationalism", the average post-war Englishman, "ill at ease when out of his environment". The strains of that reading, however, become apparent when Heaney tries to illustrate Larkin's attachment to "the speech, the customs, the institutions of England"[12] by discussing "The Importance of Elsewhere", a poem that Larkin wrote about the years he spent in Belfast in the early 1950s.

The opening lines of the poem (*The Whitsun Weddings*, 34) dramatize what is now a commonplace of theories of nationhood, namely the fact that national identity is always defined against a foreign Other. England's Other is, rather unsurprisingly, Ireland: "Lonely in Ireland, since it was not home,/Strangeness made sense." Larkin's stay in Belfast thus seems to have been a defining moment in the development of his sense of English identity. Heaney, keen as he is to describe Larkin as a poet of essential Englishness, writes that, when faced with his experience of foreign Belfast, Larkin "gave thanks, by implication, for the nurture that he receives by living among his own", that is the English.[13] It has since become clear that this does not quite correspond to Larkin's reaction to England when he came back among his fellow countrymen. In a letter that followed both his return to England and the composition of "The Importance of Elsewhere", Larkin declared he was "a bit out of sympathy with England at present. God, what a hole, what witless crapulous people ...".[14] But Heaney's reading misses more than biographical information. Indeed, Heaney characteristically misinterprets the last stanza:

> Living in England has no such excuse:
> These are my customs and establishments
> It would be much more serious to refuse.
> Here no elsewhere underwrites my existence.

What those lines tell us is that, in England, Larkin experienced an existential strangeness, a temptation to refuse which did not make sense in terms of national identity. And yet Heaney compares the poem to Hopkins's dark lament about his Irish exile from England, "wife to his creating thought", in one of his "terrible sonnets".[15] The parallel is of

---

[11] Heaney, *Preoccupations*, 150, 167, 151.
[12] *Ibid.*, 167.
[13] *Ibid.*
[14] Philip Larkin, *Selected Letters*, 245.
[15] Heaney, *Preoccupations*, 168.

course tempting, especially since Heaney regards both Hopkins and Larkin as English nationalists. But unlike Hopkins, Larkin wrote his poem while in England, not in Ireland. This is a difference that Heaney misses, and it seriously distorts his reading of Larkin's poem.

Larkin's drafts show that he had actually started a poem in which he imaginatively connected with England from his Irish exile.[16] The first lines, which he reworked considerably, read: "For all that divides us, I can feel,/Cities of England turning to the winter ..."; "Looking across the Irish sea, I sense/The English cities turning towards winter." This was followed by urban descriptions of the type that would re-emerge in other poems: "their leafless rate-supported parks" points forward to the parks of "Afternoons", "their canals of industrial water" became the "canals with floatings of industrial froth" of "The Whitsun Weddings" (*The Whitsun Weddings*, 44, 21). However, that poem did not come about; what did emerge instead was a poem in which Larkin, freshly returned to England, looked back with some envy on his Irish experience. Indeed, the crucial difference that Heaney refuses to see is that, unlike Hopkins, Larkin found that his exile had actually alleviated an underlying sense of alienation: Ireland's alterity "made [him] welcome". The drafts of the poem make this even clearer: Larkin wrote that in Ireland "loneliness was halved/Once it was claimed that home was somewhere else/And easy to accept the half it left". He also referred to his "dry return/Lonely to England. Now there is no home".[17] Far from being the quintessential post-war insular Englishman that Heaney makes him out to be, Larkin is still very close to a pre-war generation of aesthetes whose relation to England was much more complex. "The Importance of Elsewhere" points back to Cyril Connolly's essay "England, not my England", where Connolly voices feelings remarkably similar to those Larkin later experienced when he returned from Belfast: "Back in England; feel nothing but intense disgust at its stupidity", "Abroad, I was at least interesting to myself – in London I can't be even that", "It is better to be *depaysé* [*sic*] in someone else's country than in one's own."[18] In 1984, Larkin wrote an introduction to Connolly's essays, in which he explained that "there is a study to be made of this literary hatred of England

---

[16] Larkin's workbooks (catalogued as "DPL") are in the care of the Brynmor Jones Library, University of Hull. All quotations are reproduced by kind permission of the Philip Larkin Estate. For this poem, see DPL 1/4/10.

[17] DPL 1/4/15.

[18] Cyril Connolly, *The Condemned Playground: Essays 1927-1944*, London, 1985, 201, 205, 206. Larkin had in fact been much influenced by Connolly in his student days. See Andrew Motion, *Philip Larkin: A Writer's Life*, 202.

between the Wars".[19] But the "literary hatred of England" which Larkin considered with almost clinical detachment in 1984 was an attitude that he himself still shared to a large extent when he settled back in the 1950s.

Larkin's sense of isolation in England is toned down in the final version of "The Importance of Elsewhere". This has made it possible for several readers to think that Larkin really identified with his English "customs and establishments."[20] But a careful reading of the poem shows that he didn't. The "strangeness" mentioned in the first stanza is not cancelled by Larkin's return to England; Larkin's rhymes suggest that it will not go away. In the first two stanzas, Larkin uses a form of pararhyme in which only the final consonants are similar. Thus, "home" only partially rhymes with "welcome"; the same goes for the pairs "speech"/"touch", "faint"/"went", "stable"/"unworkable". The rhymes aren't perfectly identical, in the same way that Larkin does not identify with Ireland: the imperfect rhymes too "insist … on difference", they underline the fact that Larkin is "in touch" with Belfast, but different. The rhymes only work to a certain extent; like Larkin in Ireland, they are both awkward and "not unworkable". The third stanza apparently heralds a return to full rhymes: Larkin is back home in England, among the "customs and establishments" with which Heaney would have him identify. "Excuse" looks like a perfect match for "refuse", although a slight phonetic difference persists between the final /s/ of "excuse" and the /z/ of "refuse". More importantly, is "existence" a perfect match for "establishments"? There is a /t/ that insists on being pronounced in "establishments", but is not there in "existence". And unlike "refuse" and "excuse", "establishments" and "existence" do not rhyme visually either. The rhyme is not quite perfect; Larkin does not quite identify with his native customs, although Heaney would clearly like to equate Larkin's "existence" with English "establishments".

The problems that Heaney experiences in his attempt to force Larkin into a nationalist framework in "Englands of the Mind" are repeated in "The Main of Light", an essay which deals with Larkin's symbolist tendencies. Heaney starts by stressing the austerity of Larkin's epiphanies, although the underlying nihilism of Larkin's visions is clearly at odds with Heaney's own Romantic and religious inclinations: as he admits of Larkin's poem "Solar", "there is nothing … that the happy

---

[19] Introduction to *The Condemned Playground*, no page number.

[20] Andrew Motion agrees with Heaney when he comments on the last stanza of the poem: "After five years of self-imposed exile, [Larkin's] sense of nationality and nationhood began to sharpen" (*Philip Larkin: A Writer's Life*, 264). Tom Paulin also writes that Larkin's "nationalism was intensified by [his] experience of Ireland" – see his *Minotaur*, 234.

atheist could not accept". However, as in "Englands of the Mind", Heaney does find a way of recuperating Larkin's poetics for purposes more congenial to his own. Indeed, after describing the "infinitely neutral splendour" of the vision that ends Larkin's "High Windows", Heaney explains that such moments are "connected with another kind of mood" that generates "visions of the 'spiritual, Platonic old England', the light in them honeyed by attachment to a dream world that will not be denied because it is at the foundation of the poet's sensibility". This sleight of hand allows Heaney to subsume Larkin's visionary impulse under the sense of nationhood that is essential to his reading of contemporary English poetry. The "spiritual, Platonic old England" is "Geoffrey Hill's borrowing from Coleridge"; Larkin is thus made to toe the line of the neo-Romantic Englishness favoured by Heaney.[21]

Later in this chapter, I will show that the real connection between the two visionary moods that Heaney identifies in Larkin is one of radical opposition and therefore precludes Heaney's nationalist recuperation. Such a counter-analysis is made urgent by the impact that Heaney's reading has had on Larkin criticism. Before I actually turn to Larkin's poems proper, I will pause to sketch the ideological context which has caused such a problematic reading to be regarded as a seminal intervention. The reason why Heaney's view of Larkin has aroused such interest is that it answers a growing ideological need: the redefining of English nationhood in the context of devolution. Exploring the difficulties of Heaney's and others' readings of Larkin as a poet of "postcolonial" Englishness will not only correct influential views of his poetry, it will also illuminate the internal contradictions of identity thinking as a mode of literary criticism.

Heaney was not the first critic to stress the Englishness of Larkin's work. Ever since the publication of *The Less Deceived* and of the anthology *New Lines*, which set out the aims and principles of the Movement, Larkin had sometimes been regarded as a spokesman for post-war England. Hostile critics took him to task for his insularity and his attacks on modernism, and their charge of xenophobic Little Englandism later seemed both verified and intensified by what Larkin's letters and biography revealed. Others welcomed his ability to translate the new moods of the nation into a verse distinguished by a very English elegance. The critical vocabulary used by those early commentators often remained suitably vague; their assumptions were often more intuitive than demonstrable. Characteristically, Larkin's Englishness has been a favourite subject of John Bayley, a critic noted for his stress on the

---

[21] *The Government of the Tongue*, 18, 21.

ineffable nature of the aesthetic experience. According to Bayley, "Englishness in poetry, like the reaction to the poetry itself, is in the end a secret and solitary thing". Thus, if Bayley discerns that Englishness in Philip Larkin, he locates it in rather elusive qualities: he alternately ascribes it to the fact that "in Larkin's world it is the experience that matters" and claims that Larkin's "Englishness is not in the subject matter but in the way it conveys itself into our minds". The closest attempt at a definition does not yield much more than a handful of quasi-psychological traits: "something sardonic, solitary, personal, and very compelling".[22]

In 1974, Bayley's front page review of *High Windows* in the *Times Literary Supplement* featured a photograph of Larkin sitting on a milestone at the Scottish border, his elbow resting above the word "England" inscribed on a plaque. Bayley asserted that Larkin's poems were "the most refined and accurate expression possible of a national as well as universal area of awareness: they are very English in fact".[23] Shortly before this culminating moment in the making of Larkin as a national spokesman, Donald Davie had arrived at similar conclusions through a more analytical approach. In *Thomas Hardy and British Poetry*, he cast Larkin as the heir to the decent English liberalism of Thomas Hardy. Divided between its irritation at Larkin's Little Englandism and its desire to justify a "poetry of lowered sights and patiently diminished expectations" in the context of post-war England,[24] Davie's position awkwardly bridged the gap between Larkin's early admirers and detractors. However, the four-letter words of *High Windows*, its surprising symbolist flights, and the emergence of a tougher kind of English liberalism with the Thatcher revolution have since combined to render Davie's political diagnosis obsolete. At other times Davie, like other commentators, does not go very far beyond the safe observation that Larkin's landscapes correspond to "the congested England that we have inhabited day by day".[25] This suggests that at least part of Larkin's poetry were intuitively attuned to the sociological changes that took place in post-war England. Larkin was undeniably English and certainly had an eye for the details of English life. But it is another thing to argue, as several critics do, that he set out to speak for the nation. Indeed, the sweeping assertion that Larkin's poetry was one of the mirrors in which

---

[22] John Bayley, "English Equivocation", *Poetry Review*, LXXVI/1-2 (1986), 4, 5.
[23] John Bayley, "Too Good for this Life", Review of *High Windows*, *Times Literary Supplement*, 21 June 1974, 653.
[24] Donald Davie, *Thomas Hardy and British Poetry*, 71.
[25] *Ibid.*, 64.

the nation "recognized itself"[26] sits rather awkwardly with the unease that is perceptible in poems like "The Importance of Elsewhere".

Heaney's writings on Larkin partly built on the commentaries that had accumulated up to the 1970s, but they also introduced a new vocabulary and a shift of emphasis. According to Heaney, the "new sense of the shires", the "new valuing of the native English experience" which is allegedly distinctive of Hughes, Hill and Larkin results from "the loss of Imperial power, the failure of economic nerve, the diminished influence of Britain inside Europe". Post-Imperial depression and economic decline have regularly featured in historicizing analyses of Larkin, but Heaney remains silent about other sociological factors such as the Welfare State, popular culture, consumerism and the rise of the meritocracy.[27] The renewed interest in a native identity that is central to "Englands of the Mind" is in fact a consequence of a perceived transition, indicated by Heaney's subtle lexical choices, between "Britain" and "England" – a transition in which a Northern Irish nationalist has a barely-concealed interest. The sense of nationhood that Heaney ascribes to his English contemporaries is a copy of his own sense of Irishness, and although Larkin is a more implausible alter ego than Hughes or Hill, it was inevitable that the poet who separated (Northern) Ireland from England so neatly in "The Importance of Elsewhere" should have been considered as an interesting case.

The real context of Heaney's essay is not quite the changing English society of the two decades that followed the Second World War, but rather the emergence of neo-nationalism in the British Isles in the 1970s. The Northern Irish nationalism revived by the Civil Rights movement and the Troubles was obviously important, but the impact of Heaney's essay can only be properly understood by taking into account the rise of other nationalist movements such as the SNP, and the possibilities that neo-nationalism offered to left-leaning British intellectuals orphaned by the failures of Labour socialism at home and the betrayals of communism abroad.

In 1977, the Marxist historian Tom Nairn argued in *The Break-Up of Britain* that nationalism was the only way of securing a genuine transformation of the political and social structures in Britain. His position, which rests on a remarkably unreconstructed Hegelianism, is

---

[26] Motion, *Philip Larkin: A Writer's Life*, 343.
[27] Heaney, *Preoccupations*, 169. Chapter five has stressed Heaney's neglect of Hughes's and Hill's relation to Welfare State culture. Moreover, his economics do not always add up: the "failure of economic nerve" (169) is not easily squared with the threat that a certain form of "success", represented by "houses and roads and factories", poses to England's "pastoral hinterland" (168).

that "the new nationalisms of the British Isles represent a detour on the way to revolution". Nairn himself consequently joined forces with Scottish nationalism, but also conceded that the break-up of Britain would only lead to socialism if a "new left-nationalism" arose in England and supplanted the reactionary nationalism developed by Conservatives like Enoch Powell.[28] Despite Eric Hobsbawm's reassertion of the incompatibility between an enlightened Marxism and nationalist politics,[29] Nairn's call for a new nationalism set a precedent for other British radicals. Thus, in *Imagined Communities*, Benedict Anderson objected to traditional Marxist/humanist critiques of nationalism as false consciousness and emphasized the productivity and the enabling character of nationalism.[30] The fusion of English patriotism with left-wing politics is an idea that recurs in the three volumes of Raphael Samuel's *Patriotism: The Making and Unmaking of a British National Identity*. Linda Colley has also shown how patriotism and radicalism could sometimes feed each other in eighteenth- and early nineteenth-century Britain. She therefore argues that "we need to stop confusing patriotism with simple conservatism, or smothering it with damning and dismissive references to chauvinism and jingoism". Patriotism must be seen as "multi-faceted" indeed[31] – but that definition does not rid it of an ineherent political ambiguity. Moreover, Colley is too scrupulous a historian to claim that her analysis of patriotism has broad implications beyond the period which she is studying. Whether radical patriotism can be resurrected in the markedly different context of twentieth-century Britain is another matter altogether. Yet this is a hope that has clearly resurfaced in some quarters. Since the 1970s, the loss of faith in international, Marxist versions of socialism has breathed new life into more Blakean, home-grown versions of radicalism. At the same time, the rise of postcolonial nationalisms has also helped bolster the radical credentials of patriotism. More recently, in the wake of devolution, voices on both sides of the political spectrum, and both in England and in other parts of Britain, have encouraged England to cultivate its own sense of nationhood.

It is not a coincidence that Nairn's plea for a new English nationalism found an equivalent in Heaney's avuncular expression of support to a

---

[28] Tom Nairn, *The Break-Up of Britain*, London, 1977, 90, 303. See also 79 and 89.

[29] Eric Hobsbawm, "Some Reflections on *The Break-Up of Britain*", *New Left Review*, CV (1977): 3-23.

[30] Benedict Anderson, *Imagined Communities*, 15.

[31] Linda Colley, *Britons: Forging the Nation 1707-1837*, London, 1996, 392. It is worth noting that Colley analyses a patriotism that was both English and British – the very synthesis that is under attack from modern radicals interested in patriotism.

transformed English patriotism (both texts appeared within one year of each other). However, Nairn warned against hasty parallels between new nationalisms within Britain and

> contemporary national-liberation struggles in the Third World. Romantic interpretations along these lines are not lacking, of course. This is not surprising, because the conceptual language we have available is predominantly "nationalist" in just this sense .... new movements cannot help wearing old clothes.[32]

I will have ample opportunity to show how the "romantic interpretations" to which Nairn refers have informed readings of nationhood in contemporary British poetry. This is illustrated by the use of a "(post)colonial" terminology by Heaney and other critics after him. Nairn himself has more recently explained that he "would not speak ill of romanticism as such": "I doubt whether nations can exist without it."[33] The ambivalence of Nairn's nationalist position was summed up by Eric Hobsbawm, who argued that there is a "point where creating a nation-state becomes its own purpose, and the left-wing argument becomes indistinguishable from that of all the Ruritanians of the past".[34] Similarly, Anderson's idea of an "imagined community", based on the productive potential of nationalism, invites the question: can a sense of nationhood be created from scratch? The danger always exists that, in their endeavour to develop a left-wing version of nationalism, radicals will find themselves involved in a cultural project that does not differ significantly from that of reactionary nationalists. Nowhere is that danger as obvious as in literary criticism; the unconscious ambiguities of English radicals' praise of Seamus Heaney are a case in point (see chapter 5). I will now have further opportunities to explore those contradictions. Indeed, in the wake of Heaney's essay, several discussions of Larkin's work have been informed by an effort to trace the new, radical Englishness that the neo-nationalists like Nairn and others have called for.

Heaney's attention to Larkin's Englishnsess makes him dwell on "Show Saturday", a poem which celebrates a traditional English fair. He comments that the poem "beautifully expresses a nostalgic patriotism which is also an important part of this poet's make-up".[35] Heaney's

---

[32] *The Break-Up of Britain*, 127.
[33] Tom Nairn, "The Departed Spirit, or the English Quandary", *London Review of Books*, 30 October 1997, 6.
[34] "Some Reflections on *The Break-Up of Britain*", 17.
[35] *The Government of the Tongue*, 19-20.

indulgent tone reminds us that cultural conservatism is very much part of his own imagination. Yet, this has not prevented an increasing number of critics (often of a left-wing persuasion) from following Heaney in arguing that Larkin's work embodies a postcolonial sense of English nationhood. Stephen Regan thus comments that Heaney has "written impressively and revealingly about [Larkin's] postcolonial consciousness".[36] Considering Heaney's relative neglect of sociological factors, Regan's praise is rather surprising: of all Larkin critics, Regan has been most interested in placing Larkin's poetry in its changing social context. He thus insists that the reason for a continued interest in Larkin's Englishness "is not that his poems dutifully parade some ideal, conservative vision of the nation, but that they prove in the end to be so responsive to the fractures and collisions in post-war English culture".[37] Heaney's glimpse of the "spiritual, Platonic old England" in Larkin should logically be given short shrift, as should all unifying versions of Englishness. But Regan himself has paradoxically emphasized Larkin's determination to heal the rifts that divide English society, especially in later poems that exhibit a "sense of communal obligation and commitment, a desire to rebuild and renew a sense of collective life".[38]

Regan's own praise of "Show Saturday" is qualified by the nostalgic pastoralism of the poem, even though he writes that it "has the power to counteract ... the contemporary business ethic". Regan's preference goes to "The Explosion": a poem about a mining disaster is of course more likely to appeal to a left-wing critic than an agricultural show. Regan reads "The Explosion" as an "unqualified affirmation of the instinct for shared protection and mutual survival in working class communities".[39] His desire to find traces of his own left-wing agenda in Larkin blinds him to the fact that "The Explosion", in its portrayal of a closely-knit and picturesque miners' community is in fact just as nostalgic and idealizing as "Show Saturday".[40] More recent comments by Regan suggest that the

---

[36] Stephen Regan, "Larkin's Reputation", in *Larkin with Poetry*, ed. Michael Baron, Leicester, 1997, 57.

[37] *Ibid.*, 67.

[38] Stephen Regan, *Philip Larkin*, 126.

[39] *Ibid.*, 127, 141.

[40] Neil Corcoran points out that Larkin's slightly kitsch portrait of the miners was published in the year when real miners brought down Heath's government. See his *English Poetry since 1940*, 95. "The Explosion" may also exemplify William Empson's assertion that, when proletarian literature is written "about" but not "by" or "for" the people, it veers off into pastoral. See *Some Versions of Pastoral* (1935), New York, 1974, 6.

"sense of communal obligation and commitment" which he praises in Larkin has an unmistakably English dimension:

> as England's role in Europe becomes problematic and uncertain at the end of the twentieth century, Larkin's reputation will come to rest not so much on the ill fame of the letters and the biography as on the essential Englishness of his poetry, and on the many ways in which it continued to construct an England of the mind ... [41]

Regan thus proposes to exchange the Little-Englandism of Larkin's letters for another version of Englishness. Such comments form part of a broader attempt to appropriate English patriotism for radical purposes – although this radicalism may end up being appropriated by patriotism. In 1977, Nairn had complained that English cultural nationalism "has not yet come to consciousness of its own nature and purpose. Hence it has remained closer to ideas of a rather undefined socialism, politically, rather than to ideas of England. But this may not be for long".[42] Twenty years on, Regan seems to have verified Nairn's prophecy by allowing his radical aspirations to mingle with the search for an England of the mind.

Philip Larkin had variously been described as "the dreary laureate of our provincialism", the author of a poetry sustained by "parochial beliefs" and "comfortable cultural assumptions", and the letter-writer whose casual racism and reactionary views nearly ruined the poet's reputation.[43] Regan wants this picture to make way for another English Larkin: a poet endowed with a postcolonial and/or radical awareness. Yet Regan's praise of Heaney and his own reading of "The Explosion" show that the distinction between cultural conservatism and the cultivation of a postcolonial/new nationalist consciousness, between Little-Englandism and radical Englishness, all too easily becomes blurred. What Heaney describes as the "tempered English nationalism" of a poet who draws sustenance from his own "customs and institutions" may be but the flipside of the casual racist ensconced in his "comfortable cultural assumptions". Most worryingly, this warped distinction once again leaves no room for what poems like "The Importance of Elsewhere" suggest

---

[41] Regan, "Larkin's Reputation", 68.
[42] *The Break-Up of Britain*, 304.
[43] Bryan Appleyard, "The Dreary Laureate of our Provincialism", *The Independent*, 18 March 1993, 27; Lisa Jardine, "Saxon Violence", *The Guardian*, 8 December 1992 (section 2), 4.

about Larkin's actual response to English "customs and establishments": that is was anything but comfortable.

Much of the recent critical response to Larkin has depended on the possibility of identifying his England with a particular version of English nationhood. If his Englishness is one with the Little-Englandism and the jingoism of his letters, Larkin can be safely dismissed as a hopeless reactionary. On the other hand, if his Englishness can be interpreted as a form of marginal, provincial, (post)colonial consciousness, Larkin emerges as a more interesting writer. He can even become one of the writers who challenge Anglo-centricity by "devolving English literature". In his *Devolving English Literature* (a book dedicated "To Scotland"), Robert Crawford agrees with Heaney that Larkin's Englishness is "really very much of the provincial variety", and argues that Larkin is consequently as much of a "barbarian" as postcolonial or "Celtic" writers; indeed, such an Englishness makes him "all the closer to the Northern Ireland-born Heaney". Crawford thus makes much of what he calls Larkin's "defiantly 'provincial' stance at Hull", which he uses to refute identifications of Larkin with the "English cultural centre".[44] The critic finds a confirmation of his views in Larkin's poem about Hull, "Here" (*The Whitsun Weddings*, 9).

"Here" may be considered as a crucial test of Larkin's Englishness. Indeed, the last line of the poem that foregrounded Larkin's reflection on national identity, "The Importance of Elsewhere", reads: "*Here* no elsewhere underwrites my existence" (*The Whitsun Weddings*, 34. Emphasis mine). In the dialectical movement of that conclusion, Larkin's fondness for indeterminate adverbs of place crystallized round his problematic relation to England. Any serious discussion of Larkin's Englishness must explore his complex use of adverbs like "here", "somewhere", "elsewhere" and "nowhere" in the rest of his poetry. Such a work will also expose the problems of several previous readings of "Here"; Crawford's provides a convenient point of departure.

Crawford writes that the poem emphasizes the geographical remoteness of Hull, a town which can only be reached by "'swerving' aside from the main flow of the traffic".[45] Crawford's reading almost puts Larkin on a par with Tony Harrison and other poets from the North of England, whose provincialism has an obvious political dimension. However, he forgets that "Here" refers not only to Hull, but also to a very different location, namely the place where the Spurn Head peninsula

---

[44] Robert Crawford, *Devolving English Literature*, London, 1994, 277, 274, 301.
[45] *Ibid.*, 276.

turns into the North Sea ("bluish neutral distance/Ends the land suddenly"). The paradox on which the poem rests is that "Here" is in fact several places at once: not only the urban bustle of Hull, but also the point where an English stretch of land turns into something insubstantial. Larkin's treatment of Hull is fraught with complexities that Crawford entirely misses in his reading of the poem as a provincialist manifesto. One the one hand, the poem stresses Hull's separateness, but it also reduces Hull to a metonymy for England: "Here domes and statues, spires and cranes cluster/Beside grain-scattered streets ...". Hull is described as a "a terminate and fishy-smelling/Pastoral of ships up streets": "fishy" both realistically conveys the atmosphere of a sea-port and figuratively reinforces the impression that Larkin, for all his "eloquen[ce] on behalf of Hull's 'sudden elegancies'",[46] is consciously presenting a deceptive cliché. Larkin's description of Hull's "cut-price crowd, urban yet simple" also betrays a sense of class difference that Crawford's political vocabulary, based on the concepts of devolution and provincialism, cannot account for.

Moreover, the indeterminacy of "Here" is not purely geographical. Indeed, although various elements clearly identify the town as Hull (the "slave museum", for instance), Larkin's calculated refusal to name the place opens the text for multiple readings and intertextual investments that the regionalist poetics advocated by Crawford would make impossible. Thus, if the sea-port of Hull is "fishy" in a realistic sense, the figurative "fishiness" of its "pastoral" points to another poetic location. Crawford may choose to see "Here" as an expression of Larkin's dislike of metropolitan London. But Larkin's lines not only form an accurate description of Hull, they also constitute a parodic echo of Wordsworth's pastoral vision of London in "Westminster Bridge": "Ships, towers, domes, theatres and temples lie/Open unto the fields, and to the sky".[47] Intertextual echoes do not stop here: as John Goodby has noted, Larkin's description of Hull is oddly reminiscent of his own impressions of Belfast in "The Importance of Elsewhere": "Their draughty streets, end-on to hills, the faint/Archaic smell of dockland, like a stable" (*The Whitsun Weddings*, 34).[48] This does not only point to the similarities that exist between two Northern provincial cities and industrial ports of the United Kingdom. Such resemblances are in fact borne out by another intertextual

---

[46] Crawford, *Devolving English Literature*, 276.

[47] William Wordsworth, *Poetical Works*, Oxford, 1978, 214.

[48] John Goodby, "'The Importance of Being Elsewhere', or 'No Man is an Ireland': Self, Selves and Social Consensus in the Poetry of Philip Larkin", *Critical Survey*, I/2 (1989), 133.

displacement; indeed Larkin is also drawing on the urban catalogues which MacNeice provided in poems like "Belfast" and "Birmingham".[49] Most importantly, what really links "Here" and "The Importance of Elsewhere" is Larkin's aesthetic stance. His descriptions of both Hull and Belfast consist in swift enumerations of phrases, separated by commas, that briefly manage to capture some detail without suggesting close familiarity. Larkin constantly flirts with the picturesque while avoiding the greater specificity and knowingness of sheer local colour; in its mixture of loving attention and occasionally sharp irony, his response reveals the alienation of the detached observer.

This greatly complicates Heaney's attempt to distinguish between Larkin's responses to Belfast and England, as well as Crawford's insistence on the depth of Larkin's provincial sympathies. But cultural allegiances have become such an absorbing issue for a certain type of criticism that Larkin's relation to Hull and England seems bound to get simplified. Peter MacDonald describes "Here" as an "English poem with a secure sense of placing and physical context": in his view, Larkin is "untroubled by the need to name [his] home".[50] Larkin never actually names Hull in the poem, but what may otherwise be read as an ultimate expression of rootlessness gets reinterpreted as a sign of confidence. John Kerrigan similarly contrasts Larkin's treatment of Hull with Derek Mahon's response to the city in his poem "Going Home", and writes that Mahon is "determined to exclude any Larkinesque sense that, despite its grottiness, Hull might be where people belong".[51] Yet it is surely a strange kind of belonging that can speak of the "*surprise* of a large town" that one inhabits (*The Whitsun Weddings*, 9. Emphasis mine). An ingenious critical lexis has been created in which the word "Larkinesque" is synonymous with "securely English", despite textual evidence to the contrary.

Larkin's ambivalence towards Hull is not the only means by which "Here" questions Englishness and belonging. The poem's parody of Wordsworth's urban pastoral is accompanied by other intertextual subversions. In the first stanza of "Here", Larkin already provides a degraded version of previous pastoral descriptions of the English countryside. His vision travels through fields in the countryside around Hull that are "Too thin and thistled to be called meadows"; sometimes it

---

[49] Regan, *Philip Larkin*, 104. Regan's claim that Larkin "inherits an England of 'industrial shadows' and 'isolate' [*sic*] villages" from MacNeice (104) is only partly valid: MacNeice's poetry, like Larkin's, encompasses both England and Belfast.

[50] Peter MacDonald, "Michael Longley's Homes", in *The Chosen Ground: Essays on the Contemporary Poetry of Northern Ireland*, ed. Neil Corcoran, Bridgend, 1992, 65.

[51] John Kerrigan, "Ulster Ovids", in *The Chosen Ground*, ed. Neil Corcoran, 260.

stops at "a harsh-named halt". The landscape of "Here" stands in revealing contrast to those of classic English nature poems, Edward Thomas's "Adlestrop" in particular. Like Thomas's poem, "Here" takes the reader through an English landscape. Looking out of his train window, Thomas saw "Adlestrop – only the name,/and willows, willow-herbs, and grass/and meadowsweet and haycocks dry".[52] What Larkin gives us to see is a "harsh-named halt" and fields that are too bare to be called meadows. Similarly, in the last stanza, "bluish neutral distance" may recall Housman's "blue remembered hills", More crucially, Larkin is not looking back nostalgically at Housman's "land of lost content",[53] he is contemplating a vision which has remained and will remain "out of reach" and which is devoid of patriotic resonance. Housman's descriptions of the English landscape in *A Shropshire Lad* became intimately associated with English patriotism during the First World War, and Edward Thomas's description of Adlestrop was all the more poignant for having been composed in 1915. Written in the second year of the conflict, Thomas's vision "took on the meaning of a last moment of prelapsarian England".[54] Larkin's final vision, on the other hand, is situated "past the poppies". Larkin thus intriguingly prefers a "neutral" reality that he glimpses after discarding the symbol through which English patriotism commemorates the War. In "Naturally the Foundation Will Bear Your Expenses" – a poem which, like "Here", was written in 1961 – Larkin himself had satirized a certain intellectual contempt for the "mawkish nursery games" of Remembrance Day through the figure of a jet-setting academic who "outsoar[s] the Thames" (*The Whitsun Weddings*, 13). But his own longing for "bluish neutral distance" only differs from the satirized intellectual's flight from London in being metaphorical rather than literal, and in substituting a vision of nothingness for the comfortable decenterings of a cosmopolitan jet set. The contrast does not obscure the fact that both gestures amount to a rejection of England.

The irony of "Here" is that it is impossible to define the exact location of the poem. Larkin's very poetics add to this disorientation: the first stanza is characteristically made up of a drawn out series of participle

---

[52] Edward Thomas, *Collected Poems*, 71-73.

[53] A.E. Housman, *Collected Poems*, Penguin, 1956, 70.

[54] See John Lucas, "Discovering England: The View from the Train", *Literature and History*, VI/2 (1997), 45. Thomas was remembering a journey that took place in June 1914, but the poem "imbues that key minute with an implication ... which it could not have had before the events of August of that year" (45).

clauses ("Swerving ... swerving ... swerving ..."),[55] and although the syntax becomes more regular by the time Larkin's vision focuses on Hull, the rhythm of the poem hardly slackens. Only in the last stanza does the punctuation allow the reader to pause: "Here silence stands/Like heat" is the shortest sentence in the poem. But through a final irony, the last phrase – "out of reach" – denies any sense of security that a more stable syntax may have engendered.

"Here" thus also refers to a transition from various versions of Englishness that the poem subverts to the impossible point where they finally dissolve, and which foreshadows the nihilistic vision of "High Windows", with its "deep blue air, that shows/Nothing, and is nowhere, and is endless" (*High Windows*, 17). Indeed, the "nowhere" of "High Windows" can be read in the light of Larkin's comment on Hull: "I like it because it's so far away from everywhere else. On the way to nowhere, as somebody put it. And beyond the lonely country there's only the sea .... I very much feel the need to be on the periphery of things."[56] The lonely country around Hull is a station on the way to nowhere. Larkin's imagination, haunted by its inability to coincide with England, is ultimately drawn to the liminal space where that England dissolves into nothing.

Crawford's mistake is precisely to ignore that movement and try to pin down "Here" as the specific location of Larkin's "defiantly 'provincial' stance at Hull". Another reading of "Here" that founders on the indeterminacy of the poem is Tom Paulin's. Paulin shares Heaney's belief that Larkin's "nationalism was intensified by [his] experience of Ireland",[57] but he is far less sanguine about Larkin's ability to express a positive English nationalism. Like Nairn and other supporters of neo-nationalism, Paulin looks forward to an "alternative English nationalism" one embodied in "Blake's vision of Albion" and more recently observed in "the shift in public opinion in favour of a withdrawal from Northern Ireland". Paulin also appears to follow Heaney when he explains that he sees "no contradiction in revering that idea of [Platonic] England and at the same time hoping that Ireland will eventually be a united and separate country".[58] But he fails to find a confirmation of his hopes in Larkin's

---

[55] Andrew Swarbrick comments that "in a poem about emptiness, the grammar achieves its own sort of deprivation". See his *Out of Reach: The Poetry of Philip Larkin*, London, 1995, 104.

[56] Philip Larkin, *Required Writing*, 54-55.

[57] *Minotaur*, 234.

[58] Tom Paulin, "A New Look at the Language Question", in *Ireland's Field Day*, ed. Seamus Deane, London, 1985, 13; *Ireland and the English Crisis*, Newcastle, 1984, 16.

work. Indeed, Paulin's approach to Larkin radically differs from Crawford's in that he rejects the distinction between the Anglo-centric and the provincial.

According to Paulin, the significance of Hull's remoteness is that Larkin regards the whole of England as an isolated province. But this provincial Englishness is seen not as a challenge to, but rather a hangover from British Imperialism: Larkin is accused of hankering after a "rock-solid sense of national glory" that still draws on Imperialist militarism, of typifying a "terminal Englishness that feels tired and lost and out of date", of speaking for "Tebbit's England". Paulin reads Larkin's obsession with solitude as a metaphor for the sense of English insularity that Larkin both cultivates and resents. Therefore, "the maritime fastness of Hull, its bracing dinginess and unique atmosphere of being somehow Yorkshire and North European and entire unto itself, is essential to Larkin's public-private persona".[59] But when his reading turns to the minutiae of "Here", Paulin runs into self-contradiction. Indeed, his conclusion awkwardly reintroduces the very distinction between Hull and the "bluish neutral distance" which he suppressed in order to interpret solitude as a metaphor for Englishness. As he himself points out, the closing lines of "Here" "identify the value of solitude with a vision of the North Sea, so that Hull ... and the hinterland of Spurn Head build an emblem of England". But if solitude is only to be found in the final vision, what becomes of Hull and the England that Larkin has left behind? Paulin's reading leaves Larkin rather improbably poised "on watch, a prophet ... speak[ing] for the nation".[60] Paulin also fails to account for the fact that, although the first stanza of "Here" suggests an actual journey through Humberside, no observer ever gets mentioned in the poem. Moreover, the final vision of the poem, with its insistence on emptiness and unattainability, excludes any human presence.

The complexities of "Here" cause major difficulties for critics who want to cast Larkin as a spokesman for a specific sort of English identity, whether radical or conservative. Such interpretations show a deeply ingrained need to suppress the intertextual, syntactic and thematic decenterings that make "Here" a most ironically titled poem. Moreover, the fact that such analyses can read "Here" in diverging political terms reveals the hidden contradiction that lies within the discourse which causes this critical blindness. Identity thinking has not only failed to do justice to the subtlety of Larkin's poetics: it has also undone itself in the process.

---

[59] Paulin, *Minotaur*, 234, 244, 250, 237, 248.
[60] *Ibid.*, 248.

"Here" is not the only poem that lies out of the reach of those who would appropriate it for identitarian ends. Crawford indirectly imports his own concerns in another poem in the following misreading: "when [Larkin] writes, in relation to Hull, that 'Poetry like prose happens anywhere', he is making a statement which is ... important in its devolutionary impact."[61] In that comment, Larkin was echoing the last line of his own poem "I Remember, I Remember" (*The Less Deceived*, 38-39). The poem explicitly refers to Coventry, where he spent his famously uneventful childhood. Looking at his home town from a train, "Coming up England by a different line", Larkin suggested the vacancy of his early years through negatively defined experiences ("I did not invent/Blinding theologies of flowers and fruits", 38). Finally, he observed that "'Nothing, like something, happens anywhere'" (39). One year before Larkin wrote "The Importance of Elsewhere",[62] his fascination with indeterminacy had already produced this arresting conclusion. Its effect, however, is to relativize the importance of Coventry, not to entrench its local significance ("I guess it's not the place's fault" – 39). When Larkin applied the same words to Hull, he was not making a defiantly provincial point against a metropolitan Englishness. As in "I Remember, I Remember", he actually defines Hull through a series of negatives: "a place cannot produce poems. It can only not prevent them, and Hull is good at that. It neither impresses nor insists".[63] Crawford's devolutionary agenda clearly requires stronger identifications than Larkin ever subscribed to.

Larkin's description of Hull as being "on the way to nowhere" suggested that its geography helped generate his visions of nothingness in *High Windows*. But Hull was no more than instrumental in this; Larkin's longing for vertiginous "absences" predated his move to the town. It was already at work not just in "Absences", but also in "I Remember, I Remember". Here Larkin's last line, in its sudden rejection of all the particulars that the previous stanzas had accumulated, stands typographically separated from the rest of the poem, in much the same way as the last line of "Absences", "Such attics cleared of me! Such Absences!" (*The Less Deceived*, 40). In both poems, Larkin's use of rhyme reinforces the effect of his conclusion. "Absences" follows an ababcb cac d scheme which leaves the tenth line isolated in rhyme as well

---

[61] Crawford, *Devolving English Literature*, 301.

[62] "I Remember, I Remember" was written in 1954, "The Importance of Elsewhere" in 1955.

[63] Philip Larkin, *Further Requirements*, ed. Anthony Thwaite, London, 2001, 128.

as typography. The last line of "I Remember, I Remember" does fit in the poem's rhyme structure, which consists in the fourfold repetition of a nine-line abccbaabc scheme. If Larkin had opted for three-, four- or six-line stanzas, the entire poem would have been divided into equal units, but his five-line stanzas cannot accommodate his thirty-sixth and last line, which ends the poem suddenly with all the epigrammatic force it has indeed acquired.[64] Its "Nothing" is consequently invested with the quasi-symbolist quality that characterizes the last line of "Absences" – a line which Larkin described as "a slightly unconvincing translation from a French symbolist".[65] Moreover, the "foreignness" of such lines is underlined by their marginal relation to the English formal structures within which Larkin is working, and thus strengthens the thematic questioning of Larkin's relation to place.

The nothingness of boredom and vacancy in "I Remember, I Remember" blends with the nihilistic visions of other poems. Hull, in its flatness, its remoteness from the rest of England and its proximity to "nowhere", simply happened to provide the landscape that most approximated to that nothingness. But before he moved to Hull in 1955, Larkin had already glimpsed that absence in Coventry; in fact he was constantly looking out for its manifestations. One important role of this nihilistic sublime is to pit a vision of "nowhere" or of a negatively defined "here" against the "here" that, in "The Importance of Elsewhere", was England itself, with its "customs and establishments".

The development of that sublime is already traceable in *A Girl in Winter*, the novel in which Larkin looked at England through the eyes of his protagonist Katherine Lind, a foreign refugee in wartime England. Larkin's later travels through England, in poems like "Here", "The Whitsun Weddings" or "Dockery and Son", all remained indebted to this early experiment with a nationally decentered subjectivity. Katherine had first visited England in the 1930s. Looking out of a car's window as it approached and then left London, she had seen how "the rows of new brick houses were brilliantly shadowed in the sun", or

> innumerable hoardings, empty petrol drums and broken fences lying wastefully about. Occasionally she saw white figures standing at a game of cricket. These were the important things, and because of them the town never seemed distant. Only infrequently did she see things that reminded her of landscape

---

[64] It was included in the *Oxford Dictionary of Quotations* (*Required Writing*, 48).
[65] Quoted by Andrew Motion in *Philip Larkin*, 74.

paintings – a row of cottages, a church on rising ground, the slant
of a field ...

Katherine's vision gives the lie to the picture of England she had
expected: "white cottages, a very old church, grass – ".[66] The landscape
that she encounters paves the way for the similar descriptions of England
in "The Whitsun Weddings": "the backs of houses", "short-shadowed
cattle and/Canals with floatings of industrial froth", "acres of dismantled
cars", "someone running up to bowl" (*The Whitsun Weddings*, 21-23).
The country Katherine discovers is already made up of what Davie would
call "the congested England we have inhabited day by day". Such
similarities, however, force us to question Davie's sweeping assertion that
Larkin's landscapes stand metaphorically for "the seasons of the English
soul".[67] Indeed, Katherine's subjectivity remains decentered throughout
the novel. The speakers of Larkin's poems, far from being typical post-
war Englishmen, retain a sense of isolation which first manifested itself
when Larkin identified with a foreign presence in wartime England. As a
young, artistically minded intellectual cut off from the war effort, sexually
insecure and ill at ease with certain manifestations of wartime English
patriotism,[68] Larkin started articulating the consciousness of an outsider,
always at some remove from the England that he or she inhabits. The
Second World War may have done much to heighten the sense of English
nationhood in the twentieth century, but its effect on Larkin was not to
foster a strong empathy with England any more than his encounter with
Ireland later did. English experiences of war and of Ireland have
traditionally been ways of defining and enhancing Englishness, but on
both occasions Larkin's sense of national identity was actually questioned
rather than confirmed.

　　Larkin's response to the Second World War stands in sharp contrast to
the ways in which the conflict shaped the national consciousnesses of
Hughes and Hill. This shows yet again how much is left out in attempts to
see all three writers as spokesmen for an England that emerged from the
war with a modified self-image. The Second World War prompted a
besieged England to look inward and draw sustenance from its own
myths, but those myths could not always include those who stood in an
awkward or marginal relation to wartime culture: "as the nation rallied

---

[66] Philip Larkin, *A Girl in Winter* (1947), London, 1975, 78, 80, 95.
[67] Davie, *Thomas Hardy and British Poetry*, 64.
[68] For Larkin's detachment from the war effort and his occasional anti-patriotic
outbursts, see James Booth's *Philip Larkin*, Basingstoke, 1992, 16-17, and some of
Larkin's letters: "[We] stood to attention as the news bulletin was read out and sang
'God Rape the King' (I hope some fucking censor reads this)" (*Selected Letters*, 47).

around feelings of national unity in the emergency of war, it rejected those who represented difference", namely the "women and refugees" who were "its ironic opposite".[69] Whereas Hughes and Hill would keep exploring the inward-looking myths of the England of their childhood (see chapter three), Larkin expressed his own sense of alienation from English wartime culture by adopting the perspective of a female refugee – Katherine Lind in *A Girl in Winter*, or the "Polish airgirl" of "Like the train's beat". In this poem, "gestures like these English oaks/Flash past the windows of her foreign talk" (*LCP*, 288): the traditional symbols which England resuscitated in the 1940s are only evoked in Larkin's poetry to be erased by a decentered perspective. In *A Girl in Winter*, Larkin's England is a barren, wintry landscape at odds with the organic and pastoral self-representations of wartime culture.[70] As later in "Here", Larkin's decentering strategy ultimately moves towards the indeterminacy of a nihilistic sublime rather than to a culturally specific site. Katherine's nationality is never revealed; instead, she eventually identifies most with an English landscape which is both atypical and purely metaphorical:

> In most lives there had to come a break, when the past dropped away and the maturity it had enclosed for so long stood painfully upright. It came through death or disaster, or even through a love-affair that with the best will in the world on both sides went wrong .... once that break was made ... life ... became a flat landscape, wry and rather small, with a few unforgettable landmarks somewhat resembling a stretch of fenland.

Katherine's "winter landscape in neutral colours"[71] points forward in two directions: on the one hand, the "neutral" solitude of "Here" (*The Whitsun Weddings*, 9); on the other hand, the visions of boredom and of "nothing" in poems like "I Remember, I Remember" and "Dockery and Son" (*The Less Deceived*, 39; *The Whitsun Weddings*, 38). Larkin's cultivation of this nihilistic sublime somehow rids Katherine's alienated perspective of direct political relevance. Indeed, the novel itself tends to move away from the exploration of a specific historical predicament in order to articulate its central trope of emotional detachment and barrenness, which culminates in the ending's quietist vision: "Against this

---

[69] Phyllis Lassner, *British Women Writers of World War Two*, London, 1998, 17.
[70] Prominent among these were the English village, which even radical women writers like Woolf or Vera Brittain identified with the England they wanted to preserve (*Ibid.*, 30, 50).
[71] *A Girl in Winter*, 183, 184.

knowledge the heart, the will, and all that made for protest, could at last sleep."[72] This may in part explain why the novel has not prompted the kind of political interpretations that its historical context nevertheless invites.[73] On the other hand, the novelist's decision to play down the politics of *A Girl in Winter* would allow the poet to keep exploiting Katherine's detachment beyond its original wartime context. His subversions of Englishness would indeed resurface in contexts where his underlying sense of alienation was reinforced by other factors (such as his complex response to his Irish experience, class difference, bachelorhood ...).

Another equivalent of Katherine's flat landscape emerges in Larkin's discussion of Rupert Brooke (the appointed purveyor of images of England in another war). Indeed, Larkin writes that Brooke "never achieves an epigram to equal a contemporary's 'Life's so flat that you can see your own tombstone at the other end'".[74] Larkin's landscapes are even further removed from Brooke's England than from Thomas's or Housman's; the tombstone at the end of Larkin's vistas is similar to that formed by his epitaph on Brooke's England, "MCMXIV". In that poem, Larkin records the innocence of an England that stretched from mediaeval "Domesday lines" to mythical Edwardian summers, and declares it irretrievable: "never such innocence again" (*The Whitsun Weddings*, 28). Seamus Heaney writes that "Larkin's England of the mind is in many ways continuous with the England of Rupert Brooke's 'Grantchester' and Edward Thomas's 'Adlestrop'",[75] but Larkin's poetry often subverts those earlier representations of England. The significance of Larkin's preference for more austere landscapes is also conveyed in his discussion of Tennyson's poetry:

> To open the complete works of Tennyson is to enter the Victorian age itself .... The silliness and sentimentality are excruciating. We see the flash of moral indignation, and hear the rumble of received opinion: the smoke of double-think drifts obscuringly across the scene. Then suddenly we are brought up

---

[72] *Ibid.*, 248.

[73] *A Girl in Winter* does not feature in Stephen Regan's book-length historicist analysis of Larkin. Regan's discussion of Larkin's politics in the 1940s focuses on class and the influence of Thirties poetry. The political subtext of *A Girl in Winter*, centering on questions of gender and national identity, may unsettle the framework of critics concerned with the relation between poetry and traditional English left-wing radicalism.

[74] *Required Writing*, 178.

[75] Heaney, *Preoccupations*, 168.

sharp by a voice speaking of doubt; there is *a vision of fen country* on a winter evening; something robust and chuckling digs us in the ribs; finally we hear the assertive trumpets of Imperial patriotism and historic endurance.[76]

The order of Larkin's description is quite revealing. By placing the "vision of fen country" after the mention of Tennyson's anxieties, Larkin connects it with the nihilistic side of Tennyson's imagination, and contrasts it with the confidence of the Poet Laureate who could speak for the nation and flatter its prejudices.

Tennyson's darker intimations have their equivalent in Larkin's poetry. Tennyson's vision of fen country in winter is matched by Larkin's metaphor for final extinction in "The Winter Palace": "Then there will be nothing I know./My mind will fold into itself, like fields, like snow" (*LCP*, 211). And when Tennyson's Lincolnshire appears in Larkin's poetry, it is significantly bare, another apprehension of his levelling, nihilistic sublime. The journey of "The Whitsun Weddings" offers a glimpse of it: "The river's level drifting breadth began,/Where sky and Lincolnshire and water meet" (*The Whitsun Weddings*, 21). The poem progressively leaves this solitude to accumulate a near-comprehensive catalogue of England, but all the while Larkin's growing impulse to celebrate a sense of community remains checked by his awkward sense of social superiority, the singleness that haunts him and the basic alienation that he still shares with the unEnglish and withdrawn protagonist of *A Girl in Winter*. When he reaches London, the fulfilment that he has looked forward to becomes mingled with a sense of dissolution and nothingness: "a sense of falling, like an arrow-shower/Sent out of sight, somewhere becoming rain" (*The Whitsun Weddings*, 23). Larkin's most direct use of wartime English iconography (the arrow-shower in Olivier's *Henry V*[77]) dissolves in a sense of separation, a fall into an unknown "somewhere" .

"The Whitsun Weddings" is often taken to be Larkin's most appealing manifesto of post-war Englishness. John Lucas, for instance, dismisses the social fastidiousness of Larkin's descriptions of the weddings and insists on the "intensely democratic" nature of Larkin's final vision:

> there is a politics implicit in the ending of "The Whitsun Weddings", and for all the aggressive, snobbish, or merely nostalgic little-Englandism that Larkin has increasingly

---

[76] *Required Writing*, 182. Emphasis mine.
[77] See chapter one for a detailed analysis of that image.

displayed, the vision with which he brings to an end "The Whitsun Weddings" is anything but that.[78]

Lucas's dissatisfaction with *"merely nostalgic* little-Englandism" (emphasis mine) implies a belief in a more positive Englishness: Lucas too is involved in the attempt to revive a Blakean, visionary English patriotism that can be reconciled with his radical politics. But his analysis, like others treated above, remains both caught up in the contradictions of English identity thinking and blind to the complexity of Larkin's poem. As we saw in the first chapter, the patriotism of Larkin's final symbolist vision recalls not so much Lucas's radical models, but the conservative Eliot; most importantly, its short-lived outburst can mask neither its symbolist incongruity nor the persistence of Larkin's alienation. When its historical and literary contexts and its poetic ironies are taken into account, "The Whitsun Weddings" is not quite the celebration of democratic Englishness that Lucas wants to read into it. Rather, it is a poem which still contains traces of Katherine Lind's alienated perspective, and which dramatizes its own failure to translate any sense of national community onto a transcendental level.

Transcendence in Larkin's work would henceforth revert to the absolute negativity of absence, thus allowing Larkin to develop his nihilistic sublime to the full. That sublime had been fleetingly associated with a sense of past national glory in "The March Past", where the "pure marchings" of Orangemen had conjured up the memories of certain "things" that were "now ended", but which could still "awake and occupy/An absent mind" (*LCP*, 55). However, Larkin later emptied his sublime of all cultural content: the "pure marchings, pure apparitions" of "The March Past" thus became the "pure crust/Pure foam, pure coldness" proclaimed by the advertisements in "Essential Beauty" (*The Whitsun Weddings*, 42), which finally make way for the starker abstraction of death sensed by "dying smokers":[79]

> ... that unfocused she
> No match lit up, nor drag ever brought near,
> Who now stands newly clear,
> Smiling, and recognising, and going dark.

---

[78] John Lucas, *Modern British Poetry from Hardy to Hughes*, 203-4.

[79] A similar process occurs in "Sunny Prestatyn" (*The Whitsun Weddings*, 35), where all that remains of the impossible beauty of the girl on the poster ("She was too good for this life") is a mixture of Mallarméan *azur* ("some blue") and death ("Now *Fight Cancer* is there").

As it blended with the total absence of death, Larkin's sublime also acquired an ambiguous status. The fascinating visions of "Absences", "Here" and "High Windows" became associated with his terror of extinction. In "The Old Fools", the indeterminate and unreachable locations of "Here" are fused with the apprehension of death, which the human wrecks who inhabit the old people's home try to escape through memory:

> That is where they live:
> Not *here* and now, but where all happened once.
> This is why they give
> An air of baffled absence, trying to be there
> Yet being *here*.
>
> (*High Windows*, 20. Emphases mine)

"Here" is also Larkin's hospital in "The Building": a "ground curiously neutral" (*High Windows*, 24) recalling the "neutral distance" of "Here" (*The Whitsun Weddings*, 9). In comparison with its death-haunted corridors, the outside world of normal living becomes a "touching dream", "beyond the stretch/Of any hand from *here*" (*High Windows*, 25. Emphasis mine).

Larkin's "here" thus became an increasingly tangible reality, out of the reach of the living but reaching out to engulf those who get near "extinction's alp" (*High Windows*, 20). Meanwhile, "elsewhere" became an England whose importance lay once again in Larkin's ability to separate himself from it. Thus, the lighthouse-keeper of "Livings II", isolated in his tower, listens to the radio "telling [him] of elsewhere": a traditional England of "Fires in humped inns" and "Kippering sea-pictures" (*High Windows*, 14). "Livings II" suggests the possibility of escaping from England into the solitude of pure elements. The lighthouse-keeper's description of the surrounding seascape ("The sea explodes upwards,/Relapsing..." – 14) indicates that the very similar visions that Larkin had earlier developed in "Absences" ("Fast-running floors, collapsing into hollows,/Tower suddenly") were no longer entirely "cleared" of all human presences (*The Less Deceived*, 40). On the other hand, the fact that Larkin had to contrive a rather unlikely persona to inhabit that space points to a certain artificiality in the exercise. The vignettes of "Livings" thus lack the tension that arises when Larkin explores the dazzling emptiness of his negative visions, as in the title poem of *High Windows*.

That nihilistic sublime, however, can exceed the articulation of
Larkin's unease with his English identity. One should be wary of
systematically reading an obsession with nothingness as a negation of
Englishness, which is the kind of mistake Paulin makes when he
interprets solitude as a national metaphor in Larkin. David Gervais is
partly right to point out, with regard to the death-obsessed poem
"Aubade", that "there could be no finer instance of ... the 'aftermath of
England' than this surprisingly Beckettian late Larkin",[80] but one might
then suspect that Larkin's nihilistic sublime is little more than yet another
lament about "England gone". This would be to forget that his visions of
nothingness can also carry a sense of authenticity and release. His
nihilistic sublime is also the point where his work attains to a negative
humanism which carries meaning beyond the rejection of English
identity, and where England becomes only one metaphor among others.
The extinction described in "Aubade" or "The Old Fools" can happen
anywhere – England, in this case, is no more than a barely recognizable
setting. The national significance of Larkin's nihilistic sublime is in fact
subsumed in his pessimistic humanism.

It is hardly surprising that Larkin's cultivation of a nihilistic sublime
should make his work so intractable for a literary criticism informed by
identity thinking. The negativity of the sublime was what Burke, the
father of modern cultural conservatism, had to domesticate or reject in
order to praise the organic, the cultural and, eventually, the national. In
the *Philosophical Enquiry*, Burke was already careful to inscribe the
sublime into a dialectic where its negativity would always be transcended.
Terror, madness, annihilation could only be contemplated if they
enhanced self-preservation.[81] And in his seminal defence of Englishness
in *Reflections on the Revolution in France*, Burke became increasingly
wary of the negative sublime, which he identified with the excesses of the
French Revolution, the sublime spectacle against which England defined
itself.[82]

---

[80] David Gervais, *Literary Englands*, 215.

[81] The sublime is defined as a "delightful horror" which only arises "if the pain is not
carried to violence, and the terror is not conversant about the present destruction of
the person". See Edmund Burke, *A Philosophical Enquiry into the Origins of Our
Ideas of the Sublime and the Beautiful* (1759), London, 1958, 136.

[82] See Edmund Burke, *Reflections on the Revolution in France* (1790), London, 1910.
The Revolution is "astonishing", "most wonderful", a "strange chaos" (8), capable of
inspiring "exultation and rapture" in some minds (9). The theoretical speculations of
republicans are "most sublime" (61), and Burke turns with "horror" from the
spectacle afforded by the French national assembly (66).

Burke's rejection of the negative sublime in favour of a defence of English cultural identity may shed light on some of the poems in Larkin's last collection *High Windows*. Larkin's increasing fear of death and the radicalization of his right-wing prejudices combined to produce a poetics of conservatism which, in pieces like "Going, Going", works against the negative sublime that dominates the final vision of the title poem. It would be foolish to press the comparison with Burke so far as to discern a revolutionary potential in Larkin's sublime, but as we have seen, the symbolist sources of Larkin's visions of absence interestingly tend to be French rather than English. And, as James Booth has noted, the English poet whom Larkin's negative sublime recalls most is Shelley,[83] who contemplated his own absence in "Mont Blanc" and whose deep truths, like Larkin's, were imageless. Larkin's sublime is consequently at odds with that developed by conservative Romantics like Coleridge, whose contemplation of the sublime was tinged with traditional piety.

Both the poetic origins and the philosophical implications of Larkin's sublime show why Heaney is wrong to connect Larkin's visionary moments with Coleridge's vision of the "spiritual, Platonic old England", and to locate a similar vision "at the foundation of [Larkin's] sensibility".[84] The nationalist side of Heaney's imagination cannot make sense of transcendence unless it can be identified with patriotic exaltation; Heaney cannot rest content with the neutrality of Larkin's nihilistic visions. Coleridge's "spiritual, Platonic old England" most definitely belongs to the realm of the beautiful, the domesticated sublime of the *Reflections on the Revolution in France*, which Burke fuses with the idea of tradition or, to use Larkin's words, the "customs and establishments" of England.[85] It is therefore ironic that a radical critic like Regan, who rightly distinguishes between Larkin's "visions of communal solidarity" and the "lucent, nihilistic element" in his work, should insistently prefer the former.[86] The fact that poems like "Show Saturday" and "The Explosion" are about the rituals of ordinary people does not mean that Larkin was developing a potentially radical vision of England. They are poems that present Burkean, idealized pictures of the common people of England; and the fact that they have been given radical interpretations shows that a Burkean view of the nation is infiltrating left-

---

[83] James Booth, *Philip Larkin*, 162.
[84] Heaney, *The Government of the Tongue*, 21.
[85] English tradition, Burke writes, "carries an imposing and majestic aspect. It has a pedigree and illustrating ancestors. It has its bearings, and its ensigns armorial ... its monumental inscriptions; its records, evidences and titles" (*Reflections*, 32). The link between the counter-revolutionary politics of Burke and Coleridge is also obvious.
[86] Regan, *Philip Larkin*, 138.

wing criticism through the vocabularies of postcolonialism and "radical" patriotism.

Burke's critique of Imperialism and his defence of local traditions have recently caused some radicals to take an active interest in his work and to present him as a more radical figure than is commonly thought.[87] But efforts to bring out the supposedly radical side of Burke may equally betray the essentially conservative basis of the new nationalisms and postcolonial identities that contemporary criticism makes much of. Critics who analyse recent British writing in postcolonial terms should indeed think through the origins of that discourse before they rush to political conclusions. Simon Gikandi has observed that Britain "seeks to understand its unraveling (in the aftermath of Empire) using the cultural grammar (nationalism, tradition, and usable pasts) inherited from its colonies". The use of that discursive framework would seem to guarantee the emergence of an Englishness unblemished by either the Empire or backward-looking little-Englandism. But Gikandi percipiently points out that, ironically, many postcolonial nationalists were indebted to Burke; indeed they valued the concept of tradition "precisely because their English education had convinced them of its centrality in imagining nations and communities".[88] Burke's shadow thus looms equally large behind the projects of new nationalists in Britain. Thus, one could argue that Benedict Anderson's view of the nation as an "imagined community" was after all already implicit in Burke's *Reflections*.

Although Larkin's own "imagined communities" have occasionally appealed to radicals, they are also profoundly Burkean. The ideological basis of "Show Saturday" and "The Explosion" is similar to that of "Going Going" – a poem where Larkin rails against a modern, unidealized crowd and unabashedly indulges in reactionary outbursts.[89] But while all radical critics duly condemn "Going, Going", Seamus Heaney, uneasy though he often is about Larkin's four-letter words, reads it rather uncritically as an environmentalist lament about the disappearance of a certain England. The poem was indeed indirectly commissioned by the Department for the Environment, but Heaney's comment that "houses and roads and factories mean that a certain England is 'Going, Going'" glibly elides the bitter social satire with

---

[87] See for instance Terry Eagleton, "Saving Burke from the Tories", *New Statesman*, 4 July 1997, 32-33. Eagleton writes: "It is unwise ... to see a concern with cultural tradition as automatically conservative, and an adherence to universal theories as necessarily on the left" (32).

[88] Simon Gikandi, *Maps of Englishness*, New York, 1996, 3, 227.

[89] Larkin himself described it as "thin, ranting, conventional gruel" (*Selected Letters*, 452).

which Larkin infuses the poem.[90] Heaney's reading of "Going, Going" is similar to that of John Powell Ward, one of the critics who did most to develop the concept of an "English Line" in poetry. Ward writes that in "Going, Going", Larkin "anticipated Britain's environmental emergency by two decades". His placing of Larkin at the end of the "English Line" (which starts with Wordsworth) is in fact ambiguous: while Larkin's inclusion would seem to be a matter of celebration, Ward is also uneasy about the implications of Larkin's nihilism. Indeed, "it is difficult to see the English line surviving it", which is why Ward describes it as a "danger".[91] Since Heaney himself favours a version of Englishness which is conservative as well as post-Imperial, his own resistance to Larkin's nihilistic sublime is hardly surprising.

If "Going, Going" shows Larkin at his most conservative and nostalgic, his lines betray the incompatibility of this stance with his poetics of sublime forgetting. It is ironic to hear Larkin bemoan "England gone" in terms like these: "The shadows, the meadows, the lanes,/The guildhalls, the carved choirs ..." (*High Windows*, 22). In "Here", he himself had already left behind those very same paraphernalia of Englishness in his longing for "bluish neutral distance" (*The Whitsun Weddings*, 9). The clichés of "Going, Going" and the briskness with which they are enumerated show that the sense of nationhood to which Larkin sometimes clung had not emerged unscathed from his exploration of the negative sublime.

Critics who focus on Larkin's attempts to construct Englands of the mind must always reject the nihilistic sublime that deconstructs those Englands. However, the ideological implications of their preferences are not always as clear as they would wish. Thus, while supposedly radical approaches criticize the escapism of Larkin's sublime as politically sterile, the politics that they embrace instead do not resist the deconstruction that results from their engagement with Larkin's poetry. Their problem is that Larkin's sublime only presents them with a void – the "void" which, as Tom Nairn complains, denotes "something persistently missing, something absent from English national identity itself" and in which Paulin glimpses "the maybe missing centre of Englishness".[92] That void will always remain a scandal to those whose thinking is shaped by identity politics, and who can only read it either as the absence left by a defunct British Imperialism or as an emptiness that

---

[90] Heaney, *Preoccupations*, 168.
[91] John Powell Ward, *The English Line: Poetry of the Unpoetic from Wordsworth to Larkin*, London, 1991, 186, 183.
[92] Nairn, *The Break-Up of Britain*, 262; Paulin, *Minotaur*, 240.

must urgently be filled with new national myths. Its value, however, may lie in the ultimate expression of a negative humanism that transcends the internal contradictions of identity thinking and its twin, cultural conservatism.

In so far as Larkin's nihilistic sublime and his compulsive scepticism amount to sheer metaphysical pessimism, they can of course seem to lead straight into a dead end. However, they can do more than help expose the flaws of the various agendas that inform critical misreadings of his work. Their importance should also be measured by the extent to which they have penetrated and transformed other poetics.

Robert Crawford writes that "by seeing Larkin as, in some sense, a 'colonial' writer, Heaney is able both to identify and compete with Larkin, the poet of 'English nationalism'".[93] Yet, as we have seen, Heaney's identification is always either partial or highly problematic. His criticism awkwardly seeks to put Larkin on a par with Hughes and Hill, but the failure of that project is confirmed by the fact that, unlike Hill's and Hughes's, Larkin's poetry finds no echo in Heaney's poetry of Irish nationhood. In other words, the latter never "competes" with Larkin's work in any Bloomian sense: the fact that Larkin did not influence Heaney's poetics of Irishness underlines the insuperable problems of Heaney's attempt to read him as a poet of nationhood. It is only more recently that Larkin's presence has become more perceptible in Heaney's poetry. This new influence has significantly coincided with Heaney's growing detachment from the chthonic pieties and nationalist organicism of *Wintering Out* and *North*. The changes that Heaney's continued engagement with Larkin's poetry have produced in his own work may be the best illustration of the potential strength and relevance of Larkin's scepticism and of his negative sublime.

It is sometimes claimed that Heaney's early poetry responded to Larkin as well as Hughes,[94] but his first collections only exceptionally suggest the former's influence. One example may be "Scaffolding" (*Death of a Naturalist*, 37), in which the process of erecting a building is compared to the first steps in a love relationship. This somehow recalls the extended metaphors of poems in Larkin's *The Less Deceived* ("No Road", "Skin" ...), but may equally point back to many other models like

---

[93] Crawford, *Devolving English Literature*, 277.
[94] See *British Poetry since 1945*, ed. Edward Lucie-Smith, London, 1985: "In [Heaney's] earlier work some influences were visible – both Hughes and Larkin played their part" (343). John Wilson Foster also alludes to "Heaney's early affinities with Larkin" in his *Colonial Consequences*, Dublin, 1991, 74.

the Metaphysicals. Such poems grew even more scarce in Heaney's output in the 1970s. In the first part of *North*, Heaney deployed his mythologizing poetics to the full by completing his misreading of Hughes (see chapter five). Larkin's contribution to that achievement was of course non-existent. The only occasion on which Heaney uses a strategy comparable to Larkin's in *North* is in "Punishment". Indeed, Heaney's wavering response to the victimized body of the Windeby girl recalls Larkin's own agonizing attitude about the raped girl of "Deceptions". Like Larkin, Heaney has to bridge the historical distance that separates him from the period in which the girl lived: the Windeby girl was sacrificed in the Iron Age that P.V. Glob's book documents; the anonymous rape victim of "Deceptions" was inspired by the description from Mayhew's *London Labour and the London Poor* which Larkin uses as an epigraph. Both poems start with an attempt to empathize with their subject: "I can feel the tug/of the halter at the nape/of her neck" (*North*, 30); "Even so distant, I can taste the grief ..." (*The Less Deceived*, 37). Both then go on to express a form of male guilt about a female victim. But the comparison that these parallels invite also shows that Heaney's and Larkin's attitudes, beyond their obvious similarities, remain largely opposed.

   In "Punishment", Heaney initially feels a mixture of erotic titillation and pitying fondness towards the girl. The former dominates the first stanzas – the girl's nipples are compared to "amber beads" (30). Both tendencies then alternate and correct each other in the middle of the poem; the girl is described in turns as "undernourished" and "beautiful". Heaney calls her "My poor scapegoat", which is followed by the poem's turning point: "I almost love you" (31). This line shows Heaney pulling himself up in the articulation of one of his favourite phrases. Indeed, his poetry is noted for its propensity to conjugate the verb "to love", often in the first person, in contexts that are not necessarily amorous.[95] The possessive in "*my* poor scapegoat" turns out to be ambiguous. It is not only affectionate, but is revealed as quite literal when Heaney starts imagining his own passive implication in acts of tribal violence: he "would have cast ... the stones of silence". The tension that this creates prompts a damning self-indictment of his male fantasizing (he is an "artful voyeur") and of his attempt at sympathy – "love" is here vague

---

[95] The following list is not exhaustive, but gives an idea of Heaney's reliance on the verb: it appears in *Death of a Naturalist* (1, 11), *North* (twice on p. 33), *Field Work* (21, 37, 47), *Station Island* (14, 22, 116), no less than nine times in *Seeing Things* (8, 13, 16, 23, 50, 72, and thrice on p. 46), and *The Spirit Level* (15, 23, 53, 60).

enough to encompass both attitudes. But the last stanza subtly changes
the terms of Heaney's internal debate: he

> would connive
> in civilized outrage
> yet understand the exact
> and tribal, intimate revenge.

(North, 31)

The final contrast of the poem is no longer between erotic arousal at the
girl's body and an admission of guilty complicity, but between a moral
revulsion which is presented as a source of guilt (to condemn the
punishment would be to "connive") and an atavistic imperative which
gains quasi-erotic power ("intimate") from its absolution of the guilt it
first generated: the revenge is "exact" and understood as such within the
parameters of the tribe. Once again, the Goddess seems to "swallow"
Heaney's "love and terror" *(North*, 39) as female victimization finds a
rationale in the worship of female deities. Heaney's dark, sensual
sublime, where "love and terror" become hard to distinguish, underwrites
his cultural assumptions.

   In the first part of "Deceptions" *(The Less Deceived*, 37) Larkin takes
it upon himself to convey the girl's response to her rape through a series
of tentative metaphors: her grief is a "scar" that will not heal, her mind is
"a drawer of knives". In the second part, however, Larkin's metaphorical
strategy yields to self-questioning as he realizes the limits of his empathy:
"I would not dare/Console you if I could." This can be compared with
Heaney's hesitant "I almost love you/but ..." – the metaphors also grow
less prominent in "Punishment" after Heaney's admission of guilt. Larkin
suggests that, being male, he cannot help considering the girl's
experience from the point of view of male desire. His guilty complicity
blurs his previous sympathetic stance: "where/Desire takes charge,
readings will grow erratic"; one also suspects that the last word in that
line can only just keep itself from turning into the more compromising
"erotic". The only consolation that Larkin could offer to the girl is that
she was "less deceived" than the rapist, whose erotic fantasies are literally
and figuratively exploded by the unsatisfactory orgasm he has wrested
from his victim: he has "burst into fulfilment's desolate attic". The last
word also undercuts the potential thrill of the word it echoes: "erratic" is
only falsely "erotic". This metaphorical insight, however, is itself
relativized as Larkin discredits his whole stance. The blunt, plain line
"For you would hardly care" (the shortest in the poem, which wrecks any
harmony that its tentative pentameters may have worked towards) has

already made it impossible for the poem to provide consolation to anyone: rapist, girl, poet or reader. At the end of the poem, desolation is complete.

The only certainty offered by the poem is that "suffering is exact". For Heaney, by contrast, what is "exact" is the "revenge": not the suffering itself, but the terrible forces that have caused it. Heaney's imagination is enamoured of resolutions; although "Punishment" shows him aware and apprehensive of the costs they imply, his cultural mystique tends to override his scruples. If "Punishment" is partly a response to "Deceptions", it is a response that allowed Heaney to articulate doubts about his mythologizing method, but overcame them as it cancelled the desolate bleakness of Larkin's irresolution. In his critical prose, Heaney has definitely tried to construe "Deceptions" as a more optimistic poem than it actually is. In "The Main of Light", he defensively claims that he has "no doubt that Larkin would have repudiated any suggestion that the beauty of the lines ... is meant to soften the pain", but he nevertheless argues that "the blank tenderness at the heart of the poem takes it beyond irony and bitterness, though all the while keeping it short of facile consolation".[96] The "light" of "Deceptions" is an "unanswerable" light that "forbids the scar to heal" (*The Less Deceived*, 37), but it was apparently not unanswerable enough to keep Heaney from investing it with a healing tenderness. Heaney's own imagination cannot leave open the wounds it explores: in "Punishment", the girl's "blindfold" is also "a soiled bandage" (*North*, 30), while the slashed throat of the "Grauballe Man" is a "cured wound" (*North*, 28).

In order to support his critical misreading of "Deceptions", Heaney resorts to a rather far-fetched comparison with Wordsworth. He draws a parallel between "Deceptions" and Wordsworth's "The Ruined Cottage", and finds that both poems revolve round an "image of tranquillity" that helps reconciles one to human suffering.[97] It is not a coincidence that Heaney should turn to Wordsworth here: his likening of Larkin to a conservative English Romantic ties in with his attempt to force Larkin into a nationalist framework. The way in which he misreads "Deceptions" parallels his awkward attempt to connect Larkin's visionary moments with Coleridge's "spiritual, Platonic old England" in the same essay.[98] However, Heaney wrote "The Main of Light" at a critical moment in his career (1982). Compared with "Englands of the Mind", the essay shows a greater (though rather grudging) willingness to concede the insistent neutrality of Larkin's visions, although Heaney ultimately feels he must

---

[96] *The Government of the Tongue*, 18, 19.
[97] *Ibid.*
[98] *Ibid.*, 21.

connect these visions with a "blank tenderness" or with the "honeyed" light of Coleridge. But the collections that have appeared since *North* also show traces of Heaney's fascination with the possibilities that Larkin's negative sublime affords.

In *Field Work* already, one poem introduces a new note in Heaney's work. The end of "Casualty" develops a poetics of indeterminacy in order to question the tribal attachments that held Heaney's imagination captive in *North*. The casualty of the title is a Catholic man who was "blown to bits" in an IRA bomb blast, "Out drinking in a curfew/Others obeyed" (22). As with the girl of "Punishment", Heaney considers that this acquaintance also "broke [their] tribe's complicity". But instead of invoking tribal allegiances, Heaney prefers to recall a moment he shared with the dead man while out fishing on a boat. Heaney had "tasted freedom with him" on the sea, as he found a "rhythm/Working you, slow mile by mile,/Into your proper haunt/Somewhere, well out, beyond ..." (24). In his earlier collections, Heaney had preferred the guttural waters that sprang from the Irish soil. This poem now shows him drawn to the anonymity of oceanic waters. In the same way that Larkin could not find his "*proper ground*" (*The Less Deceived*, 16) except in imaginary seascapes from which he remained absent, Heaney is beginning to long for a "proper haunt" other than those where his dark atavisms had previously led him. The "somewhere" of "Casualty" is quite comparable to the indeterminate adverbs that Larkin used to strategic effect in his poetry; such adverbs have significantly multiplied in Heaney's later collections.

Station Island is generally considered as a pivotal moment in Heaney's development. One poem stages an imaginary encounter with Joyce, where Heaney lets his Irish master voice a radical questioning of the philological and mythological poetics of Irish nationhood that had informed *Wintering Out* and *North*:

> ... You are raking at dead fires,
> a waste of time for somebody your age.
> That subject people stuff is all a cod's game,
> infantile, like your peasant pilgrimage.
>
> (*Station Island*, 93)

There are of course other voices in *Station Island*, and not just in the eponymous central section where Heaney is listening to dead voices. In "Making Strange", the voice that Heaney overhears is still the voice of his native landscape, which commands him to "be adept and be dialect" (32). The tension between local pieties and their relativization is dramatized in the next poem, "The Birthplace", which relates a visit to Thomas Hardy's house. Heaney remembers how he once avidly read Hardy's *The Return of the Native* at one go – an enthusiasm that points yet again to his preference for the regionalist side Hardy's work. But he also asks: "Everywhere being nowhere,/who can prove/one place more than another?" (35). The voice that challenges Heaney's nativist outlook here does not speak with Joyce's inflection, but with the accents of a poet whose response to Hardy differed radically from Heaney's. Larkin's deliberate rootlessness is echoed in Heaney's temptation to "resist/the words of coming to rest", like "*birthplace*" (35).

Heaney's creative interest in Larkin's poetics is part of a dialectic that questions the chthonic earthiness and Romantic organicism of his early style. These still have their appeal in the first part of *Station Island*; indeed "The Birthplace" is set between "Making Strange" and the thoroughly Wordsworthian "Changes", which concludes a pastoral vision with the words:

> 'Remember this.
> It will be good for you to retrace this path
> when you have grown away and stand at last
> at the very centre of the empty city.'
>
> (37)

The tension between those two competing outlooks is one that Heaney would often explore in his later work. Understanding Larkin's role in that reflection is important not just to grasp Heaney's poetic development, but also to correct his early misreading of Larkin.

In *The Haw Lantern*, Heaney took one step further away from his early poetics, in the direction of a more ethereal and abstract style. As Henry Hart comments "Heaney's later landscapes become more overtly psychological than geographical". At the heart of those landscapes of the mind, the chthonic and mythological certainties of the vowel of earth have increasingly been replaced by dazzling absences – a change for which Heaney could indeed "draw supportive examples from Philip Larkin".[99] If "The Main of Light" (1982) still unconvincingly struggled to impose conservative Romantic interpretations on Larkin's visionary moments, *The Haw Lantern* (1987) shows that Heaney himself can sometimes yield to the negative sublime whose emptiness otherwise disturbs him.

---

[99] Henry Hart, *Seamus Heaney: Poet of Contrary Progressions*, 177.

Words like "absence" and "nothing" have now become part of
Heaney's poetic stock (*The Haw Lantern*, 14, 21), and there are two
moments in *The Haw Lantern* where Heaney seems to be more
specifically echoing Larkin's nihilistic sublime. "In Memoriam: Robert
Fitzgerald" (22) describes how an arrow "travels out of all
knowing/Perfectly aimed towards the vacant centre". As John Wilson
Foster has noted, the image recalls the closing vision of "The Whitsun
Weddings".[100] Heaney's arrow is sent "out of all knowing", just as
Larkin's arrow shower was sent "out of sight" (*The Whitsun Weddings*,
23). Heaney's closing metaphor is also contrasted with the earlier
Hughesian image of a "Doorway to a megalithic tomb" (22). The poem
thus summarizes the direction which Heaney's poetics have followed in
the 1980s, and which leads away from his early primitivist archaeologies
and towards a contemplation of absence.

Some lines in Heaney's sequence "Clearances" have also prompted
comparisons with Larkin. Most of the poems are elegies for the poet's
dead mother, but its closing sonnet strikes a more general note and
provides an insight into the changes that have occurred in Heaney's
poetics. The very title of the sequence, as Michael Allen comments,
"rings bells first touched in Larkin's line 'Such attics cleared of me! Such
absences!'".[101] In the last poem, Heaney feels drawn to "a space/utterly
empty", while the natural symbols of his early poems, "deep planted and
long gone", become a "bright nowhere/A soul ramifying and
forever/Silent" (32). While the phrase "bright nowhere" strongly recalls
Larkin, the word "soul" may suggest that, as Michael Allen writes,
Heaney is "pressing this Larkinesque agnostic intensity in his own
directions".[102] Heaney's latest essay on Larkin in *The Redress of Poetry*
still betrays a religious imagination's unease with radical scepticism: this
time, Heaney expresses his dissatisfaction with Larkin's outlook through
a disappointed reading of "Aubade", a poem that offers a haunting and
unconsoling view of death.[103] But if religiousness is still distinctive of
Heaney's writings, it has partly been pruned of the cultural and political
associations of Irish Catholicism and of his early Hughesian primitivism.

---

[100]   John Wilson Foster, *Colonial Consequences*, 193.
[101]   Michael Allen, "Holding Course: *The Haw Lantern* and its Place in Heaney's
Development", in *Seamus Heaney: A Collection of Critical Essays*, ed. Elmer
Andrews, London, 1992, 200.
[102]   *Ibid.*, 200. Stan Smith also finds Heaney's "nowhere" here quite similar to
Larkin's. See Stan Smith, "The Distance Between: Seamus Heaney", in *Seamus
Heaney: A Collection of Critical Essays*, ed. Michael Allen, 238.
[103]   See "Joy or Night" in *The Redress of Poetry*, London, 1995.

In an interview given in 1980, Heaney explained that what interested him in Hughes's poetry was its

> linguistic energy, arrest and power, textures and surfaces. What I searched for ... was that kind of texture and richness. I had a notion of poetry being like stained glass almost, although now I would like to be able to write a poetry that was like window glass.[104]

Heaney's stained glass was not only Hughesian; it also pointed to the deeply ingrained Irish Catholicism of his early poetry.[105] Since then, Heaney has examined his cultural allegiances with more critical distance, and the poetic changes that have accompanied that questioning show that he has also started to fulfil his ambition to create a poetry as luminous and transparent as window glass. In order to achieve this, he could hardly have turned to a more inspiring model than the poet whose high windows opened onto bright nowheres (*High Windows*, 17).

Heaney's view of Larkin remains problematic. Although Larkin makes a startling appearance at the beginning of *Seeing Things*, Heaney's description of him as a "nine-to-five man who had seen poetry" (7) is still imbued with the sense of disappointment that pervaded "The Main of Light"; the line remains something of a back-handed compliment. Heaney can still show a preference for the more pastoral side of Larkin's work: the Larkin whom he and Hughes present to children in the anthologies they co-edited tends to be a rather pious poet of nature.[106] The more sceptical or nihilistic sides of Larkin are still a source of resistance; and indeed "Joy or Night" points to an enduring philosophical quarrel. But if Heaney's critical writings on Larkin consistently point to the divide that separates their imaginations, his poetic response – culminating in *The Haw Lantern* – suggests a different story. The fascination exerted by Larkin's negative sublime has not only forced Heaney to leave behind the crude misreading of Larkin as a poet of English nationalism that he had

---

[104] See John Haffenden, *Viewpoints*, 74.

[105] There is an implicit contrast in the interview between that stained glass and the "kind of Presbyterian light" that Heaney discerns in the poetry of Iain Crichton Smith (Haffenden, 70). James Booth misses the religious connotations of Heaney's metaphors when he adapts Heaney's rhetoric to argue that, if Heaney's poetry is "clear glass, Larkin's [poetry is] stained" ("The Turf Cutter ...", 384).

[106] The poems are "At Grass", "Cut Grass", "Days", "The Explosion", "The North Ship", "Livings II" (*The Rattle Bag*, eds Seamus Heaney and Ted Hughes, London, 1982), and "Wedding-Wind" (*The School Bag*, eds Seamus Heaney and Ted Hughes, London, 1992).

developed in "Englands of the Mind". It has also made him recognize that Larkin's lights had less to do with a nostalgia for an ideal England than with a neutral, humanist sublime that can question both Larkin's sense of identity and Heaney's own nationalist attachments. Heaney has increasingly questioned his early chthonic mystique to develop a more austere visionary mode based on bright nowheres. This poetic and ideological development can perhaps best be traced through his shifting relation to his English contemporaries. While his misreading of Hughes's and Hill's troubled poetics of English nationhood had enabled the mythologizing approaches of *Wintering Out*, *Stations* and *North*, his early, purely critical misreading of Larkin has been replaced by a greater openness to poetic influence, and the change has coincided with Heaney's move away from his myths of Irish nationhood. The unlikely poetic alliance that has been tentatively forged in *The Haw Lantern* is a momentous reversal, and it proves perhaps more than anything else that Larkin is often not a Laureate of Englishness, but a poet whose visions of absence have relevance beyond the national boundaries that they both blur and exceed.

CONCLUSION

By definition, misreadings distort. But those distortions inevitably leave traces, which can in turn yield a wealth of insights, both about the ideological assumptions of misreaders and about the texts that are being misread. Moreover, misreadings need not be fixed – as Heaney's example shows, they can develop, subject as they are to the changing needs of misreaders and to the ironies of poetic influence. In this capacity for transformation, poetic misreadings may also hold a lesson for critical practice.

The pressures of recent history have resulted an increased concern with national identity that has left its mark on our perceptions of many a body of poetic work. Questions surrounding England and Englishness are now being asked with renewed insistence and from many perspectives. There is often an unmistakable sense of urgency in those questions and in the answers that criticism tries to provide, notably through its treatment of English poetry. But poems about England can raise more questions than they answer, and even these questions will not aways coincide with contemporary preoccupations. Many late twentieth-century critics still tended to regard Larkin, Hughes, Hill as "contemporary" poets who all wrote about the experience of "post-war England". But as a new century begins, the time may now be ripe for a reassessment of our literary-historical categories. The "post-war period" has come to encompass various phenomenons that only partly overlap, as the changing nature of the debate on English nationhood illutrates. Thus, many of the concepts used in recent analyses of those poets derive from the conceptual matrix of identity thinking and postcolonial studies, namely critical paradigms that met the ideological needs of the 1980s and 1990s. But I have shown that the questions raised by poets who rose to fame in the 1950s issued from ideological configurations which, while contiguous with later preoccupations, can nevertheless unsettle the critical framework of late twentieth-century readers. Thus, while the influence of postcolonialism means that the end of the British Empire and its aftermath remain central to the agendas of many critics, the variety of responses to the Second World War and a latent unease with Welfare State values were all shaping factors that are now often underrated, simplified or misunderstood.

While acknowledging the impact of a renewed attention to nationhood in the light of postcolonial thinking, I have also emphasized the interactions of those different historical factors. I have thus placed the current preoccupation with English nationhood into its own historical perspective by tracing the shifts that have transformed the question of

England in the post-war period. By historicizing present-day questions surrounding English identity, I also hope to have gestured towards a context in which it will be possible to assess the benefits and the shortcomings of such questions. This book would clearly not have come about if I had not believed that these questions offered great potential as ways of reading texts; yet it also springs from a conviction that the questions have often been asked in ways that do not do justice to modern English poetry. My aim was to restore some of that poetry to the density of its various historical and literary contexts and to stress its resulting aesthetic complexity. But this critical strategy also has political implications. It can also point up the limitations of a critical discourse which not only foregrounds the politics of national identity, but often defines itself as an active intervention in the current debate on identity politics in Britain. The theoretical flaws inherent in that discourse are betrayed by the silence that it often imposes about other dimensions of political experience such as class or gender, and by the political contradictions that its misreadings reveal. The distinction between "radical" and "conservative" expressions of English nationhood does not resist the deconstructions that follow from the interaction between Heaney, Hughes and Hill, or from the contradictory readings of Larkin as a poet of radical Englishness or of terminal Little-Englandism. My hope is that those deconstructions will have contributed to a critical reflection on the theoretical paradigms that have made cultural and national identity so central to English studies. The dominance of those paradigms obviously owes much to broader ideological considerations. Literary criticism has little influence over these, but critical practice can at least help refine or question the concepts that such considerations have bequeathed. It can certainly challenge the claims made for or against literary texts which are being used in contentions about the meaning of Englishness. Literary criticism has often joined those contentions with a willingness that betrays a desire for political relevance, but its political role should also lie in a close and sceptical scrutiny of the agendas for which literature is appropriated. As this book shows, this need not imply a retreat into aestheticism – a strategy that would be all the more untenable when many poems register how important the question of English identity was to their authors. What it does argue for is a better understanding of historical contexts and of how they interact with the development of English poetry.

By re-reading such key poets as Larkin, Hughes and Hill in the light of their complex relation to their national identity, this book is obviously meant as a contribution to the history of twentieth-century English poetry. "English" could here be used in a narrow sense, but Heaney's responses to his English contemporaries shows that the poetic misreadings which run through that history can cross national borders, even when what is stake in those misreadings is nothing other than a poet's very sense of nationhood. The interaction between Heaney and his various English models exposes the limits that inhere in the idea of national canons and traditions; it also questions the relevance of a strictly postcolonial analysis of contemporary Irish poetry and unsettles the political lessons that such an analysis suggests. English and Irish poetics of nationhood do go on meshing, and the results of those exchanges are often too unpredictable to justify the political reputations that various Irish and English poets have earned over the last decades. Critical blindness towards that interaction can only warp our view of both English and Irish literature, and of the creative tensions that go on existing between both countries.

Misreadings are poetic relationships, and as Henry James well knew, relationships stop nowhere – neither in space nor in time. The misreadings of "post-war" poets affect earlier writers of various periods, who will often turn out to have been misreaders in their turn. Tracing the development of poetic ideas of nationhood through a history of misreadings can lead us much further back in time than the period with which this study was concerned. As I have hinted, contemporary debates on nationhood eventually turn out to recycle oppositions that were defined in the Romantic era – postcolonialism itself may owe much more to Burkean thinking than is often realized. On the other hand, the concept of misreading itself originates in a Bloomian theory that regards much modern poetry as inevitably post-Romantic. The coincidence is largely fortuitous, but it should alert us to the potential for further work on poetic treatments of nationhood in the last two centuries. Many other misreadings remain to be traced, reassessed and recontextualised before we gain a fuller understanding of the interaction between poetry and nationhood in the longer perspective. Such work would also contribute to a genealogy of our ways of thinking about national identity, at a time when the issue retains a central place in cultural, and indeed wider political debates.

Larkin, Hughes, Hill and Heaney all produced work which has invited critical reflection on their treatment of nationhood, and which I argue can be placed in a history of poetic misreading. The debate on nationhood does not look likely to die down; what will happen to the poetic histories to which they contributed is less certain. The future will show if those poets' successors will in their turn misread their Englands and take them into new directions. One might alternatively speculate whether processes of poetic misreading still operate in a postmodern age, whether ideas of England will still make poetic sense, or whether English poetry can retain enough eminence within the contemporary cultural landscape for its responses to issues of nationhood – or indeed any other issue – to go on warranting attention. By and large, the poets discussed here still have the canonical status, the critical respect and (with the exception of Hill) the fairly wide readership that guarantee prolonged discussion. It is therefore all the more important that criticism should refine its perception of a poetry which undeniably speaks to its concerns, but with accents which the urgency of those concerns sometimes makes difficult to hear.

BIBLIOGRAPHY

Unpublished Material

Manuscripts of Philip Larkin [DPL]. The University of Hull. Brynmor Jones Library. DPL 1: Poetry Workbooks (DPL 1/4/10 and DPL 1/4/15: Ms. drafts of the poem "The Importance of Elsewhere").

Works Cited

Allen, Michael, "Holding Course: *The Haw Lantern* and its Place in Heaney's Development", in *Seamus Heaney: A Collection of Critical Essays*, ed. Elmer Andrews, London, 1992, 193-208.

Allen, Michael, ed., *Seamus Heaney: A Collection of Critical Essays*, London, 1997.

Alvarez, Al, ed., *The New Poetry*, London, 1962.

Anderson, Benedict, *Imagined Communities*, London, 1983.

Andrews, Elmer, ed., *Seamus Heaney: A Collection of Critical Essays*, London, 1992.

Annwn, David, *Inhabited Voices: Myth and History in the Poetry of Geoffrey Hill, Seamus Heaney and George Mackay Brown*, Frome, 1984.

Appleyard, Bryan, "The Dreary Laureate of our Provincialism", *The Independent*, 18 March 1993, 27.

Appleyard, Bryan, *The Pleasures of Peace*, London, 1989.

Arnold, Matthew, "On the Study of Celtic Literature" (1867), in *Lectures and Essays in Criticism*, Ann Arbor, 1962, 291-386.

Auden, W.H., *The English Auden*, London, 1986.

Barfoot, C.C., ed., *In Black and Gold: Contiguous Traditions in Post-War British and Irish Poetry*, Amsterdam, 1994.

Barnes, Julian, *England, England*, London, 1998.

Baron, Michael, ed., *Larkin with Poetry*, Leicester, 1997.

Bayley, John, "English Equivocation", *Poetry Review*, LXXVI/1-2 (1986), 4-6.

Bayley, John, "Too Good for this Life", Review of *High Windows* by Philip Larkin, *Times Literary Supplement*, 21 June 1974, 653-55.

Bedient, Calvin, "On Geoffrey Hill", *Critical Quarterly*, XXIII/2 (1981), 17-26.

Bedient, Calvin, "The Pastures of Wilderness: Geoffrey Hill's 'An Apology for the Revival of Christian Architecture in England'", *Yearbook of English Studies*, XVII (1987), 143-65.

Beers, Henry. *A History of English Romanticism in the Eighteenth Century* (1899), New York, 1968.

Bentley, Paul, *The Poetry of Ted Hughes: Language, Illusion and Beyond*, London, 1998.

Bloom, Harold, *The Anxiety of Influence*, New York, 1973.

Bloom, Harold, *A Map of Misreading*, New York, 1975.

Bloom, Harold, "The Voice of Kinship", Review of *Field Work*, by Seamus Heaney, *Times Literary Supplement* 8 Feb.1980, 137-38.

Booth, James, "Philip Larkin: Lyricism, Englishness and Postcoloniality", in *Larkin with Poetry*, ed. Michael Baron, Leicester, 1997, 9-30.

Booth, James, *Philip Larkin: Writer*, Basingstoke, 1992.

Booth, James, "The Turf Cutter and the Nine-to-Five Man: Heaney, Larkin and 'the Spiritual Intellect's Great Work'", *Twentieth Century Literature*, XLIII/4 (1997), 369-93.

Bradshaw, Graham, "Hughes and Shakespeare", in *The Achievement of Ted Hughes*, ed. Keith Sagar, Manchester, 1983, 52-69.

Brandes, Rand, "Behind the Bestiaries: The Poetry of Lawrence and Hughes", in *D.H. Lawrence's Literary Inheritors*, eds Keith Cushman and Dennis Jackson, London, 1991, 248-67.

Brooker, Peter and Peter Widdowson, "A Literature for England", in *Englishness: Politics and Culture 1880-1920*, eds Robert Colls and Philip Dodd, London, 1986, 116-63.

Burke, Edmund, *A Philosophical Enquiry into the Origins of Our Ideas of the Sublime and the Beautiful*, 2nd edition (1759), London, 1958.

Burke, Edmund, *Reflections on the Revolution in France* (1790), London, 1910.

Cannadine, David, "The State of British History", *Times Literary Supplement*, 10 October 1986, 1139-40.

Clarke, Austin, *Collected Poems*, Dublin, 1974.

Clausen, Christopher, "Tintern Abbey to Little Gidding: The Past Recaptured", *Sewanee Review*, XCIV/3 (1976), 405-24.

Coleridge, Samuel Taylor, *Anima Poetae*, ed. Ernest Hartley Coleridge, Boston and New York, 1895.

Colley, Linda, *Britons: Forging the Nation 1707-1837* (1992), London, 1996.

Collini, Stefan, *English Pasts: Essays in History and Culture*, Oxford, 1999.

Colls, Robert and Philip Dodd, eds, *Englishness: Politics and Culture 1880-1920*, London, 1986.

Connolly, Cyril, *The Condemned Playground: Essays 1927-1944*, with an introduction by Philip Larkin, London, 1985.

Conquest, Robert, ed., *New Lines*, London, 1956.

Conrad, Joseph, *Heart of Darkness* (1902), London, 1983.
Cooper, John X., *T.S. Eliot and the Ideology of Four Quartets*, Cambridge, 1995.
Corcoran, Neil, ed., *The Chosen Ground: Essays on the Contemporary Poetry of Northern Ireland*, Bridgend, 1992.
Corcoran, Neil, *English Poetry since 1940*, Harlow, 1993.
Corcoran, Neil, *Seamus Heaney*, London, 1986.
Corr, Chris, "Matthew Arnold and the Younger Yeats: The Manoeuverings of Cultural Aesthetics", *Irish University Review*, XXVIII/1 (1998), 11-27.
Crawford, Robert, *Devolving English Literature*, London, 1994.
Davie, Donald, *Purity of Diction in English Verse* (1952), London, 1967.
Davie, Donald, *Thomas Hardy and British Poetry*, London, 1973.
Davie, Donald, *Under Briggflats*, Chicago, 1989.
Davie, Ian, ed., *Oxford Poetry 1942-1943*, Oxford, 1943.
Deane, Seamus, *Celtic Revivals*, London, 1985.
Deane, Seamus, *Heroic Styles: The Tradition of an Idea*, Derry City, 1984.
Deane, Seamus, ed., *Ireland's Field Day* (1983), London, 1985.
Deane, Seamus, "Seamus Heaney: The Timorous and the Bold" (1985), in *Seamus Heaney: A Collection of Critical Essays*, ed. Michael Allen, London, 1997, 78-94.
Dodsworth, Martin, "*Mercian Hymns*: Offa, Charlemagne and Geoffrey Hill", in *Geoffrey Hill: Essays on His Work*, ed. Peter Robinson, Milton Keynes, 1985, 49-61.
Dodsworth, Martin, "Ted Hughes and Geoffrey Hill: An Antithesis", in *The New Pelican Guide to English Literature: 8. The Present*, ed. Boris Ford, London, 1983, 81-93.
Douglas, Keith, *Selected Poems*, ed. Ted Hughes, London, 1964.
Eagleton, Terry, "Saving Burke from the Tories", *New Statesman*, 4 July 1997, 32-33.
Easthope, Antony, *Englishness and National Culture*, London, 1999.
Easthope, Antony, "How Good is Seamus Heaney?", *English*, XLVI/184 (1997): 21-36.
Eliot, T.S., *After Strange Gods*, London, 1934.
Eliot, T.S, *Collected Poems 1909-1962*, London, 1974.
Eliot, T.S., *The Idea of a Christian Society*, London, 1948.
Eliot, T.S., *Notes Towards the Definition of Culture*, London, 1948.
Eliot, T.S., *On Poetry and Poets*, London, 1957.
Eliot, T.S., *Selected Prose of T.S. Eliot*, ed. Frank Kermode, New York, 1975.

Ellis, Steve, *The English Eliot: Design, Language and Landscape in Four Quartets*, London, 1991.

Empson, William, *Some Versions of Pastoral* (1935), New York, 1974.

Everett, Barbara, "Eliot's *Four Quartets* and French Symbolism", *English*, XXIX/133 (1980), 1-37.

Everett, Barbara, "Philip Larkin: After Symbolism" (1980), in *Poets in Their Time*, London, 1986, 230-44.

Faas, Ekbert, *Ted Hughes: The Unaccommodated Universe*, Santa Barbara, 1980.

Forster, E.M., *Howards End* (1910), Penguin, 2000.

Foster, John Wilson, *Colonial Consequences*, Dublin, 1991.

Foster, John Wilson, "Getting the North: Yeats and Northern Nationalism", in *Yeats Annual 12*, eds Warwick Gould and Edna Longley, London, 1996, 181-212.

Foster, Paul, *An Arundel Tomb*, Chichester, 1987.

Fowler, Alastair, "Geoffrey Hill: Refined, Furious - and Great?", *Times Literary Supplement*, 4 April 1986, 363.

Fowles, John, "On Being English But Not British", *Texas Quarterly*, VII/3 (1964), 154-62.

Gardner, Helen, *The Art of T.S. Eliot*, London, 1949.

Gardner, Helen, *The Composition of Four Quartets*, London, 1978.

Gervais, David, "Ted Hughes: An England Beneath England", *English*, XLII/172 (1993), 45-73.

Gervais, David, *Literary Englands*, Cambridge, 1993.

Ghosh, Peter, "How We Got Where We Are", *London Review of Books*, 28 November 1996, 18-19.

Gifford, Terry, "Gods of Mud: Hughes and the Post-Pastoral", in *The Challenge of Ted Hughes*, ed. Keith Sagar, 1994, 129-41.

Gifford, Terry and Neil Roberts, "Hughes and Two Contemporaries: Peter Redgrove and Seamus Heaney", in *The Achievement of Ted Hughes*, ed. Keith Sagar, Manchester, 1983, 90-106.

Gikandi, Simon, *Maps of Englishness*, New York, 1996.

Giles, Judy and Tim Middleton, eds, *Writing Englishness 1900-1950: An Introductory Sourcebook on National Identity*, London, 1995.

Glen, Heather, "Geoffrey Hill's 'England of the Mind'", *The Critical Review*, XXVII (1985), 98-109.

Glob, P.V., *The Bog People*, London, 1969.

Goodby, John, "'The Importance of Being Elsewhere', or 'No Man is an Ireland': Self, Selves and Social Consensus in the Poetry of Philip Larkin", *Critical Survey*, I/2 (1989), 131-38.

Gordon, Lyndall, *Eliot's Early Years*, Oxford, 1977.

Haffenden, John, *Viewpoints: Poets in Conversation with John Haffenden*, London, 1981.
Halpern, Susan, *Austin Clarke: His Life and Works*, Dublin, 1974.
Hart, Henry, *Seamus Heaney: Poet of Contrary Progressions*, Syracuse, 1992.
Haughton, Hugh, "How Fit a Title ... : Title and Authority in the Work of Geoffrey Hill", in *Geoffrey Hill: Essays on His Work*, ed. Peter Robinson, Milton Keynes, 1985, 129-48.
Heaney, Seamus, "Celtic Fringe, Nordic Fringe", *The Listener*, 21 Aug. 1969, 254-55.
Heaney, Seamus, *Death of a Naturalist*, London, 1966.
Heaney, Seamus, *Door into the Dark*, London, 1969.
Heaney, Seamus, "Envies and Identifications: Dante and the Modern Poet", *Irish University Review*, XV/1 (1985), 5-19.
Heaney, Seamus, *The Government of the Tongue*, London, 1988.
Heaney, Seamus, *The Haw Lantern*, London, 1987.
Heaney, Seamus, Interview with Frank Kinahan, *Critical Inquiry*, VIII/3 (1982), 405-14.
Heaney, Seamus, "The New Poet Laureate", in *Critical Essays on Ted Hughes*, ed. Leonard Scigaj, New York, 1992, 45-46.
Heaney, Seamus, *North*, London, 1975.
Heaney, Seamus, "Now and in England", Review of *The Sleeping Lord* by David Jones, *The Spectator*, 4 May 1974, 547.
Heaney, Seamus, "Place and Displacement: Reflections on Some Recent Poetry from Northern Ireland", in *Contemporary Irish Poetry*, ed. Elmer Andrews, London, 1992, 124-44.
Heaney, Seamus, "Place, Pastness, Poems: A Triptych", *Salmagundi*, LXVIII-LXIX (1985-1986), 30-47.
Heaney, Seamus, *Preoccupations: Selected Prose 1968-1978*, London, 1980.
Heaney, Seamus, *The Redress of Poetry*, London, 1995.
Heaney, Seamus, *Seeing Things*, London, 1991.
Heaney, Seamus, *The Spirit Level*, London, 1996.
Heaney, Seamus, *Station Island*, London, 1984.
Heaney, Seamus, *Stations*, Belfast, 1975.
Heaney, Seamus, *Sweeney Astray*, London, 1984.
Heaney, Seamus, "Unhappy and at Home", Interview with Seamus Deane, in *The Crane Bag Book of Irish Studies 1977-1981*, eds Mark Patrick Hederman and Richard Kearney, Dublin, 1992, 66-72.
Heaney, Seamus, *Wintering Out*, London, 1972.
Heaney, Seamus and Ted Hughes, eds, *The Rattle Bag*, London, 1982.
Heaney, Seamus and Ted Hughes, eds, *The School Bag*, London, 1997.

Hederman, Mark Patrick and Richard Kearney, eds, *The Crane Bag Book of Irish Studies 1977-1981*, Dublin, 1992.

Henley, W. E., *Poems*, London, 1898.

Hill, Geoffrey, *Canaan*, Penguin, 1996.

Hill, Geoffrey, *Collected Poems*, Penguin, 1986.

Hill, Geoffrey, "Dividing Legacies", *Agenda*, XXXIV/2 (1996), 9-28.

Hill, Geoffrey, "Gurney's Hobby", *Essays in Criticism*, XXXIV/2 (1984), 97-128.

Hill, Geoffrey, "'I in Another Place.' Homage to Keith Douglas", *Stand*, VI/4 (1964), 6-13.

Hill, Geoffrey, Interview with Blake Morrison, *New Statesman*, 8 February 1980, 212-14.

Hill, Geoffrey, *The Lords of Limit*, London, 1984.

Hill, Geoffrey, *The Triumph of Love*, Penguin, 1998.

Hobsbawm, Eric, "Some Reflections on *The Break-Up of Britain*", *New Left Review*, CV (1977), 3-23.

Holloway, John, "The Myth of England", *The Listener*, 15 May 1969, 670-72.

Homberger, Eric, *The Art of the Real*, London, 1977.

Hooker, Jeremy, "Seeing Place", in *In Black and Gold: Contiguous Traditions in Post-War British and Irish Poetry*, ed. C.C. Barfoot, Amsterdam, 1994, 27-44.

Hopkins, Gerard Manley, *The Poems of Gerard Manley Hopkins*, eds W.H. Gardner and N.H. MacKenzie, Oxford, 1970.

Hopkins, Gerard Manley, *Selected Prose*, ed. Gerald Roberts, Oxford, 1980.

Housman, A.E., *Collected Poems*, Penguin, 1956.

Howes, Marjorie, *Yeats's Nations: Gender, Class and Irishness*, Cambridge, 1996.

Howkins, Alun, "The Discovery of Rural England", in *Englishness: Politics and Culture 1880-1920*, eds Robert Colls and Philip Dodd, London, 1986, 62-88.

Hughes, Eamonn, "Representations in Modern Irish Poetry" (1990), in *Seamus Heaney: A Collection of Critical Essays*, ed. Michael Allen, London, 1997, 64-77.

Hughes, Ted, "An Address Given at the Memorial Service at St. Martin-in-the-Fields", in *Henry Williamson: The Man, the Writings. A Symposium*, ed. B. Sewell, Padstow, 1980, 159-65.

Hughes, Ted, *Birthday Letters*, London, 1998.

Hughes, Ted, *Crow* (1970), London, 1972.

Hughes, Ted, *Flowers and Insects*, London, 1986.

Hughes, Ted, *Gaudete*, London, 1977.

Hughes, Ted, *The Hawk in the Rain*, London, 1957.
Hughes, Ted, *Lupercal*, London, 1960.
Hughes, Ted, *Moortown*, London, 1979.
Hughes, Ted, *Moortown Diary*, London, 1989.
Hughes, Ted, *New Selected Poems 1957-1994*, London, 1995.
Hughes, Ted, *Poetry in the Making* (1967), London, 1969.
Hughes, Ted, *Rain-Charm for the Duchy and Other Laureate Poems*, London, 1992.
Hughes, Ted, *Remains of Elmet*, London, 1979.
Hughes, Ted, *River*, London, 1983.
Hughes, Ted, "The Rock", in *Writers on Themselves*, ed. Herbert Read, London, 1964, 86-92.
Hughes, Ted, *Season Songs*, London, 1975.
Hughes, Ted, *Shakespeare and the Goddess of Complete Being*, London, 1992.
Hughes, Ted, *Tales from Ovid*, London, 1997.
Hughes, Ted, "Ted Hughes and *Crow*", Interview wih Ekbert Faas (1970), in *Ted Hughes: The Unaccommodated Universe*, Santa Barbara, 1980, 197-208.
Hughes, Ted, "Ted Hughes and *Gaudete*", Interview with Ekbert Faas (1977), in Ekbert Faas's *Ted Hughes: The Unaccommodated Universe*, Santa Barbara, 1980, 208-15.
Hughes, Ted, *Three Books: Remains of Elmet, Cave Birds, River*, London, 1993.
Hughes, Ted, *Winter Pollen: Occasional Prose*, ed. William Scammell, London, 1994.
Hughes, Ted, *Wodwo*, London, 1967.
Hughes, Ted, *Wolfwatching*, London, 1989.
Hulse, Michael, "The Laureate Business or the Laureateship of Englishness", *Quadrant*, XXIX (1985), 45-49.
Jardine, Lisa, "Saxon Violence", *The Guardian*, 8 December 1992 (section 2), 4.
Jones, David, *The Anathemata* (1952), London, 1955.
Jones, David, *In Parenthesis* (1937), with an introduction by T.S. Eliot, London, 1953.
Jones, David, *The Sleeping Lord*, London, 1974.
Joyce, James, *Ulysses* (1922), Penguin, 1992.
Kearney, Richard, "Myth and Terror", in *The Crane Bag Book of Irish Studies 1977-1981*, eds Mark Patrick Hederman and Richard Kearney, Dublin, 1992, 273-87.
Keith, William J., *The Rural Tradition*, Hassocks, 1975.

Kelleher, John V., "Matthew Arnold and the Celtic Revival", in *Perspectives of Criticism*, ed. Harry Levin, New York, 1970, 197-221.

Kennedy, David, *New Relations: The Refashioning of British Poetry 1980-1994*, Bridgend, 1996.

Kerrigan, John, "Ulster Ovids", in *The Chosen Ground: Essays on the Contemporary Poetry of Northern Ireland*, ed. Neil Corcoran, Bridgend, 1992, 235-69.

Knottenbelt, E. M., *Passionate Intelligence: The Poetry of Geoffrey Hill*, Amsterdam, 1990.

Larkin, Philip, DPL - Poetry Workbooks (See Unpublished Material).

Larkin, Philip, *Collected Poems*, ed. Anthony Thwaite, London, 1988.

Larkin, Philip, *Further Requirements*, ed. Anthony Thwaite, London, 2001.

Larkin, Philip, *A Girl in Winter* (1947), London, 1975.

Larkin, Philip, *High Windows*, London, 1974.

Larkin, Philip, *The Less Deceived*, Hull, 1955.

Larkin, Philip, ed., *The Oxford Book of Twentieth Century English Verse*, Oxford, 1973.

Larkin, Philip, *Required Writing*, London, 1983.

Larkin, Philip, *Selected Letters*, ed. Anthony Thwaite, London, 1991.

Larrissy, Edward, *Reading Twentieth Century Poetry: The Language of Gender and Objects*, Oxford, 1990.

Lassner, Phyllis, *British Women Writers of World War Two*, London, 1998.

Lawrence, D.H., *Complete Poems*, vol. 1 (1964), eds Vivian de Sola Pinto and Warren Roberts, London, 1967.

Lawrence, D.H., *England, my England and Other Stories*, ed. John Lawton, London, 1998.

Lloyd, David, "'Pap for the Dispossessed': Seamus Heaney and the Poetics of Identity" (1993), in *Seamus Heaney: A Collection of Critical Essays*, ed. Michael Allen, London, 1997, 155-84.

Lloyd, J.F., *Geoffrey Hill and British Poetry, 1956-1986*, unpublished D.Phil thesis, University of Oxford, 1991.

Lodge, David, "Philip Larkin: The Metonymic Muse", in *The Modes of Modern Writing: Metaphor and Metonymy and the Typology of Modern Literature*, London, 1977, 212-20.

Longley, Edna, "'Inner Emigré' or 'Artful Voyeur'? Seamus Heaney's *North*" (1986), in *Seamus Heaney: A Collection of Critical Essays*, ed. Michael Allen, London, 1997, 30-63.

Longley, Edna, *The Living Stream: Literature and Revisionism in Ireland*, Newcastle, 1994.

Lucas, John, "Discovering England: The View from the Train", *Literature and History*, VI/2 (1997), 37-55.

Lucas, John, *England and Englishness: Ideas of Nationhood in English Poetry 1688-1900*, London, 1990.

Lucas, John, *Modern British Poetry from Hardy to Hughes*, London, 1986.

Lucie-Smith, Edward, ed., *British Poetry since 1945*, London, 1985.

MacDonald, Peter, "Michael Longley's Homes", in *The Chosen Ground: Essays on the Contemporary Poetry of Northern Ireland*, ed. Neil Corcoran, Bridgend, 1992, 63-83.

Marshall, Alan, "England and Nowhere", in *The Cambridge Companion to T.S. Eliot*, ed. A. David Moody, Cambridge, 1994, 94-107.

Molino, Michael R., "Flying by the Nets of Language: Seamus Heaney, the 'English Language' and Ulster's Troubles", *Modern Philology*, XCI (1993), 180-201.

Morrison, Blake, *The Movement*, London, 1986.

Morrison, Blake, *Seamus Heaney*, London, 1982.

Motion, Andrew, *Philip Larkin*, London, 1982.

Motion, Andrew, *Philip Larkin: A Writer's Life*, London, 1993.

Nairn, Tom, *The Break-Up of Britain*, London, 1977.

Nairn, Tom, "The Departed Spirit, or the English Quandary", *London Review of Books*, 30 October 1997, 6.

O'Brien, Sean, *The Deregulated Muse*, Newcastle, 1998.

Orwell, George, *Inside the Whale and Other Essays*, Penguin, 1971.

Pagnoulle, Christine, "Music Alone Survives? Collapsing Faith in Some Sonnets by Gerard Manley Hopkins and Geoffrey Hill", *Cahiers Victoriens et Edouardiens*, XLII (1995), 91-107.

Parker, Michael, "Hughes and the Poets of Eastern Europe", in *The Achievement of Ted Hughes*, ed. Keith Sagar, Manchester, 1983, 37-51.

Parker, Michael, *Seamus Heaney: The Making of the Poet*, London, 1993.

Paul, Anthony, "The Poet Laureate's National Poet", in *Reclamations of Shakespeare*, ed. A. J. Hoenselaars, Amsterdam, 1994, 159-72.

Paulin, Tom, *Ireland and the English Crisis*, Newcastle, 1984.

Paulin, Tom, *Minotaur: Poetry and the Nation State*, London, 1992.

Paulin, Tom, "A New Look at the Language Question", in *Ireland's Field Day*, ed. Seamus Deane, London, 1985, 3-18.

Paulin, Tom, *Thomas Hardy: The Poetry of Perception* (2nd edition), London, 1986.

Paxman, Jeremy, *The English: A Portrait of a People*, London, 1998.

Perl, Jeffrey, *Skepticism and Modern Enmity*, Baltimore, 1989.

Perse, Saint-John, *Collected Poems*, with translations by W.H. Auden, Hugh Chisholm, Denis Devlin, T.S. Eliot, Robert Fitzgerald, Wallace Fowlie, Richard Howard and Louise Varèse, Princeton, 1971.

Pittock, Murray, *Spectrum of Decadence*, London, 1990.

Plath, Sylvia, *Collected Poems*, ed. Ted Hughes, London, 1981.

Pollard, A.J., *The Wars of the Roses*, London, 1988.

Regan, Stephen, "Larkin's Reputation", in *Larkin with Poetry*, ed. Michael Baron, Leicester, 1997, 47-69.

Regan, Stephen, *Philip Larkin*, London, 1992.

Rhodes, Neil, "Bridegrooms to the Goddess: Hughes, Heaney and the Elizabethans", in *Shakespeare and Ireland*, eds Mark Thornton Burnett and Ramona Wray, London, 1997, 152-72.

Robinson, John, *In Extremity: A Study of Gerard Manley Hopkins*, Cambridge, 1978.

Robinson, Peter, ed., *Geoffrey Hill: Essays on His Work*, Milton Keynes, 1985.

Sagar, Keith, ed., *The Achievement of Ted Hughes*, Manchester, 1983.

Sagar, Keith, *The Art of Ted Hughes*, Cambridge, 1975.

Sagar, Keith, ed., *The Challenge of Ted Hughes*, New York, 1994.

Sagar, Keith, "Fourfold Vision in Hughes", in *The Achievement of Ted Hughes*, ed. Keith Sagar, Manchester, 1983, 285-312.

Samuel, Raphael, ed., *Patriotism: The Making and Unmaking of British National Identity*, 3 volumes, London, 1989.

Scigaj, Leonard, ed., *Critical Essays on Ted Hughes*, New York, 1992.

Scigaj, Leonard, *Ted Hughes*, Boston, 1991.

Scruton, Roger, *England: An Elegy*, London, 2000.

Sherry, Vincent, *The Uncommon Tongue*, Ann Arbor, 1987.

Smith, Stan, "Darkening English: Post-Imperial Contestations in the Language of Seamus Heaney and Derek Walcott", *English*, XLIII/175 (1994), 39-55.

Smith, Stan, "The Distance Between: Seamus Heaney" (1992), in *Seamus Heaney: A Collection of Critical Essays*, ed. Michael Allen, 1997, 232-52.

Smith, Stan, "Wolf Masks: The Early Poetry of Ted Hughes" (1975), in *Critical Essays on Ted Hughes*, ed. Leonard Scigaj, New York, 1992, 67-81.

Spiering, M., *Englishness: Foreigners and Images of National Identity in Postwar Literature*, Amsterdam, 1992.

Stuart, Robert, "Ted Hughes", in *British Poetry since 1970: A Critical Survey*, eds Peter Jones and Michael Schmidt, Manchester, 1980, 75-84.

Swarbrick, Andrew, *Out of Reach: The Poetry of Philip Larkin*, London, 1995.

Thomas, Edward, *Collected Poems*, ed. R. George Thomas, Oxford, 1978.

Thomas, Edward, *The Heart of England* (1906), Oxford, 1982.

Thomas, Edward, *A Language Not to Be Betrayed: Selected Prose of Edward Thomas*, ed. Edna Longley, Manchester, 1981.

Thwaite, Anthony, *Poetry Today*, London, 1996.

Tolkien, J.R.R., *The Lord of the Rings* (1954-55), London, 1968.

Tolley, A.T., *Larkin at Work: A Study of Larkin's Mode of Composition as Seen in his Notebooks*, Hull, 1997.

Tomlinson, Charles, "The Middlebrow Muse", *Essays in Criticism*, VII (1957), 208-17.

Trotter, David, "Modernism and Empire: Reading *The Waste Land*", *Critical Quarterly*, XXVIII/1-2 (1986), 143-53.

Ward, John Powell, *The English Line: Poetry of the Unpoetic from Wordsworth to Larkin*, London, 1991.

Watt, R.J.C., "Seamus Heaney: Voices on Helicon", *Essays in Criticism*, XLIV/3 (1994), 213-44.

Wiener, Martin J., *English Culture and the Decline of the Industrial Spirit 1850-1980* (1981), London, 1985.

Williamson, Henry, *Tarka the Otter*, Penguin, 1937.

Wordsworth, William, *Poetical Works*, Oxford, 1978.

Yeats, W.B., *Essays and Introductions*, London, 1961.

Yeats, W.B., *The Poems*, ed. Daniel Albright, London, 1990.

INDEX